T0197013

Profiting from Uncertainty

Also by Paul J. H. Schoemaker

Decision Traps
Ten Barriers to Brilliant Decision Making

Decision Sciences
An Integrative Approach

Wharton on Managing Emerging Technologies

Winning Decisions
Getting It Right the First Time

Peripheral Vision
Detecting the Weak Signals That Will Make or Break Your Company

Chips, Clones, and Living Beyond 100
How Far Will the Biosciences Take Us?

Brilliant Mistakes
Finding Success on the Far Side of Failure

Profiting from Uncertainty

Strategies for Succeeding No Matter What the Future Brings

Paul J. H. Schoemaker

With Robert E. Gunther

ATRIA BOOKS

New York • London • Toronto • Sydney • New Delhi

ATRIA BOOKS
A Division of Simon & Schuster, Inc.
1230 Avenue of the Americas
New York, NY 10020

First Atria Books hardcover edition May 2013

ATRIA BOOKS and colophon are trademarks of Simon & Schuster, Inc.

For information about special discounts for bulk purchases, please contact Simon & Schuster Special Sales at 1-866-506-1949 or business@simonandschuster.com.

The Simon & Schuster Speakers Bureau can bring authors to your live event. For more information or to book an event, contact the Simon & Schuster Speakers Bureau at 1-866-248-3049 or visit our website at www.simonspeakers.com.

Designed by Paul Dippolito

Manufactured in the United States of America

1

The Library of Congress has cataloged the Free Press edition as follows:

Schoemaker, Paul J. H.
Profiting from uncertainty: strategies for succeeding no matter what the future brings/ Paul J. H. Schoemaker with Robert E. Gunther.
p. cm.
Includes bibliographical references and index.
1. Strategic planning. 2. Uncertainty. 3. Management. I. Gunther, Robert E. II. Title.
HD30.28 .S3455 2002 2002024394

ISBN 978-1-5011-6175-9

I dedicate this book to my children, Kim and Paul, in the hope that they will navigate life's uncertainties with resilience, intelligence, honor, and humor.

Acknowledgments

Those who aim high usually stand on the shoulders of others. This book tackles a very challenging and increasingly important subject, in a way that is accessible to managers. I wish to acknowledge here the shoulders my feet rested on. To properly apportion my intellectual debt, I offer a brief chronological account of the interesting journey that led me to this book.

My interest in uncertainty traces back to my undergraduate days as a physics major. This field taught me that common sense serves us well in the middle of the spectrum (where Newtonian physics reigns), but that to understand the extremes of the spectrum, we need *uncommon* sense. From the enigma of the big bang to the indeterminacies of quantum physics, the edges force us to confront ourselves, our own mental models, and the sense-making process we engage in. The same applies to uncertainty in the economic realm—above all we face ourselves as we stand naked before the unknown with little to hold on to for comfort or support.

In graduate school my interests shifted to economics and finance and later to decision making as an intriguing subject of study. I wrote my doctoral thesis at Wharton on the limitations of expected utility theory, the prevailing model of choice under risk at the time. Here I benefited much from the keen minds of Howard Kunreuther (my adviser), Paul Kleindorfer, and later Jack Hershey. I fondly recall the stimulating dialogues with Howard and Paul as we teamed up to write our graduate text *Decision Sciences* (Cambridge University Press, 1993). With Jack Hershey I published several academic papers probing the nature of people's risk attitudes, especially their biases and sensitivity to context.

Around 1979 I moved to the rarified halls of the University of Chicago, where I joined the newly formed Center for Decision Research. This research group was led by the late Hillel Einhorn, a gifted scholar in behavioral science. Operating in the shadows of finance and economics, our fledgling group advanced heretical notions about bounded rationality and flaws in human judgment. I befriended

Jay Russo, from whom I learned much about cognitive psychology and with whom I wrote *Decision Traps* (1989) and later *Winning Decisions* (2002). I also learned much from my other behavioral colleagues, notably Robin Hogarth, Josh Klayman, and George Loewenstein. Our workshops with guest speakers were always fun and spirited as we listened to and debated the best minds in the field.

After I was promoted to associate professor at the University of Chicago, I thought it wise to look at how the real world deals with uncertainty. In 1982 I took an extended sabbatical with the planning group of Royal Dutch/Shell in London that had been pioneering scenario planning under the inspired leadership of Pierre Wack and Ted Newland. At Shell I was privileged to work with Arie de Geus, Kees van der Heijden, and Peter Schwartz, all of whom later wrote significant books about planning under uncertainty. Like Chicago, Shell was fermenting with novel ideas as a constant stream of creative visitors passed through. The Shell experience painted a sharp contrast between theory and practice and increased my respect for the complexity and importance of context in real-world decision making.

Upon my return to Chicago, I turned my attention from decision making to strategy, a field that was still in its infancy and had little legitimacy at the University of Chicago. I was fortunate that Dan Schendel, founder and director of the Strategic Management Society (SMS), visited us for a sabbatical year, and I much enjoyed our frequent lunches. With Raffi Amit, who was then at Northwestern University, I started to explore the behavioral foundations of the resource-based view of strategy. In 1993 we published a joint article in the *Strategic Management Journal* titled "Strategic Assets and Organizational Rent." This work was later honored with SMS's best paper award and forms the basis for Chapters 4 and 5 of this book. While at Chicago I also got involved in various consulting engagements that further challenged the pristine models of academia. I am much indebted here to the numerous executives I worked with across a variety of functions and industries.

In the mid-1990s, as my interest and focus shifted to my company Decision Strategies International, we moved to Philadelphia, where I reconnected with friends and colleagues at the Wharton School. I teamed up with George Day, who had started to study emerging technologies through a center composed of multiple disciplines. I was invited to join this group as a part-time research director and later edited with George Day the book *Wharton on Managing Emerging Technologies* (New York: John Wiley, 2000). The subject of uncertainty is front and center when studying emerging technologies, and I benefited greatly from the stimulating discussions of our core faculty group, which consisted of George Day, Bill Hamilton, Harbir Singh, Jitendra Singh, and Sid Winter. Also, the executives who joined our research center as industry partners are thanked for their spirited discussions and valued experiences, especially Larry Huston (Procter & Gamble) and Terry Fadem (DuPont).

I have learned much from my colleagues at Decision Strategies International (DSI), who helped conduct many of the consulting projects on which this book is based. In particular, Michael Mavaddat and Roch Parayre proved to be very stimulating colleagues who blend a curious mind with a pragmatic orientation. Stephen Dull and Doug Randall also have been valued DSI colleagues. In addition, various executives in our client organizations also helped shape my thinking, especially Mary Jean Connors (Knight-Ridder), Gabriel Gedvilla (Weyerhaeuser), Leon Mandel (Lagoven), Nanty Meyer (Berkeley's Haas School of Business), Michael Packanowski (W. L. Gore), Anil Patel (U.S. Army Corps of Engineers), Howard Rosoff (NatWest Bank), Steve Rossi (Knight-Ridder), Franck Schuurmans (Credit Union Executives Society), Sue Sheuerman (Household Finance), Dean Taylor (Ross Products), and Randy Woelfel (Shell Oil), as well as my academic and consulting colleagues from the McKinsey Forum.

Several friends and colleagues have offered valuable commentary on earlier manuscript drafts, for which I thank them greatly. They are Stephen Dull (DSI), Terry Fadem (DuPont), Paul Kleindorfer (Wharton), Jeff Kuhn (Columbia University), Howard Kunreuther (Wharton), Michael Mavaddat (DSI), Hugh Courtney (McKinsey), Roch Parayre (DSI), Anil Patel (U.S. Army Corps of Engineers), Doug Randall (DSI), Franck Schuurmans (Credit Union Executives Society), Gabriel Szulanski (Wharton), and Michael Tomczyk (Wharton). In addition, I am much indebted to those whom we interviewed and quote in the pages of this book: Russ Ackoff, Louis Arnitz, Tom Borger, Eric Brooks, George Day, Terry Fadem, Tom Graham, Mike Hostetler, Alberto Ibargüen, Paul James, Dave Landsberg, Michael Mavaddat, Jack McAdoo, Roch Parayre,

Rudy Pereira, Jay Russo, Franck Schuurmans, Scott Snyder, Jeff Yass, and Jeff York. Also, I am grateful for the wise counsel, moral support, and seasoned editorial judgment rendered by Robert Wallace from the Free Press. Furthermore, we thank Celia Knight for her meticulous editing, and Michel Dijkstra for his help with the artwork.

A great measure of debt is owed to Robert Gunther, who helped shape and hone a large collection of academic papers, client reports, and consulting experiences into the present book. Robert and I spent many hours at my white board sketching and reworking the concepts, principles, and examples that constitute the core of this book. His sharp mind, good cheer, strong work appetite, and gifted pen made it a pleasure to write this book. Although his original role was to be that of a writer, he ended up being a valued intellectual collaborator as acknowledged on the title page. Nonetheless, the usual caveat applies—any flaws remain mine alone.

Finally, I thank my dear wife Joyce for creating a stable and loving home environment, with two active teenagers, which allowed me to complete this third book in the space of just three years. Also, she offered careful commentary on various chapter drafts and debated with me the deeper premises of the book from her more scientific perspective. She has proved to be a wonderful soul mate for many seasons, and my gratitude to her is great.

Contents

New Preface

Are You Ready for Yet More Upheaval and Global Turmoil?

There is nothing stable in the world; uproar's your only music.
—JOHN KEATS (1795–1821), BRITISH POET

When I was finishing the writing of *Profiting from Uncertainty* around 2000, it was clear that uncertainty was on the rise and that managers lacked good tools to deal with it. The collapse of the dot-com bubble in 2000; the subsequent terrorist attacks on September 11, 2001, in the United States; the precipitous decline of the biotech sector; and the recession of 2002 all helped make the case for rising uncertainty strongly. But in some sense my 2002 book was published six years too soon—much stronger evidence was yet to come. The global financial crisis of 2008 that originated in the housing sector, several Arab Spring revolutions, and deep fault lines in the European Union made the case more strongly yet. And so have increases in extreme weather events, such as Hurricane Katrina, vast polar ice melting, mega floods in Pakistan in 2011, and Hurricane Sandy's battering of the northeast coast of the United States in 2012. Uncertainty is here to stay and will likely increase. Sadly, our political, social, economic, and personal strategies often fall short because we are ill prepared and often blind.

Newspaper headlines remind us daily that many things do not play out as expected in business and government, and that often there is no good plan B available as backup. The World Economic Forum's *Global Risks Report* periodically identifies significant uncertainties facing our global economy and world order, as listed in the appendix to this preface. It is a long and somewhat depressing list covering economic, geopolitical, environmental, societal, and technological threats. But in each category, numerous companies have been able to profit from these risks and uncertainties. In the economic realm, those trading pollution rights profit from environment uncertainty, and large players like GE, with its multipronged ecomagination strategies, are carving out promising opportunities. Growing shortages of fresh water—with its many unforeseen consequences—are shouting out for better desalination technologies. Advances in genomics and proteomics are opening many new doors for biotech and pharmaceutical companies. As my book argues, managers need to reframe uncertainty as a friend and recognize that without it no company can really create new economic rent. Uncertainty is a necessary condition for superior performance precisely because it upsets the apple cart and tosses equilibrium solutions out the window. It is healthy to reshuffle the social and economic deck at times, such that animal spirits awaken and entrepreneurs take risks.

Unfortunately, many managers remain shackled to flawed linear forecasts produced by traditional planning and budgeting systems. The world they operate in has not only become more risky, it has become far more uncertain as well. Businesses can handle cases of risk reasonably well. These are situations in which managers have decent probability estimates for various outcomes that can materialize, reflecting past experience or rigorous analysis. Managers can use decision trees, Monte Carlo simulations, portfolio modeling, and Bayesian updating as proven methods in the risk management tool kit. But when it comes to those pesky cases of uncertainty, where they don't have solid probabilities to rely upon, and perhaps may not even be aware of important possibilities, they too often fall back on gut feelings and hope. Unfortunately, hope is not a strategy. But rising uncertainty should not lead to despair, as it can actually be turned to advantage. Conceptually speaking, any investment entails an uncertain distribution of possible returns. Net present value analysis looks at the expected return and then adjusts the projected cash flow for systematic risk. This model is self-limiting in that it does not handle uncertainty well, but if tweaked properly, it can still be valuable. By using scenario planning, flexible strategies, real options analysis, and early warning systems, managers can protect downside risk better and find new opportunities to fully capture upside returns.

The wide range of uncertainties listed in the appendix holds much promise for entrepreneurial companies. The *frequency* of surprises, as well as their *magnitude*, will increase over time. This trend will likely continue even if many companies are not ready for the turmoil ahead. Nassim Nicholas Taleb discusses this very issue in his books *The Black Swan* and *Antifragile*. He argues that managers should not waste much time predicting change but instead create organizations that can handle anything. But this argument goes too far in my view. Some trends can be projected and many uncertainties can be analyzed and bounded. Still, our global system is indeed becoming more complex due to higher interdependency, new technologies, clashing value systems, religious conflicts, terrorism, climate change, and overpopulation inter alia. And this can create various wild cards ranging from environmental disasters and new diseases to nuclear war and power grabs by maniacal leaders of mafia states. The key is to prepare for what can be anticipated while also leaving room for a significant dose of surprises.

Our global system can probably handle any one of the challenges identified in the World Economic Forum reports reasonably well. But a deeper problem is that we may face several of these major challenges at once. Policy makers and business leaders are justly concerned about the fragility of our financial and economic systems, since crises can spread overnight and companies can lose substantial value in a single week. How robust our circuit breakers are remains an open question, especially since market psychology and mass hysteria can play a major role in eroding confidence. The wisdom of the crowd can quickly turn into collective madness and mass delusion as well. Many of the risks described above are interconnected, and it is not clear that our financial and economic systems can easily handle the confluence of stresses they may impose on our fragile regulatory systems. The occurrence of multiple low-probabilities events, with hidden interconnections, is typically what causes perfect storms or black swans that few spot in time.

So, the challenge is not just one of uncertainty (i.e., not knowing what may happen) but also one of complexity (i.e., not understanding how things are linked). This is the difference between playing poker or chess (a case of uncertainty) versus managing a crisis—such as that of 2008—while operating at the edge of our collective knowledge (a case of complexity). As mathematical genius John von Neumann noted, "If people do not believe that mathematics is simple, it is only because they do not yet realize how complicated life is." Our limited ability to grasp the complexities that surround us has justly reached the popular press, with bestselling books like *Freakonomics, Predictably Irrational, Nudge, The Black Swan,* and *Thinking, Fast and Slow*. Behavioral economics and decision psychology properly highlight why the quirks and foibles of the human mind often lie at the root of great disasters and tragic choices. My book *Winning Decisions* (written with Jay Russo) explains how we can counter various decision traps at the individual level. *Profiting from Uncertainty* does the same for organizations, with a special focus on how smart leaders can turn seemingly unwelcome uncertainty into a competitive edge by better mastering various tools and methods for navigating the unknown.

It is a daunting challenge indeed to manage any single big uncertainty, such as global warming, regulatory change, new technologies, disruptive new business models, or shifting consumer preferences. What makes the bigger picture yet more challenging is that many of these uncertainties are interconnected at a deep level that we only partly understand. The Great Recession of 2008 was in part due to regulators, investors, and risk managers underestimating the high levels of systematic risk embedded in our global economic system, as well as the perverse incentives created by moral hazards. Positively correlated risks will bring about greater market swings and more fragile fault lines. As a consequence, companies operating across geographic or industry boundaries need to be prepared for a roller-coaster environment. Unfortunately, many are not prepared. In fact, we can all do better. I'll close this preface with some questions I was asked by the *Harvard Business Review* online, since the answers I gave there provide a short prelude to the issues examined in detail in this book.

If we haven't already prepared for higher levels of turmoil, is there still time?

Yes, there is still time for those companies that did not overcommit. The key to dealing with turmoil is to have flexibility in your strategy. In addition, you need to detect the changes quickly and respond accordingly. This requires good peripheral vision, i.e., the ability to pick up weak signals outside your area of focus. Few companies do this well, and often they get blindsided unnecessarily, as documented in my book *Peripheral Vision* (written with George Day). If your company did stick its neck out dangerously far, as some of the smartest financial firms did by overbetting on subprime mortgages, then you may wish to unwind some of these commitments or pursue hedging strategies that will mitigate your downside exposure. All companies should stress test their strategies by putting them into the wind tunnel of wide-ranging future turmoil to see how robust they are. As Darwin observed, it is not the strongest or smartest who survive, but those who are most adaptive to change. Don't box yourself in.

Should companies that have engaged in scenario planning go back and revise some of their assumptions?

Ideally, such revisions should occur routinely as part of an ongoing monitoring and scanning system. It was easy for Shell's scenario experts to recognize that they needed to rethink their conceptual frameworks after the Berlin Wall came down, since a new geopolitical world order was about to emerge. The challenge is to do such revisions ahead of time, when the signals are weaker. Cognitive science shows that managers often overreact to changes in symptoms or surface features, such as a spike in sales revenue or a drop in interest rates, but underreact to more fundamental regime change, which often happens more gradually (and thus can sneak up). By designing scenario-based monitoring systems and executive dashboards, leaders can track which scenarios have become more or less likely. And, as important, they can track signals that are emerging that do not fit any of the scenarios. If this bucket of aberrant signals gets crowded, it is time to go back to the drawing board. Don't ignore the warning signs or run through red lights.

What are some best practices that companies should follow?

Here is my favorite list in a nutshell. Ideally, these practices operate as a highly integrated system with numerous cross synergies as illustrated in this book.

1. Use **scenario planning** to improve your organization's insight and foresight about the future. Make sure the scenarios tell engaging and insightful stories about changes yet to come. The aim is create strategic dialogue and change people's mental models.
2. Devise **adaptive strategies** that have sufficient flexibility built in to deal with the unexpected, including future-proofing your plans. Keep some options open and appreciate the value that flexibility and additional information can bestow.

3. Design a **dynamic monitoring** system to track the external world in real time, as well as to pick up internal warnings about strategies and plans not being executed well. Also, make sure to scan for the unexpected by developing strong peripheral vision.
4. Improve your **organization's agility** by adjusting rigid structures, tedious processes, misguided norms, and reward systems that favor the status quo. The aim is to design in sufficient flexibility to change the strategy and plans when trouble hits the fan.
5. Enhance your **information and decision-making** procedures to remain vigilant as well as focused on the most important overall objectives of the organization. Decisions are where rubber hits the road daily; make sure your teams master the necessary skills.
6. Foster **strong leadership** at multiple levels in the organization to deal better with crises and other unexpected circumstances. When all hell breaks loose, this is your last resort and leadership capacity cannot be developed overnight. It needs to ripen.

We shall likely continue to live in periods of great upheaval and global turmoil. This in turn will place special challenges on managers who have to deliver reliable results and make the numbers. Only a prepared mind that knows how to adapt can do so well. Just as sea captains have to deliver their cargo without sinking the ship, even when facing violent storms, ruthless pirates, and tough sea currents, senior leaders must do likewise. This requires state-of-the-art navigational equipment, up-to-date maps, a well-trained crew, and the ability to change midcourse if circumstances so dictate. Companies with superior navigational ability, as proposed in the book, can succeed where others fail. But you do have to turn on your radar and know when to trust your equipment, just as good pilots do. In times of turmoil, the spoils will be especially great for those with a prepared mind and the ability to maneuver quickly in the face of change.

Paul J. H. Schoemaker, Ph.D.
December 7, 2012

Appendix: More Uncertainty Ahead as Well as Much Hidden Opportunity

Economic: Rising food, water, and energy prices; sustainability of growth in China, India, etc.; insufficient funding for pensions and health care in developed countries; crosscurrents in credit, housing, and other asset markets; weakness in capital markets to finance growth; weak insurance regimes to protect against catastrophes.

Geopolitical: Continued terrorism; spread of nuclear weapons; regional conflicts and failed or failing countries (Taiwan, Middle East, Iran, Pakistan, North Korea, Horn of Africa, fragile countries in Latin America); expansion of organized crime (drugs, weapons) and mafia states; backlash against globalization; human rights violations; clash of civilizations; cooling relationships with Russia; rising instability in Pakistan.

Environmental: Extreme weather (cyclones, floods, droughts); ecosystem degradation (water shortages, deforestation, irreversible loss of biodiversity, natural catastrophes (earthquakes, seaquakes, inland flooding, category-5 hurricanes hitting major cities, global-warming fallout).

Societal: Global pandemics; infectious diseases (HIV/AIDS, TB, malaria); rising obesity, diabetes, cardiovascular disease in developed countries; spread of U.S.-style liability regimes; underinvestment in growth; wealth polarization; overpopulation; transportation constraints (airports, highways, harbors, public systems).

Technological: Failures of critical infrastructures (energy grids, Internet, emergency management); health effects due to nanoparticle exposure (in paint, cosmetics, health care) or cell phones (brain tumors?); ethical lapses in use of biosciences (misuse of cloning, stem cells, and genetic engineering); cyber terrorism; nuclear confrontations; bio-warfare.

Preface

Tumultuous Times

I was in the midst of writing this book when the events of September 11, 2001, dramatically raised the level of uncertainty in the world, both real and perceived. Following the terrorist attacks on the World Trade Center and the Pentagon, book buyers cleared the shelves of works by Nostradamus in hopes of finding clues as to what might happen next. Most people crave certainty, yet we live in an increasingly uncertain world. Since it is not possible to know much for certain anymore, we must become skilled at sailing into the unknown.

It is hard to look uncertainty in the eye without blinking. Three weeks before the September 11 terrorist attacks, I was working with managers from a major property and casualty insurance company on scenarios for their business. There was a heated discussion about whether to include in the scenarios major catastrophic losses from terrorist acts or other disruptions. Some argued that such risks were already priced into the premiums and that adequate reserves existed to cover them. Time will tell whether property and casualty insurance companies, and their reinsurers, were in fact sufficiently well capitalized to absorb the shocks from various catastrophic events. (In November 2001, Warren Buffett blamed a large loss at Berkshire Hathaway on what he called a "huge mistake" by its insurance companies in not anticipating the need to collect extra premiums for terrorist acts before September 11.)[1] But I am sure that we gave it far less weight in our discussions than we would today.

Life is inherently uncertain—from the moment of our birth to the unknown moment of our death—and yet we hate uncertainty, particularly in business. Business leaders traditionally have viewed uncertainty as the enemy. Skilled management is often seen as the process of avoiding unpleasant surprises. Uncertainty is something to be nailed down and rooted out, an evil that detracts from one's ability to manage with control. Uncertainty creates obstacles for the organization in generating profits and ensuring consistent performance.

As managers, we seek to reduce uncertainty. We gather facts and figures. We turn to experts for predictions. We hope to pin down uncertainty like a butterfly in a scientific collection. We use insurance to buffer uncertainty. We use denial to avoid uncertainty. And we put gates around our communities and our lives to keep risk at bay. We long for certainty with such passion that we very often bend reality to fit our desires. Instead of looking at the complex and chaotic soup that is reality, we make up a story, and we stick to that story under cross-examination, no matter how much the facts argue otherwise. We believe that our business is just on the verge of an upswing—until the movers come in and begin carting out the furniture. We believe our current business model will be successful in the future—it always has been—and so we fail to see that the world has shifted and that new competitors have arrived.

Uncertainty cannot be pinned down or coaxed into cages. It is only partly tamable, and we must learn to live with the beast. We cannot avoid surprises. Instead, we must be ready for them when they come. We need to be able to manage surprise and roll with the punches.

Certainty has never been more elusive than in today's tumultuous times. In recent decades we have lived through shocks such as the fall of the Berlin Wall, the explosion of the space shuttle Challenger, the mapping of the human genome, mad cow disease, Asian financial and political crises, Balkan wars, introduction of the euro, the boom and bust of the dot-coms, electricity blackouts and brownouts in California, and terrorist attacks of various kinds. Technology, deregulation, and other shifts in the global competitive environment continue to reshape the world in unpredictable ways.

Some shocks come completely out of the blue. When I was at Royal Dutch/Shell in the 1980s, our planning group in London had anticipated a major shift in the Soviet Union if a rather obscure bureaucrat named Mikhail Gorbachev came to power. But the Shell scenarios completely missed the subsequent fall of the Berlin Wall and its repercussions for the world (as did Gorbachev and most of the U.S. intelligence community). There will always be surprises, and the most difficult uncertainties for managers are those unimagined and those deemed to be possible but unlikely. But while we cannot fully know the future, we can better anticipate and prepare for the possibilities that we can foresee, factoring them into our strategies.

The silver lining of our turbulent environment is that we need uncertainty to create profit. Only modest profits can come from taming traditional uncertainty such as life insurance risks. Common risks lead to common returns. Consider the financial markets. If we knew the future income stream of a company for certain, its stock price would be largely fixed. There would be little opportunity to buy or sell at a significant profit or loss. In the end, the opportunity to profit comes from uncertainty. Of course, some companies do earn high profits in environments of high predictability, but these profits are drawn from having a better hand of cards or superior execution, not from mastering uncertainty. However, the vast value created by innovation, through distinctive strategies that set a company apart from its rivals, depends upon knowing how to profit from uncertainty.

Profiting, in this context, is different from profiteering. The goal is not to profit by capitalizing on tragedy and hardship, but rather to profit from anticipating different futures and preparing better for them. Such profit can be in the form of money, but it can also take nonpecuniary forms such as universities being better prepared for distance learning, hospitals staying abreast of technological change, and churches anticipating better the evolving needs of their parishioners. The strategies and methods we discuss extend far beyond the for-profit enterprises that constitute our primary focus.

Profiting from Uncertainty offers frameworks and approaches that help business leaders prepare for uncertain futures and find opportunities within them. The following pages offer a systematic approach for understanding uncertainty and capitalizing on it. The book is based upon a comprehensive approach—using scenario planning, options thinking, dynamic monitoring, and other strategies—pieces of which have been employed by major corporations around the world to think about and prepare for the future. This book shows how these approaches can be used not only to cope better with ambiguity but also to profit and prosper from it as well.

Paul J. H. Schoemaker
Villanova, Pennsylvania

Profiting from Uncertainty

Chapter 1

Embracing Uncertainty

"The only 'risk' which leads to a profit is a unique uncertainty. . . . Profits arise out of the inherent, absolute unpredictability of things."
—FRANK KNIGHT, UNIVERSITY OF CHICAGO ECONOMIST, 1921[1]

On March 17, 2000, a lightning bolt ignited a fire in Albuquerque, New Mexico, destroying a Philips semiconductor plant. Across the globe in Scandinavia, both Nokia and Ericsson depended on the factory for key chips in their cellular phones, and this chance disaster threatened to choke off their production. Nokia responded fast and flexibly, recognizing the problem thanks to its dynamic monitoring. Even before it was told of the plant shutdown, the company quickly patched together a solution. Ericsson, however, was less well prepared and moved slowly, losing an estimated $400 million in potential revenue, contributing to a corporate operating loss of about $1.86 billion in 2000 and ceding an increasing share of the global mobile phone market to Nokia. As Jan Ahrenbring, Ericsson's marketing director for consumer goods, told *The Wall Street Journal,* "We did not have a Plan B."[2]

Ericsson lost some $400 million in sales—a serious price to pay for not having a plan B. While it may be easy to understand how managers can be blindsided by a random lightning strike half a world away, this represents one of the simpler forms of uncertainty that managers face. It concerns a known risk with a very low probability and high potential cost—against which managers can use insurance or contingency planning. The more challenging uncertainties that managers face are those they haven't a clue about—when they wake up one day to find that the Berlin Wall has crashed to the ground or to recognize that the Internet has emerged or faded as a powerful new market space. Such uncertainties have the potential to create or destroy billions of dollars in market value:

- Cisco Systems very adroitly surfed the rising tide of the Internet to build one of the most successful information technology businesses in the world. Its market value skyrocketed for thirteen consecutive quarters and by April 2000 topped $550 billion, surpassing Microsoft and General Electric. Investors and managers began to believe it was a sure thing. Cisco, whose sophisticated Web-enabled accounting system allowed it to close its books hourly in a "virtual close," seemed to have the kind of tight rein on its business that would help avoid surprises. But then the tide of uncertainty turned against the company. In 2001 Cisco hit a downturn in the market that it had failed to anticipate. Its backward-looking accounting system turned out to be a highly polished rearview mirror that failed to keep the company from running off a cliff. It was also locked in to contracts and other commitments that made it hard to shift its strategy. Its revenues and share price plummeted over 70 percent, and worse, it had to take a $2.5 billion write-off for excess inventory. Cisco CEO John Chambers compared the slump to "a 100-year flood." He said, "It's something you don't expect to see in your lifetime. We never built models to anticipate something of this magnitude."[3] But had the collapse of the Internet bubble and the ensuing recession really been that unpredictable? Or was the company so caught up in the euphoria of the moment that it had been slow to see the cross-currents swelling just below the surface?

- Even Nokia, the Finnish wireless equipment maker that grew to become the world's largest manufacturer of mobile phones by skillfully riding uncertain and turbulent market conditions—and dodging occasional lightning strikes—found itself blindsided by the ephemeral wireless market. In June 2001 it suddenly halved its forecasts for growth in handset sales, projecting lower second-quarter profits, and its share price fell by 23 percent.[4] Is there any way it could have better prepared itself for this eventuality?

- The spectacular failure of Long-Term Capital Management (LTCM) in 1997 shows that even the brightest thinkers cannot fully anticipate the future.[5] In this case, Nobel Prize–winning economists teamed up with savvy Wall Street traders using sophisticated computer models, but a future they did not bank on came to pass. They were blindsided by an unusual confluence of circumstances outside their mental frames. The failure of LTCM was also perhaps the result of sheer hubris, an unreasonable confidence in the team's ability to outsmart the market. As this elite team learned the hard way, the market can behave less rationally than their sophisticated models assumed.[6] In the end, trading remains a very human business, fraught with the quirks and foibles that set us apart from machines.

So how do you come up with a plan B, and perhaps a plan C, when many uncertainties lurk around the corner? What will allow you to prepare for the lightning strikes or to capitalize on the gold strikes that occur with ever-increasing frequency in today's world? Uncertainty is ultimately the only source of superior profits, yet it entails a highly dangerous game. This game is where tremendous value is created—and destroyed. How can you profit from the upside of uncertainty while managing the downside? How can you position yourself to win, no matter what the future holds?

The point of these examples is not to deride the companies involved for poor planning under uncertainty. It is easy to see the right path today, with twenty-twenty hindsight, when we know for certain what future came to pass; it is much harder to chart the right course in the midst of rapid change and high uncertainty. The point of these examples is first of all to show that the stakes are high. As economist Frank Knight points out in the quotation that opens this chapter, significant profit and loss are found in uncertain times. Cisco and Nokia, as well as other companies such as Microsoft and Amazon, all built tremendous wealth by charting a course across choppy seas that swamped many other boats. When more traditional players—such as IBM, AT&T, and Sears—struggled, the new kids on the block seized the opportunity. As 19th-century British banker Nathan Rothschild observed, "Great fortunes are made when the cannonballs are falling in the harbor, not when the violins play in the ballroom."

The second point of the examples above is to underscore that often the future that most rapidly undermines a business is the one that its managers

Preparing for the Unthinkable: Surviving Enron's Collapse

What if Enron went away? When strategy consultant Roch Parayre posed this question during a scenario-planning workshop at the Enron Federal Credit Union in 1999, it seemed ludicrous.* "Nobody ever dreamed of Enron collapsing," observed Jack McAdoo, president and CEO of the credit union, in early 2002. "A year ago, we were in fast times. Everything Enron touched turned to gold." The credit union rode the wave, with deposits increasing by 20 percent per year over five years. When bonuses were paid in February 2001, the credit union booked $40 million in direct deposits in one night. Nonetheless, their 1999 scenarios entertained the possibility of "Starting Over" (the actual title of one of the four scenarios) even though everybody gave it very low weight.

By mid-2001, when Enron's stock price had fallen sharply, the "Starting Over" scenario started to get more weight. Then Enron released its numbers for the third quarter of 2001, sending the corporation into a tailspin. The credit union, even though it is a completely separate organization, was deeply affected. When Enron filed for bankruptcy on December 3, 2001, McAdoo and other senior managers spent five perilous days at a table in front of the Enron Federal Credit Union, reassuring members who snaked in a long line through the front door. The executives managed to prevent a full-scale run on the branch, but still lost $22 million, a third of their deposits.

McAdoo and other leaders were stunned by the precipitous downfall of the nation's seventh-largest corporation. But the scenario-based planning process, started at the credit union in 1999 and updated in the middle of 2001, allowed them to react quickly and effectively. "I think we would have been totally blindsided by this whole thing if we hadn't done scenario planning," McAdoo said. "We were better prepared when this happened. Not that we weren't in shock, but we would not have been in any position to weather the challenges of the storm that hit us literally overnight."

The shift in strategy that had already occurred as a result of exploring different scenarios is seen most dramatically in the kind of capabilities they deemed most important at the beginning and end of the process. In 1999, senior management believed that the most important capability for future success was the credit union's relationships with Enron. By 2001, after exploring diverse potential scenarios, including the one called "Start-

*Roch Parayre, Ph.D., is a Senior Fellow at the Wharton School's Mack Center for Technological Innovation and a strategy consultant with Decision Strategies International, Inc. He served as project leader for this DSI scenario-planning engagement.

ing Over," credit union leaders realized they had to expand their fields of membership. They recognized that their most important capabilities for the future concerned their relationship with customers. The credit union built systems to engage in needs analysis and targeted marketing. After Enron collapsed, these capabilities allowed the credit union to send out customized mailings to reassure former and current Enron employees about the absolute safety of their deposits, develop plans for marketing to other employee groups and work to lure back lost deposits. Credit union leaders also quickly ramped up to open a branch outside the Enron corporate offices, shelved plans to develop new branches in Enron office buildings, and started to develop a new independent brand name.

"The whole planning process opened our eyes to the fact that our future is not really that certain," McAdoo said. "We cannot predict where we are going to be in two years, three years, and five years. Although we didn't anticipate it perfectly, we were much better prepared thanks to scenario planning." As Parayre reflects on the roller-coaster ride of Enron, he is struck by the importance of developing unusual scenarios as well as the importance of close monitoring. Because the credit union had contemplated a world without Enron, admittedly with considerable disbelief at first, they were primed to recognize this reality faster once key indicators turned south and deal with it much more decisively than they would have otherwise.

fail to see or cannot imagine clearly enough to prepare for. It is well documented in behavioral decision research that we tend to become locked in our current frames, seeing what we are conditioned to see. Cisco may have seen things through rose-colored glasses long after the rest of the world had accepted that the U.S. economy was entering a downturn. As human beings, business leaders tend to be overconfident about their predictions of the future, especially if they have been successful in the recent past.

Why is it important to focus on uncertainty? First, it affects the part of the business that managers very often don't even try to manage—the external environment—and this is where much of the potential value of the business is created or destroyed. Second, the level of uncertainty in the business environment appears to be increasing significantly. And third, human beings have inherent limitations in dealing with uncertainty. To set the stage for the rest of the book, I'll explore each of these issues in more detail.

Leaving Half the Business to Fate

While managers concentrate most of their energies on the existing business, the management of external uncertainty may have far more potential for creating value. Studies across a wide variety of industries reveal that firm-specific actions account for just over half the value of a firm. About half of the variance in return on investment is attributable to general economic and industry conditions, as illustrated in Exhibit 1-1.[7] As we sometimes note (only half-jokingly) in our executive teaching programs, the surest way to managerial success is to find an industry in the early stage of a spectacular growth spurt and hang on for the ride. From there on, 80 percent of success is "showing up" (as Woody Allen dryly noted) and keeping your nose clean.

Many managers view the external environment as something beyond their control, like John Chambers's "100-year flood." But here they often adopt a double standard. They tend to take credit for all the good news

Exhibit 1-1: Half the Business Is Left to Fate

Typical Management Focus	Opportunities to Profit from Uncertainty		
		35%	**External Effects** (General Economic & Political Conditions, Plus Random Noise)
		10%	**Industry Effects**
		55%	**Firm-Specific Actions**
		(18%)	(Corporate Level)
		(37%)	(Business Unit Level)

Note: The percentages refer to how much of the variance in return on assets is due, on average, to various influences. The data reflect over 100 US manufacturing firms consisting of at least two strategic business units covering 160 industries.
Source: *Jaime Roquebert et al., "Markets vs. Management: What 'Drives' Profitability?"* Strategic Management Journal, *Vol. 17 (8), 1996.*

(as if they had much more control than they do) and blame most of the bad on the environment (as if they had no control). A study of *Fortune 500* quarterly reports found that in good quarters 79 percent of performance was attributed to internal factors—implying that success was due to what managers did. In bad quarters, however, 75 percent of the blame was attributed to external factors.[8]

Managers who can get better at managing this external uncertainty—learning how to protect against the downside and position for the upside—can start to harvest that half of the company's value that is otherwise left to the whim of the environment. Cisco's value was not lost because of poor operational management of its existing business. The company was one of the tightest real-time operations in the world, which many other firms sought to emulate. Cisco lost so much of its value because it was unable to effectively navigate the uncertainty of its environment, to see even the possibility of the "100-year flood" that washed it off course.

I am not saying that you can *control* the environment or *predict* the future. You can't. But all firms can learn how to *prepare* better for uncertainty and proactively manage the part of the business that they too often leave to fate. There is great leverage in improving how an organization assesses and negotiates the external environment. It will require, however, a change in mindset as well as the mastery of new approaches and tools.

In general, managers tend to look backward even though most of the new opportunities and threats for companies lie in the future. Informal surveys by Gary Hamel and C. K. Prahalad suggest that senior managers devote less than 3 percent of their time and energy to building a collective vision of the future.[9] The inherent uncertainty of the future makes people uncomfortable, and for a variety of reasons that we explore later in the book, people don't like to think about it much. Most of us prefer to stay within our comfort zone, which is the past and present. Looking backward feeds the illusion that our world is orderly and predictable; in hindsight things are so much clearer.[10]

Just consider where you are focusing your attention: Are you managing the relatively certain current business, or are you anticipating the uncertain possibilities and dangers of the future? Do you have a grasp of where the key uncertainties lie in your industry and beyond so you can profit from them if they occur? Through scenario planning, by placing yourself into the future and looking backward, you can actually increase your capacity to imagine the future. This ability to engage in prospective hindsight is increasingly important as the tide of uncertainty rises.[11]

Increasing Uncertainty

The rise in uncertainty is driven by a variety of factors. An ideological shift in politics and business from centralized planning toward free-market dynamics is resulting in much more complex socioeconomic systems. In addition, new technologies are accelerating change, often in a highly disruptive way.[12] Furthermore, profound demographic changes and value shifts are occurring. All these forces combined result in much greater complexity.

A simple chart of the fluctuations (the spread for each year divided by the mean) of the Nasdaq index indicates a strong increase in uncertainty over the past two decades, as shown in Exhibit 1-2. Relative volatility—when measured in terms of range—rose from 6 percent in 1984 to 74 percent in 2001.[13]

Individual stock prices also provide indication of rising volatility. Data collected by Susquehanna International Group, a large private options trading firm in Philadelphia, show that the implied volatility of individual stocks (as inferred from the observed price of call options) has greatly

Exhibit 1-2: Signs of Increasing Volatility of Nasdaq

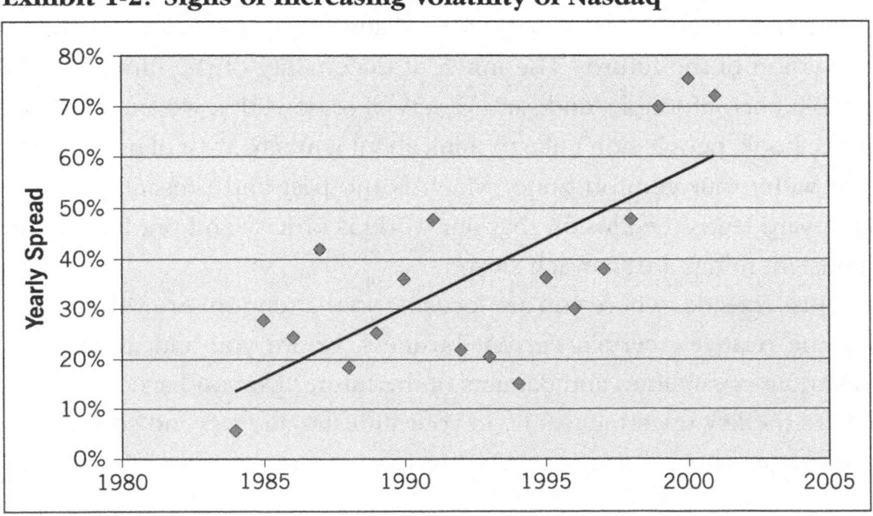

increased over the past decade.[14] A variety of indicators, from decreasing CEO tenure, compressed cycles of technology and new product development, increasing globalization, and regulatory change are also pointing to increased uncertainty.

The Nature of Uncertainty

It is not just the magnitude of uncertainty that creates challenges but also its shifting nature. As illustrated in Exhibit 1-3, there is a wide knowledge spectrum that ranges from certainty to chaos and ignorance. The left-hand side of the spectrum is the most manageable and amenable to analytic approaches. This is where great strides have been made in academia

Exhibit 1-3: A Shift Toward Greater Ambiguity

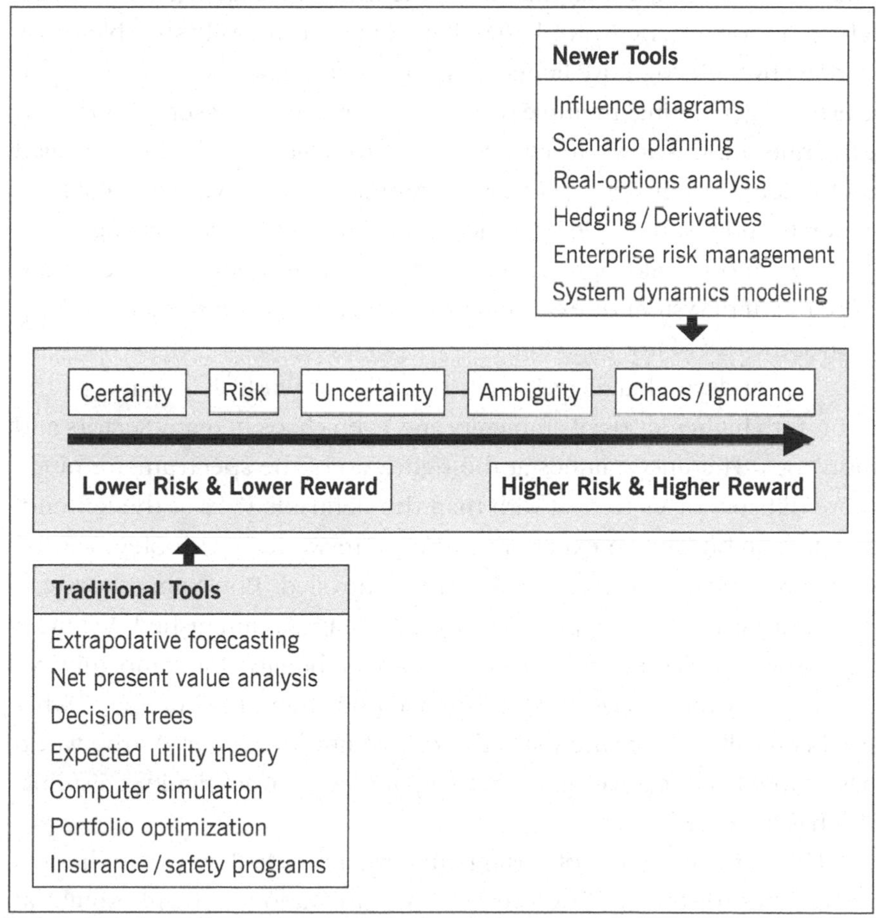

and industry, using such tools as decision trees, Bayesian statistics, expected utility theory, portfolio analysis, and Monte Carlo simulation (see Appendix B). In the middle of the spectrum we encounter ambiguity, for which our present tools and techniques are less well developed. Here we must rely more on creativity and learning than on analytic deduction. The challenge in the middle is less one of computational complexity than of cognition, to make sure that we frame the issues correctly and ask the right questions. Scenario planning, options thinking, and influence diagrams can be especially helpful here, as well as a healthy dose of humility about what is knowable.

At the far right we encounter terra incognita, like the prospect facing early explorers who sailed "off the end of the Earth." We don't really have very good tools yet to manage chaos and ignorance. Without a clear structure and good data, it is hard to tackle the problem analytically. And when left to our own devices, we know that humans can easily stumble or be trapped by their cognitive limitations. On the far right, the focus has to be more on generating multiple views, surfacing deep assumptions, and exploring the unknown terrain. Systems dynamic modeling has proved useful here since it helps portray our mental models. Also, the ability to generate and test multiple hypotheses quickly to enhance learning is key. And even more philosophical approaches, such as identifying the nature of our inquiry system or examining the structure of arguments, can help reduce the risk of not knowing.[15]

Our modern challenge is that, overall, the world is moving to the right, with higher levels of ambiguity and even chaos in many sectors and industries. The uncertainties at the right end of the spectrum are much more difficult for us to deal with than the definable risks at the left end. The less ambiguity we experience, the more we feel a problem can be structured, managed, planned for, and controlled. But competitors can do this as well, so the opportunity for advantage is diminished. We must learn how to welcome and indeed embrace ambiguity. With ambiguity we face not only the risk of the decision itself but something deeper—what has been called *epistemic* risk—the risk of not knowing.[16] As the world has moved from relative certainty to higher levels of ambiguity, epistemic risk has increased.

This environment of rising uncertainty challenges traditional approaches to strategy. The provocative observation by Frank Knight at

Sources of Superior Profit

Where do superior profits come from? Over the years, researchers have proposed a number of different views.[17]

1. Structural Advantage Profit stems from having a superior hand of cards that allows a firm to exploit its structural advantage. This advantage can be in the form of having cheaper supplies, lower-cost manufacturing, loyal customers, valuable intellectual property, superior management, strategic partnerships, channel control, excellent brands, or even privileged relationships with governments or regulators. Michael Porter's well-known work on strategy falls within this realm.[18] Frank Knight and others, however, recognized a key point: most competitive advantages are short-lived. As hypercompetition has taken hold in many markets, industrial giants such as General Motors, AT&T, Sears, and even IBM were brought to their knees by competitors who eroded their advantages.[19] They sought to identify other sources of superior profits.

2. Operational Excellence Profit here stems not from a better hand of cards but from a superior ability to play any hand of cards. The source here is organizational, ranging from process reengineering to cross-functional teams to agile organizational forms to a learning culture. Once hypercompetition became the norm and eroded structural advantage for many firms, attention shifted to doing a few things very well (such as focusing on core competencies). Southwest Airlines has been a master of operational excellence, creating distinctive systems and processes that allowed it to succeed in the very competitive airline industry.

3. Business Reinvention After operational excellence was increasingly mastered and started to yield diminishing marginal returns, the next source of profit was changing the game. Major external changes, such as deregulation, globalization, and new technologies, created new opportunities for those willing to take a fresh look at their business. For example, CNN reinvented broadcasting, using cable and twenty-four-hour news. Prahalad and Hamel especially highlighted the need to "compete for the future."[20]

4. Profiting from Uncertainty Whereas business reinvention may be occasioned by a new state of nature or an external shock, such as deregulation or genomics, it seems that we are now entering an unprecedented phase of continuous quantum change. Instead of occurring once every decade or so, reinvention may be the order of each day. In that case, companies that learn faster how to continuously manage and navigate uncertainty, in all its guises and forms, may reap superior profits as long as they stay ahead of the curve. How to do so is the focus of this book.

The above sources of profit are not mutually exclusive, and they overlap. Internal control systems that lead to operational excellence can turn into a structural advantage. Or a business reinvention, such as online shopping, can result in superior execution. At different times and depending on the industry, firms will emphasize different sources. But it is a safe bet that improving the management of uncertainty can be an important source of profit or, at a minimum, prevent the destruction of firm value.

the opening of this chapter—that uncertainty is the only true source of profit—may at first seem counterintuitive. After all, companies derive profits from specialized assets such as brand names, superior products, patents, and efficient manufacturing. Knight, an economist in the 1930s at the University of Chicago who helped shape that institution's distinctive school of economic thought, drew a sharp distinction between risk and uncertainty. In his view, the former can be anticipated and priced in competitive markets—like life insurance risks—and thus any profits associated therewith are competed away. Uncertainty, on the other hand, concerns the unforeseeable elements in markets, and by definition those things are not fully priced or factored into a firm's decisions. Assuming a competitive market, in the long run everything gets competed away except these unanticipated aspects. They alone are left when the carnage of full competition is completed. And they alone explain why some firms end up winners and others end up losers, at least according to Knight. This represents a different view of the sources of superior profit than those of the traditional schools of strategy, which focus on structural advantage, operational excellence, or business reinvention (see box).

While Knight viewed the ultimate source of profit to be random, beyond the control of companies, this book advances a different view. I propose that firms can shift the boundaries of what they control and don't, through superior anticipation, flexible strategies, and dynamic monitoring. I believe that firms can be favored by chance and that you can design organizations that profit from, or perhaps even create, serendipity. If all firms were to master these skills equally, then Knight is right and only luck would set them apart. But that is unlikely to happen in our lifetime.

Our Difficulty with Uncertainty

This rising tide of uncertainty—and ambiguity—exacerbates some existing human limitations. Humans face some inherent obstacles when it comes to handling uncertainty. Years of behavioral research have identified a variety of pitfalls that we encounter in addressing uncertainty and ambiguity.[21] Our limitations (described in more detail in Appendix A) fall into two broad categories, relating to how we perceive risks and how we act on them. In a nutshell, we tend to have *myopic eyes* and *timid souls.*

Our myopic eyes see only a limited range of uncertainties out there. Failures of imagination in envisioning future pathways, anchoring on current estimates, and overweighing readily available information all feed our tendency toward overconfidence.[22] We are often "frame blind," meaning that we don't easily recognize our implicit assumptions and we have difficulty challenging our mental models (discussed in Chapter 2). We suffer from skewed attention, giving more weight to the automobile accidents in the daily headlines than to the less visible but more deadly risk of cancer. And we suffer from high sensitivity to context effects, so our answers to questions change based on how the questions are posed. For example, people are much more likely to wear seatbelts if the chance of being in a car accident is expressed as a 30 percent probability in fifty years than if it is expressed as a 0.001 percent probability per trip, even though these statements are statistically equivalent.[23]

In addition to our cognitive myopia, we tend to have timid souls, preferring the sure option over a riskier course, even if the expected payoff is higher.[24] One reason is that we are more sensitive to losses than to gains: few of us would volunteer to flip a fair coin for $1,000. This risk aversion persists even if we are offered a sure $100 just for trying. People also dislike ambiguity, preferring a well-defined risk to a better but more ambiguous one.[25] Finally, we suffer from an isolation bias. We look at each uncertainty in separation from others and may not recognize the full portfolio. Many would judge an accountant who invests in bonds to be more risk averse than a business person owning stocks—until we learn that the accountant is an avid bungee jumper. We seldom look at the whole picture.

These limitations of myopic eyes and timid souls mean that we navigate uncertain environments with much the same difficulty that pilots face in flying through rain and fog. We can no longer rely upon our vision and instinct. We need, instead, to turn to more sophisticated tools and frameworks to guide us through the murkiness of uncertainty. These frameworks and tools, described in the remaining chapters of this book and summarized on the top right of Exhibit 1-3, can augment our limited human capabilities in addressing uncertainty. For example, a study of managers who used scenario planning showed that merely laying out alternative scenarios significantly reduced their overconfidence bias.[26]

While I refer to tools listed in Exhibit 1-3 throughout the book, my focus here is not primarily on delving into the technical details of these tools. My goal is to consider the broader shift in mindset, frameworks, and processes that are required to effectively plan amid uncertainty. Managers need to change their view of and organizational approach to uncertainty. Instead of trying to control and master it, they should explore, navigate, and exploit uncertainty when the time is ripe. This is the premise underlying the framework, methodology, and management philosophy expressed in this book.

Without this broader context, the specific tools for addressing uncertainty are much less valuable. I describe the available tools in more detail in Appendix B and also refer the reader to Hugh Courtney's book *20/20 Foresight* as an excellent starting point for exploring these tools and when to apply them.[27]

Why Not Just Trust Your Instinct?

Given the difficulty of anticipating the future in an environment of high uncertainty, some managers choose to move forward on gut or instinct. This can be very attractive, because human intuition often lets you cut through a lot of complexity when making decisions. But while this approach may be appealing in an increasingly complex environment, it also presents a real danger.

The danger is that our instincts may be wrong. Our instincts, by and large, are based upon our *past* experiences. This is what makes a seasoned manager so valuable to an organization—the ability to get right to the heart of the matter and know what to do. To the extent that the future environment will be like the past, our instincts often serve us well.[28] But an environment of disruption and uncertainty makes it very likely that the future *will not* be like the past. In a changed world, our old instincts and past experience can sometimes be worse than no experience at all.

For example, in the September 11 terrorist attacks of 2001, the experience and training of flight crew and passengers all pointed to complying with terrorist demands and not offering resistance. Based on past experience, this was the right thing to do. But the attacks fell outside of past experience. The passengers on the United Airlines flight that crashed in western Pennsylvania realized that they were in the middle of a very different scenario after speaking to family and friends by cell phone. Based on this insight, they were able to take heroic actions to stop the terrorists. Passengers and crew on subsequent flights have also been able to act out of this new experience and change their "instinct" for dealing with threats on board planes. But could this experience and new instinct have been gained before the initial tragedies?

This leads us to a very important use of scenarios—exploring the future in order to develop a new set of instincts. The purpose of developing scenarios is not to pinpoint the future, but rather to experience it. (I cannot stress this enough. Many well-grounded managers still view scenario planning as a process of determining what is going to happen. They reach the end of the planning process with the wrong question: Which scenario are we going to pick? This misses the point of preparing for *multiple* futures. Scenario planning is not really about planning but about changing people's mindsets to allow faster learning and smarter actions.)

The process of developing scenarios is one of gaining *experience* in a simulated future. Just as you build instinct in stable environments through past experience, you build an instinct about future environments by living through different scenarios. It is similar to what happens to a soldier in boot camp. What if you are lost in the middle of a hostile territory? What if you are under attack? What if you have to make an assault on a secure position? The goal is to hone the instincts of the soldiers. They will never face the exact scenarios they live through in training, but these anticipatory experiences develop their reflexes and skills for the future. An important difference, however, is that boot camp presents a fairly routine set of experiences whereas the scenarios generated through the planning process should be far from routine.

When you feel the future deep in your bones, you gain a set of instincts that allow you to respond quickly and effectively to new challenges as they unfold. The process enlarges the repertoire of responses available to managers based on superior pattern recognition. In an uncertain and changing environment, faster learning is the only lasting source of competitive advantage, and scenario planning is a powerful way to accomplish this elusive goal.[29]

A Compass for the Future

One of the basic laws of cybernetics holds that as the external environment becomes more complex, systems need to become more complex as well to prosper.[30] A simple thermostat, with a basic reactive feedback loop mechanism, can maintain room temperature at the desired level provided the changes in the room's airflow are not too complex. But if many people move in and out of the room, if windows are opened and closed, and if multiple heat ducts are present, this simple device just will not do. The greater aerodynamic complexity in the room will require a more sophisticated control system, with multiple sensors, predictive intelligence, and automated vent controls. What holds for living organisms and machines also holds for organizations. Complex challenges require greater sophistication.

Instead of cutting down the world to fit our problem-solving ability, we need to increase the sophistication of our own decision making. It used to be, in the words of F. Scott Fitzgerald, that the "test of a first-rate intelligence" was the capacity to hold two opposing ideas in the mind at the same time and still function.[31] Today we need to be able to hold three or four conflicting views of the world in our collective mind, while still being able to function adroitly. Tools and frameworks can help us in this process.

Finding a Compass

In his book *The Riddle of the Compass,* Amir D. Aczel argues that the development of the compass and other navigational tools led to great prosperity in medieval Europe. At the end of the 13th century, with the widespread use of the compass in maritime navigation, "the world saw a dramatic rise in trade, and with it, increased prosperity for maritime powers such as Venice, Spain, and Britain. A single invention—the magnetic compass—made this possible." As a pioneer in shipbuilding and applying the compass to navigation, Venice grew from a small fishing community to one of the largest and most prosperous cities in western Europe, with a larger population than the city of Paris. The compass opened the door to the Age of Exploration, as explorers such as Columbus and Magellan were able to make their way across uncharted seas around the globe.[32]

Like these early explorers, managers today face uncharted seas. Unprecedented technological innovations, global geopolitical threats, and economic swings may cause some managers to hug the coastline. They may fear, with good reason, that it is too dangerous to chart a bold course across those choppy seas. But with the right tools, we have an opportunity to move ahead confidently and dynamically into the unknown, even without a fixed set of stars to point the way.

The approaches presented in this book—including scenario planning, key success factors, robustness analysis, strategic vision, options thinking, and dynamic monitoring—are intended to serve as a new compass for navigating today's uncertain business environment.

The Nuclear Age and the Rise of Scenarios

Scenario planning arose in response to increasing complexity and uncertainty. It is perhaps not surprising that the first awakenings of scenario planning were by-products of one of the most complexity-fraught initiatives of our age: the Manhattan Project. The development of nuclear weapons posed some of the most tangled technological and moral challenges ever faced by our civilization. Even the science involved was far from straightforward.

In 1944 some scientists feared that detonating nuclear weapons might ignite the Earth's atmosphere, sending the entire planet into fiery oblivion. This in itself was a troubling scenario, but as the scientists struggled with it, they realized something even more frightening: they could not determine the chance of this happening. They first tried to solve the problem through analytic means, by trying to work out very complex heat exchange equations, but this approach proved intractable. So instead they turned to a set of simulation models and subjected them to different inputs. In effect, their computers calculated millions of different futures and based on this they concluded that the probability that the atmosphere would burst into flames was very low. Fortunately for humankind, they were right.

Like large-scale computing, which was originally created to determine ballistics trajectories, the tools created for the military were soon churning away at peacetime applications in business. Herman Kahn at the RAND Corporation is credited with applying social systems theory to create the first scenarios for the future. The Club of Rome issued dire scenarios of ecological and population disasters that riveted attention and reshaped public opinion. Pierre Wack established Royal Dutch/Shell as a center for the development and dissemination of corporate scenarios. Shell has used scenarios since 1969 as part of its process for generating and evaluating strategic options,[33] helping to make the company consistently better in its oil price projections than other major oil companies. Applications of scenario planning have since been wide ranging in business and politics.

Articles by Pierre Wack, Peter Schwartz's *The Art of the Long View,* and a variety of other works have excited managers about the prospects for using scenarios in their own planning.[34] But the actual practice of building scenarios is much more problematic, and the ability to integrate them into a systematic planning process for creating, implementing, and continuously updating strategy is particularly difficult in large organizations.

A Systematic Process

I had the pleasure of working with Arie de Geus, Kees van der Heijden, Peter Schwartz, Pierre Wack, and other leaders of scenario planning at Royal Dutch/Shell during an extended sabbatical from the University of Chicago in the early 1980s. As I later helped other companies with scenario-based strategic planning, however, I came face to face with the challenges of transferring this process beyond Shell's gifted individual practitioners. Over time I developed a more systematic framework for building scenarios and integrating them into an end-to-end process for strategy development and implementation.

Scenarios are just part of a more extended framework for exploring what it will take to win in the future and for implementing those strategies effectively. Scenarios also are only a means to an end. While they can be as captivating and creative as an engrossing novel, we need to be careful. Sometimes, in the heat of the process, managers become enticed by a given view of the future. They use scenarios to predict *the* future rather than exploring *multiple* futures. This is why disciplined analysis and multiple perspectives are so important in this process. Like Ulysses, we need to listen to the siren song of the future but tie ourselves to the mast so we don't end up on the rocks of one scenario. Accepting any given scenario as *the* future—or making the pursuit of a single future your goal—is the surest way to end up stranded in the wrong future. For the process to work, both imagination and discipline must be combined.

The broader approach described in this book, summarized in Exhibit 1-4, incorporates scenarios into a framework for understanding the strategies we need to pursue today to be successful in the future. We use scenarios to envision the future and embrace uncertainty. We then identify

Exhibit 1-4: Strategic Compass

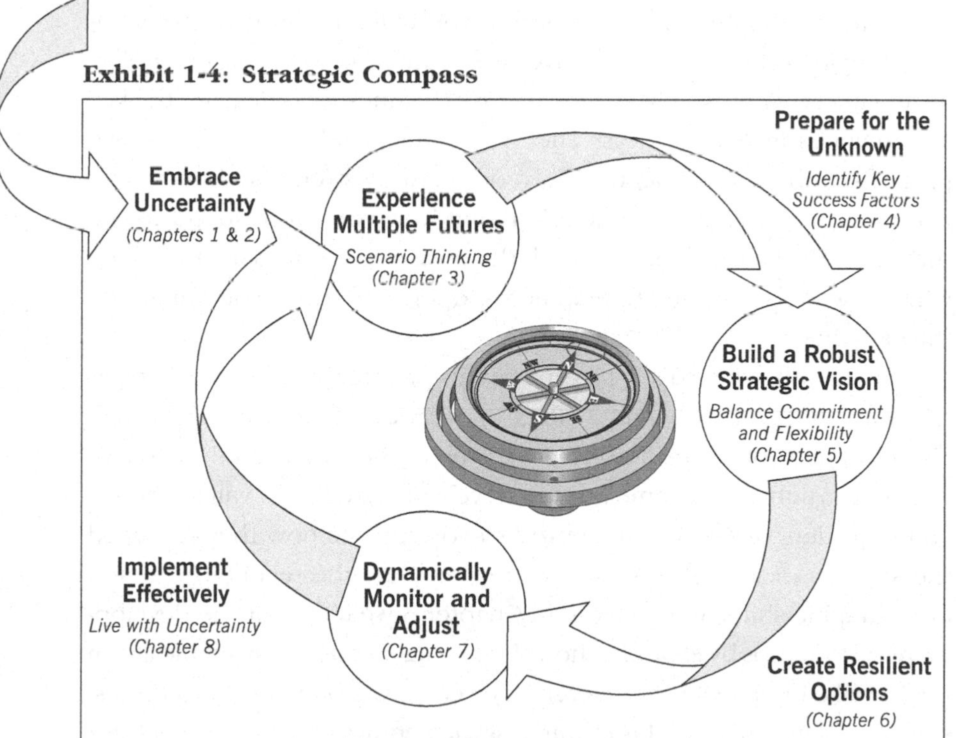

key success factors across the various scenarios and use them as a basis for a strategic vision. The vision in turn is used to generate strategic options. Managers then continue to monitor the ever-changing environment to test and adapt their strategies, and finally they effectively implement the strategies and options. This, in a nutshell, is how managers can profit from uncertainty.

My approach is more than a process for planning. It entails a profound shift in perspective. Managers often see uncertainty as an evil that detracts from an organization's ability to generate profits in the future. Companies have spent millions of dollars on gathering the information they need to reduce uncertainty. They base their investments on net present value calculations or hurdle rates that assume the world will be reasonably predictable, even in the face of solid evidence that it will be highly uncertain. We continue to look for Newtonian precision in a Heisenberg world of quantum uncertainties. (There are, however, promising developments in how organizations address risks and uncertainty—see box.)

Instead of trying to fit this complex world into a narrow box—essentially lopping off complexity to *make* it fit—my approach takes complexity and uncertainty as a given. First you ask the question: What are the key uncertainties in our business? Then you immediately ask: How can we profit from those uncertainties given our existing strengths? Uncertainty is no longer the enemy. You aren't asking how you can respond to the threat of the Internet—or beat back the invasion. You instead are asking what new doors these developments open and how you might go through them.

On the following pages, I'll explore this path to profiting from uncertainty in more detail. Chapter 2 offers an overview of the process through the examples of a small German travel agency that used scenario-planning insights to become a major travel software firm. I will introduce you to leaders of *The Miami Herald* so you can see how they reshaped the strategy of a large, established firm to meet the technological and demographic shifts in its region. In Chapter 3 we'll look at the development of scenarios by exploring how the manager of a pharmaceutical firm might wake up in two very different futures. In Chapter 4, using a discussion of polar explorers, I'll examine what companies need to pack for their journey (Key Success Factors for the future) when they can't be sure

Beyond Risk Management

The developing field of enterprise risk management (ERM) has made great strides in taking a more holistic perspective of uncertainty in organizations. For companies that have already invested in creating ERM systems, the approaches discussed in this book can deepen this work by giving more attention to the upside opportunities of uncertainty (in addition to downside risks) and addressing less easily quantified forms of uncertainty.

Businesses have a long history of risk management dating back at least as far as the maritime insurance developed for sailing ships in the 17th century.* The tools of risk management have become increasingly sophisticated in addressing financial risks. In recent times, the development of enterprise risk management has created an even broader focus, addressing operational and even strategic risks across the entire organization. It pays attention to issues such as improving internal communication, information sharing and coordinated action in managing risk. Two separate streams of risk management, namely insurance and corporate finance, are starting to merge.†

Nonetheless, ERM still has several areas of weakness. First, because of its origin in risk management, it focuses primarily on managing the downside risk. It pays much less attention to the *opportunities* that can be created from uncertainty. A truly integrated approach would examine both the upside as well as the downside risk. The ERM decision maker often views risks as a given, considering them by-products of strategic and operational decisions already taken or about to be made. New risks (such as hedges or derivatives) are usually created to better manage the existing portfolio of risks, and a price is paid to third parties to shift or transfer risk. Within this approach, risk is not viewed as a source of profit but as potential danger to be controlled.

Second, as it is currently practiced, ERM focuses mostly on risks that are easily quantified, such as financial and operational risks. A survey of 200 senior finance and risk management executives by MCC Enterprise Risk and the Economist Intelligent Unit found, however, that 53 percent

---

* For a historical overview, managers may wish to read Peter L. Bernstein's marvelous book *Against the Gods: The Remarkable Story of Risk* (New York: John Wiley, 1996). Scholars may prefer Ian Hacking, *The Emergence of Probability* (London: Cambridge University Press, 1975) and Stephen M. Stigler, *The History of Statistics* (Cambridge, MA: Harvard University Press, 1986).

† For an excellent overview of the state-of-the art in this field, see Neil A. Doherty, *Integrated Risk Management: Techniques and Strategies for Managing Corporate Risk,* 2000.

identified the inability to measure intangible risks as a major problem with their ERM strategies.‡ Examples of such intangibles are damage to a firm's brand, regulatory changes, competitive actions, technological innovation, and changes in business climate.

The approach outlined in this book offers the potential to extend ERM by emphasizing the profit-generating potential of uncertainty. It is focused not only on managing or controlling risk but also on navigating and exploiting uncertainty. In addition, because this approach is scenario-based and qualitative (although there are ample opportunities to build quantitative models), it is not limited to addressing easily quantified risks.

In this way, it can be used to enhance an organization's ERM initiatives. At the same time, the systems companies have developed for risk assessment and monitoring as part of ERM can be valuable in developing scenarios and even strategies for profiting from uncertainty.

‡ *Enterprise Risk Management,* The Economist Intelligence Unit Ltd, 2001. My thanks to Clinton T. Brass, a Wharton MBA student, for pointing out some key connections with ERM.

where they will land. In Chapter 5 we'll examine how these scenarios and Key Success Factors can form the basis of a coherent vision. We'll explore the challenges Monsanto faced with its bold vision of a shift to life sciences. In Chapter 6 we'll discuss how an online startup in the utilities business kept its options open in an environment of change. We'll then explore how companies can create and assess flexible strategic options. In Chapter 7 we'll meet with leaders of a successful options-trading firm, who have built a profitable business by recognizing patterns in the environment better than their peers. We'll consider a variety of approaches for dynamic monitoring. In Chapter 8 we'll examine strategies and pitfalls of implementation, drawing upon the experience of a number of companies, including DuPont and Royal Dutch/Shell. Finally, in Chapter 9 I'll pull all these approaches together to look at how the board and top management of the Hughes Aircraft Employees Federal Credit Union redesigned their business, their vision, their capabilities, and even their name to fly through the turbulence of defense downsizing, technological revolutions, and financial services deregulation.

In an environment of increasing ambiguity, the risks of ignoring uncertainties are greater than the risks of tackling them head-on. And the rewards of actively addressing and mastering uncertainty may be greater than ever. More than any other capability, the skill of addressing uncertainty is one of the key metacompetencies companies need to achieve future success. It will help ensure that you are prepared when that lightning bolt of opportunity or disaster descends from the heavens, as it surely will at some time or other in the future.

Chapter 2

Preparing the Mind

"Where observation is concerned, chance favors only the prepared mind."
—LOUIS PASTEUR

Like many young entrepreneurs, Louis Arnitz wanted to start a business when he graduated from college in 1977. He had worked at a travel agency as a student, so he set up his own agency on Opernplatz in Frankfurt, Germany. But unlike many travel agency owners, Louis Arnitz ultimately saw a bigger future. It was a vision that led him to use new Internet technology to create a thriving corporate travel software company that rose to a market value of 1 billion deutsche marks after going public in 1999. How did he see and act on this possibility?

Arnitz first participated in a scenario-planning process at the Wharton School in the fall of 1994 as one of several dozen corporate travel agents who were members of Woodside Travel Trust, a global network of travel agencies offering special airline, hotel, cruise, and car packages. Arnitz's business was one of countless small travel agencies around the world confronted with the challenges of caps on airline commissions and more efficient booking models. Through a chance booking of a European rock band tour, his agency, Flugbüro am Opernplatz (FAO), had become Europe's leading agency for booking rock band tours, including a monumental 125-day tour by Tina Turner in 1989. This led to making arrangements for corporate sponsors, which in turn brought him into the thriving corporate travel business. But his fifteen-person business was just about to begin its greatest rise.

The scenario-planning session at the Wharton School, which was Arnitz's first systematic planning process for his company, didn't immediately lead to a shift in direction. It did, however, open his mind to new possibilities. Arnitz organized a follow-up scenario-planning session for his own management team in the summer of 1995 in Barcelona. There he and his staff came up with a radically new vision of the future: corporate travelers would be able to book flights on their own. At the time they came up with this "book it yourself" model, the Internet was barely on the radar screen. Netscape was ramping up for its IPO, and CompuServe was the leading commercial service offering access to the Internet.

"We figured out that, in reality, people should be able to book their travel by themselves. We felt this concept was very compelling," said Arnitz, now forty-three, at a trendy café near his winter retreat in Miami's South Beach. With his dark hair brushed back from a broad forehead, he is tanned, with engaging green eyes, covered today by sunglasses after corrective laser surgery.

When Arnitz developed this vision, he knew what he was looking for. "A couple of months later, we gained access to the Internet for the first time. It was clear that this was the network," he said. "When the Internet came out, the scenario we had looked at became real."

Even then, however, the future was very uncertain. There were just faint stirrings of impending change out there, and no one really understood where this new technology would lead. Indeed, there was great uncertainty about what, if anything, would develop, and even more about what this new technological innovation would do to the travel industry. "People were talking about 'the Internet' as if there was going to be a 'Ministry of Internet' or a 'Mr. Internet,'" Arnitz recalled. "The prevailing idea was that the Internet was going to do your job. If you sold books, the Internet would sell them. If you sold cars, the Internet would sell them. If you sold travel, the Internet would sell it. Gradually people realized, however, that someone has to sit in the driver's seat here because the Internet is only a vehicle. In 1995 very few people looked at it this way, but we did."

As they looked more closely, this future also was disturbing. "In the process, we realized the Internet was going to be helpful in automating the contact not between the consumer and the travel agent but rather between the consumer and the vendor. We understood as a travel agency that we would not be a player in the Internet game. We had this great vision for the future, but we would not be a part of it unless we changed."

And change they did. They realized that they could create a new type of service by developing software to aid corporate clients in making online travel bookings. Arnitz didn't initially bet the company on this scenario of "book your own" travel. But he kept moving steadily ahead of the pack, creating options for the future that would allow him to move quickly as the technology emerged and was adopted. FAO opened a website in 1995 and the next year became the first company in Germany to take online bookings. Arnitz took more than a year, from early 1995 to the summer of 1996, to explore the new vision before he figured out what to do and how to position the company. As he worked with the idea, he steadily increased the bench strength of his programming staff, started developing software, and watched industry developments. At the time of the decision to go full-steam ahead in 1997, about a quarter of FAO's forty-person staff was involved in programming or related technology. By the end of the decade, the company—renamed i:FAO—had more than 110 employees, with about seventy working in the technology division.

It was not until the middle of 1997, when the Internet was much more of a sure thing, that Arnitz dove in headfirst. To do so, he also had to rethink his approach to financing, in a country in which venture capital was labeled with the somewhat derogatory term "risk capital." With a major infusion of capital from British investors, he moved the company aggressively into creating software for online business bookings.

His scenario planning again came in handy when Arnitz had to sell the company's vision of the future of travel to investors. The IPO in March 1999 started at a valuation of more than $100 million and climbed to over $250 million in its first year.

A Blurry Vision

As we sat together in that Miami Beach café, it seemed natural for Arnitz, who had undergone laser eye surgery that morning, to use the analogy of vision to describe the impact of scenario planning on his thinking. "The most important benefit of scenario planning from my point of view is that when you do it, you get a blurry picture permanently in your head, which consists of the many different parts of the scenarios you've developed and the drivers. It is all there, but it is still very blurry. Once a little portion of one scenario becomes reality, then this blurry picture becomes very crisp instantaneously."

Like laser vision correction? "Almost," he said with a smile, "but it doesn't require a procedure. You recognize something as being part of a much bigger whole very, very quickly, and that gives you a big advantage. That to me is the point. I think the value is that you have all the pieces in mind and no plan yet. Then, suddenly, when a little bit more of the puzzle is revealed, you quickly comprehend it and have the opportunity to react first or at least to be a very fast follower."

Today Arnitz continues to prepare for new futures. He has held follow-up planning retreats in Berlin and the Florida Keys with a new American partner, Trip.com. His new "blurry vision" is a sense that the complicated forms that characterize online travel today will be swept away by a point-and-click visual interface. Pictures will replace forms, mouseclicks will replace keyboards, and calendars will replace date fields—opening the experience to many people who do not have the time for reading or typing. This "traveler of the future" was envisioned already in the i:FAO 1999 annual report:

> Imagine: Our traveler of the future has to travel to London on a business assignment. He opens the calendar on his computer desktop and clicks on next Wednesday. He uses his mouse to drag the date over the travel icon and drops it there. The travel software is automatically launched and opens with a map of Europe. He clicks on London and the software, connected to more than 700 airlines through the Internet, returns a list of available flights, flagged by company preference. Another click secures a seat on the 8 A.M. service. One more click on Thursday, and the intelligent booking software automatically displays return flights for his selection.
>
> As soon as the traveler has made these choices, the application displays a city map of London, pinpointing the corporation's headquarters and several other important points of interest. More so, the software also displays hotels on the city map that fit two criteria: They are approved by corporate travel policy and have rooms available. Upon contact with the cursor, the little hotel icons open a window which displays name, rate, facilities and amenities of the selected property. Upon a single click a room is booked.
>
> The application returns a complete travel itinerary and at the same

time performs a number of transactions in the background. These transactions secure the traveler's preferred seat and meal, take care of payment procedures and enlist in frequent traveler programs. The traveler is not bothered by these transactions—they are all controlled by his detailed profile, which is governed by the corporate profile his online system uses. The traveler drops the itinerary onto the calendar for future reference and e-mails several copies to other staff members, his contacts in London and to his family.

Upon request, the online system will start a special agent software that will pull together a "Smart Itinerary" for his trip. This itinerary will contain recent currency exchange rates, weather forecasts, a map of the hotel's vicinity and up-to-date information on cultural and sports events. It will be automatically e-mailed to him in good time for his trip.

With projections that $38 billion in travel will be booked online by 2003 in the United States alone, the realization of this vision could offer i:FAO a path to a very profitable future. Arnitz isn't sure exactly how this vision will play out or what new shifts will come along that will create additional twists on the story. But when this new future arrives—in whatever form—he'll know it when he sees it. "It is a different blurry image right now," he said. "But at some point in time, it may become crisp again." And when it does, his mind will be prepared to profit from this chance before others do. This edge in the speed of recognition is crucial in a fast-changing and uncertain world, where the only sustainable source of competitive advantage is faster organizational learning.

Breaking the Stalemate in Mature Organizations

Preparing a gifted individual mind such as Louis Arnitz's is an easier challenge than reshaping the thinking of a large organization. Established firms are encumbered by their traditions and often suffer from inertia. The venerable *Miami Herald* is a case in point. This organization was deeply steeped in tradition and past success: it was as unchanging as its looming marble-walled offices. The production of a metropolitan newspaper is a gritty ink-on-paper business designed to fire off hundreds of thousands of daily editions onto waiting doorsteps with the efficiency and rapidity of a combustion engine. Yet at its heart it has always been about more than business: it has been about uncovering the truth and serving the community. It has, in short, been an institution, and institutions are not easily transformed.

This institution faced a hurricane of change and uncertainty during the decade of the 1990s. Like other papers, *The Miami Herald* faced problems of rising newsprint costs and declining circulation, rapid shifts in technology and new competitive realities. But the *Herald* also faced fundamental changes in the demographics of its community, with Hispanics rising to more than half the population of Miami.

By the mid-1990s, the company was against the ropes, under attack from within and without. In 1997 *Time* magazine commented that the *Herald,* once the most profitable newspaper in the Knight-Ridder empire, was "a shell of its former self." Between 1985 and 1989 *Miami Herald* circulation fell by more than 13 percent. Turnover in the newsroom was high, and morale was low. The situation looked so bleak that when Knight-Ridder decided in 1998 to move its corporate offices from the *Herald* building in Miami to San Jose, California, there were rumors that the paper might be put up for sale.

The company's inability to make a decision about spinning off the Spanish-language edition, *El Nuevo Herald,* was the poster child of its numerous dilemmas. The Spanish-language newspaper had been an insert to the *Herald* since its inception in 1976. Establishing a separate publication appeared to be the future for reaching the region's growing Spanish-speaking audience. Yet its introduction would clearly cannibalize circulation for *The Miami Herald* at a time when it could ill afford to lose subscribers and advertisers (who desire reach and penetration). The company spent two decades debating the decision. It was such a complex and gut-wrenching decision that it even became the subject of a 1994 Harvard Business School case.[1]

The company instituted a series of initiatives designed to shape a new vision—which its peers in the press derided as a sign of desperation, and some felt the company was selling its soul. It struggled with inertia, both internally and in the industry. "We're getting shelled in a 'culture war,' pitting those willing to change vs. those who will never change," publisher David Lawrence wrote in a 1996 article. "The resisters are powerful. They blame most of our problems on corporate coin changers. However convenient that may be to say, our challenge is far more complex."[2]

Organizations like this one tend to eat strategic consultants alive (or keep them alive, depending on your perspective). A string of consultants were paraded into the spacious *Miami Herald* headquarters building, lined up against the wall, and promptly gunned down. Each time it was harder for management to build faith in the process. Different factions became deadlocked—editorial on one side, commercial on the other. Processes that take an internal focus are guaranteed to inevitably become bogged down in navel staring, finger pointing, and endless debates.

The best antidote to us-against-us battles is to look outward, so that the struggle becomes us-against-the-world. The value of scenario planning is that it begins by looking outward. Managers begin to contemplate how and why the world is changing, and to think about how they need to recreate their organization to meet these new challenges and opportunities. Different groups need to see that they are in the same boat—and that it is either sailing out of port or sinking. This is the perspective that is encouraged by the scenario-planning process.

In 1997, *The Miami Herald* embarked on a scenario-planning process (as discussed in more detail in Chapter 3).[3] The scenarios were initially built around two key uncertainties, namely whether technology would disintermediate the newspaper and whether the growing Hispanic population in greater Miami would erode the reader base. Then other key uncertainties and trends were added in to create four starkly different images of the future. The initial scenarios were discussed with the employees as well as readers of the newspaper. Managers wrestled with issues such as: What if the Latin American economies collapse and as a result trade all but halts? What would things look like if those same economies blossomed? What might happen if the Internet took over the news business or if "disintermediation" were more gradual? And what will happen to Miami when Fidel Castro dies?

Different answers to these and other questions presented *Miami Herald* managers with four very different views of the world (as shown in Exhibit 2-1). Here they are in a nutshell:

- *Hong Kong of the Americas:* In 2005 Miami's reputation as the northernmost city in Latin America is widely accepted. Because Latin American economies are enjoying a mild boom, Miami's economy is also on the upswing. The firmly established Latin community in Miami attracts

Exhibit 2-1: Deeper Structure of *Miami Herald* Scenarios

		SOUTH FLORIDA'S ECONOMY?	
		Upturn	**Downturn**
DISINTER-MEDIATION?	**Low**	Hong Kong of the Americas	Falling Behind in the New Century
	High	The New World Order	To Have and To Have Not

upper-crust Latin Americans and their money. While the Internet has grown in acceptance and availability, it remains something of a niche medium. Most people still turn to the newspaper, radio, or TV for information.

- *The New World Order:* In 2005 South Floridians are connected to the world as never before. What we once knew as the Internet is now largely invisible. Anyone with a TV or a phone is connected seamlessly to endless worlds of information, entertainment, and commerce. Readers download stories and print them on high-quality home printers. They expect sharply focused information, tailored to their interests. At the same time, driven by strong Latin American economies, South Florida's economy is booming. Wages are rising, and Miami's downtown is reviving.

- *Falling Behind in the New Century:* In 2005 South Florida is receiving a steady stream of refugees from Central America and the Caribbean. South Florida's economy is in a slump, unable to create enough jobs or educate the newcomers. Miami has lost trade business to more aggressive ports. South Florida is also behind the nation in the acceptance and usage of the Internet and online services. Crime is rampant, and drugs poison the city and its government.

- *To Have and To Have Not:* In 2005 a severe economic crisis in South America's major nations sweeps Miami into a deep recession. Those who can afford it are living in a new era of information consumption. A quarter of Dade County residents and half of Broward residents regularly access electronic information. But with a relatively low Internet penetration in greater Miami, the technological revolution is limited to upper-income groups. National readership of mass-market, English-language newspapers continues to fall as customers migrate to TV and Web-based reporting.

In the scenario-planning process, the leaders of the newspaper explored what it would take to win in each of the four scenarios, a process described in more detail in Chapter 4. What capabilities would be needed in "Hong Kong of the Americas"? What different capabilities would be needed for the "New World Order"? Some capabilities are only important in a single scenario, while others are robust across multiple scenarios. The rapid emergence of new technology might call for deeper capabilities in electronic business and erode the value of printing capabilities. But customer relationships and data-mining are more robust capabilities—since they are of value in all the scenarios. They would be critical in both an upturn or a downturn scenario—in one case to grow the customer base, and in the other to hold on to the existing business and develop new niche markets. Managers then explored how these insights could contribute to the development of a strategic vision for succeeding across the range of possible scenarios, as discussed in more detail in Chapter 5. Finally, they began to create flexible strategic options for the scenarios, as examined in Chapter 6.

In June 1998, managers presented their strategies in view of the scenarios developed. But two months later, the process ended when David Lawrence, who had led the paper to four Pulitzer Prizes, resigned abruptly as publisher.

The revolution, however, was already under way. The first sign was the separation of the Spanish-language *El Nuevo Herald* as an independent publication. It rapidly became one of the fastest-growing U.S. newspapers of any language. While circulation of *The Miami Herald* did fall as a result, total circulation of the company's publications increased. After Lawrence's resignation, Alberto Ibargüen, publisher of *El Nuevo Herald,* was named to lead the company, becoming the first Hispanic publisher in the paper's ninety-six-year history. More significant, perhaps, was the shift in leadership from a journalist to a businessman. Ibargüen stressed that the best guarantee of the survival of good journalism was the commercial success of the enterprise. The organization, which had limped along at an average of 1 percent revenue growth for the previous fifteen years, grew by 3.5 percent in 1999 and grew by more than 5 percent in 2000, paying an extra week's pay as a bonus to every employee. *Columbia Journalism Review* listed *The Miami Herald* among its top 20 U.S. papers and Al Neuharth of *USA Today* ranked it second among the nation's newspapers.

Although the scenario-planning process was stopped short by Lawrence's departure, more than a dozen of the new initiatives developed through the process were ultimately integrated into Ibargüen's new set of strategies. The company moved aggressively onto the Internet, developing the Miami.com and Broward.com sites and online publications. It expanded direct marketing using the most comprehensive data base in South Florida. It built event marketing and sponsorship opportunities. It created targeted free weekly publications, such as the edgy *Street* and the *Jewish Star Times.* It moved into custom publications, such as in-room hotel visitor guides and airline magazines. And it expanded its Latin American products, building on its international edition. More important, the perspective on the world created during that process continues to shape the company's vision for the future.

David Landsberg, then CFO, described the scenario-planning process as "an out-of-body experience" for the organization. It can be a powerful way to break through a stalemate in an organization, created by power struggles or vision conflicts. These deadlocks can be resolved either through brute force, such as a palace coup, or through dialogue. Scenario planning is a structured way to build a shared vision about the future. If it is done well, all voices are represented in the different scenarios.

A Good Liberal Education

Although Ibargüen was not part of the *Miami Herald* scenario-planning team, he was an active participant in a similar process at its corporate parent, Knight-Ridder, before he took charge of the *Herald.* Here the results were even more dramatic. After actively considering the company's future in the Internet age, Knight-Ridder decided to move its corporate headquarters from Miami to San Jose, California—a shift in location reflecting a recalibration of its view of the world.

The broad windows of Ibargüen's office on the fifth floor of the *Miami Herald* building offer a sweeping vista of Biscayne Bay. Beyond the lights of boats bobbing on the water is a region undergoing a fundamental demographic upheaval. A technological revolution is challenging every aspect of the print empire Ibargüen is leading.

But where *The Miami Herald* once was battered by the change, it is now harnessing this uncertainty. Where it once braced itself against change, it is now advancing to meet the future.

On the coffee table in his office, Ibargüen spread out publications like a roadmap as he traced his course through uncertain terrain: the newly redesigned flagship publication, the new free niche papers, and an insert on a Pulitzer Prize–winning investigative series on corruption at the Miami International Airport. He conveyed a sense of excitement about the many options the company had developed for a brighter future.

Great uncertainty remains about what may unfold at the paper and in the world it serves. The only certainty is that the scenarios will change. As Ibargüen paused to reflect on the value of the scenario-planning process, he said its value lay less in the specific static views of the world it created than in the broad perspectives and ongoing learning it generated. "This is the strategic planning equivalent of a good liberal education," he said. "It teaches you how to always keep on learning. It gives you that nice broad base so very little is going to be a total surprise. It's not that the world is not uncertain; it's that we have done things not imagined three years ago and that gives people confidence to look the future in the eye."

Seeing the Opportunity

Many travel agencies saw the Internet as a tremendous threat to their businesses; Louis Arnitz was able to see it as an opportunity. *The Miami Herald* initially saw the changing demographics of its region and advancing technology as a threat to its readership and advertising base. Then it was able to shift its frame to see these changes as opportunities. The challenge is to see the future with fresh eyes: instead of recognizing the present in the future, the key is to re-cognize the potential of the future without mental baggage.[4]

The problem with most linear approaches to planning is that they lock business leaders into a single view of the world, so that they prepare for just one specific future. We all carry mental models in our heads that represent how we think the world works. While these models help us make sense of reality, our mental images are often imperfect and quite incomplete. Unfortunately, we may not realize this: we confuse our mental map with the territory.[5]

Our frames can keep us from seeing both threats and opportunities. A classic example is the Big Three automakers, which in the early 1970s had their noses buried in Detroit. As a result, they failed to anticipate the pending oil crisis in the Middle East and the rising Japanese competitors that would radically transform their world. As they watched their Japanese rivals build market share, they tended to discount their market pene-

How Frames Distort What We See

Mental frames guide our thinking in an overly complex and otherwise chaotic world, helping our minds to make useful connections and not be distracted by irrelevant ones. But frames can also play tricks on our minds. Here are some of their built-in dangers:

- **Frames filter what we see.** They control what information is attended to and, just as important, what is obscured. Remember, no single window can reveal the entire panorama.
- **Frames themselves are often hard to see.** Just as we have to step back from a window to see that it's there, so too do we have to "step back" from our frame to see that we are viewing the world through a particular perspective.
- **Frames appear complete.** Frames simplify the world. They do not capture all of reality, leaving gaps. But since our minds tend to fill in such gaps, we usually don't even notice that anything is missing.
- **Frames are exclusive.** We typically see one frame at a time. It's hard, after all, to simultaneously look out the windows on both the north and west sides of a room.
- **Frames can be "sticky" and hard to change.** Once we are locked into a frame, it can be difficult to switch, especially without conscious effort. When people have emotional attachments to their frames, changing frames can seem threatening.

Source: J. Edward Russo and Paul J. H. Schoemaker, *Winning Decisions: Getting It Right the First Time* (New York: Doubleday, 2002).

tration because it did not fit their Detroit-centric frame. They also didn't see the havoc that could be wreaked on their business by oil ministers in the Middle East. By the time the Big Three woke up after the jolt of the oil crises of 1973 and 1979, it was too late. The U.S. car industry had gone from an export surplus to a $60 billion import deficit in twenty years. Imports rose from 1 percent in 1955 to over 30 percent in 1987.

Although many factors played a role in the auto leaders' strategic blind spots, the deeper assumptions underlying their prevailing mindset are high on the list of culprits. GM's assumptions about itself and the world in the early 1970s presumed an isolated U.S. market, an abundance of cheap gas, a dominance of styling over technology, alienated workers and unions, and limited environmental concerns. These assumptions, which worked when technology was simple and gas was cheap, kept executives from noticing the many signals that the world was profoundly changing.[6]

Our minds have a way of hiding the gaps and filling the holes in our mental frames so that we fall prey to an illusion of completeness. We focus on those parts of the world that fit, and we conveniently ignore, distort, or simply forget those that don't. The plasticity of our frames makes it difficult for us to see when the world has changed, since we bend reality to fit our mental models rather than vice versa. We see the world as we would like to see it, or as we expect it to be, and not necessarily the way it really is. Few of us truly appreciate how our mental models distort reality by filtering what we pay attention to (see box).[7]

Double Vision

As a visual illustration of this important framing phenomenon, consider the two different ways of looking at the visual image in Exhibit 2-2. It is an ambiguous figure that can be interpreted multiple ways—like the continually changing reality we face day to day. What do you see?

Most people see either a mouse or a human face. Once they are locked in, they may not see the other possibility. The human mind searches for meaning and, like a guided missile, locks onto whatever image it sees. Once we ascribe meaning to an ambiguous figure, a subtle and largely unconscious process takes over that accentuates the features that fit while suppressing those that don't. That's the bad news, since it restricts our vision. The good news is that we can change the mental image if we work at it.

Exhibit 2-2: What Do You See?

By suppressing just a few features of the figure and highlighting others, we can change the fundamental gestalt or meaning of the drawing; Exhibit 2-3 shows side by side the two meanings that people normally see. Note how just a few judicious changes in the detail (amounting to less than 5 percent of the total picture) can radically alter the meaning from man to mouse or vice versa. And herein lies the power of scenario planning. By deliberately weaving various future trends and uncertainties into a coherent story about the future, a distinct tapestry of meaning emerges that leads to a certain set of strategies and options to be pursued. But if a different tapestry is woven from these same threads, another image may emerge that calls for different strategies and options. By weaving multiple scenar-

Exhibit 2-3: A Man or a Mouse?

ios, leaders can canvass the future and explore which strategies make sense across multiple scenarios and which are unique to just one future.

This visual analogy underscores the power of frames: they cause us to lock into one specific image, like the man or the mouse. The broadest opportunities, however, come from being able to look at the patterns of the world and see both images at once, to tell the stories of multiple scenarios about how the world may unfold, keeping alive the possibilities. The challenge is to live with double vision. Then, when more details fall into place, you can much more quickly see, and take advantage of, whatever picture emerges.

The Prepared Mind

The processes used by Louis Arnitz and *The Miami Herald,* in essence, allowed them to look at both the man and mouse simultaneously. By living with different scenarios and exploring their implications, business leaders can better prepare for multiple futures. Then if one pattern or another actually emerges, they are prepared to succeed—no matter what.

As a way to create meaning, exploring scenarios is closer to good storytelling than to building abstract models of multivariate relationships. But of course, a good story must have a compelling structure and plot line. It has to be internally consistent. And it has to be written so that it has some kind of happy ending (such as profits) for the protagonist.

Describing multiple scenarios simultaneously is just the first step in the process. Business leaders then have to live with the possibilities depicted in the different pictures of the future. If a "mouse" emerges, what should we do? Build a better mousetrap? If a "man" emerges, what should we do? Try to make him a customer?

More seriously, Louis Arnitz did not consider the possibility of a high-tech future for the travel industry idly. He began actively identifying and building the capabilities he might need to sustain a successful business. He continued to monitor the environment, and he developed a set of options that allowed him to move quickly when the Internet and other opportunities emerged more clearly from the fog of uncertainty. He created capabilities and options that could be deployed flexibly. He created a strategic vision and worked to implement that vision and adjust it as the world continued to change—transforming his company in the process.

So too *The Miami Herald* launched a wide range of experiments that gave the company options for the future, depending on how quickly the technology emerged and the demographic shifts transformed its markets. Its Spanish-language edition gave it insights into the rapidly expanding Spanish-speaking market and honed its capabilities for responding to deepening demographic shifts. Its niche publications offered it opportunities to address shifting readership patterns, and its online publications allowed it to capitalize on a potential migration of readers to the Internet. The development of scenarios was not an end in itself but rather a springboard for developing flexible and dynamic strategies for the future.

This broader process, which goes far beyond scenarios themselves, is the subject of this book. It involves envisioning future scenarios, identifying Key Success Factors and segments across the scenarios, creating a shared strategic vision, developing strategic options, and engaging in dynamic monitoring and flexible implementation. It is an organizational process that prepares the corporate mind to succeed no matter what the future holds. It was this very process that prepared both Arnitz and Ibargüen to seize the opportunities to profit when they emerged.

To a nimble player, there are no good or bad scenarios per se, just good and bad strategies. If you are willing to look ahead, engage in change, and take a risk, you can thrive in any future (as indeed someone will). This book invites you to examine and explore the multiple uncertainties surrounding your own business and then position yourself to derive profit from them. Instead of fearing or avoiding uncertainty, we want you to embrace uncertainty as a necessary condition for superior performance. Louis Arnitz and Alberto Ibargüen aren't looking for a way to hold back uncertainty. They are searching for ways to capitalize on the changes ahead. You can and should do the same.

Chapter 3

Experiencing Multiple Futures

If you do not think about the future, you cannot have one.

—John Galsworthy, *Swan Song*

Amid the crowded and overhyped advertising of football Super Bowl 2000, Nuveen Investments ran a television commercial that actually turned heads. The ad looked into the future, predicting that science would develop cures for AIDS and cancer and achieve victory over spinal cord injuries. These medical predictions were rather expected—until the shocking conclusion to the commercial, which showed actor Christopher Reeve walking onstage to receive an award. The computer-generated image of the paraplegic actor stepping up to the lectern to celebrate the development of a cure for his spinal injury was jarring and controversial. It also graphically illustrated how effective one concrete image can be in making the future real.

Making the Future Real

Studies have shown that concrete, vivid examples have far more impact than does abstract information. Real experience is weighed far more heavily than abstract analysis. For example, suppose that you are in the market to buy a car: you are thinking about choosing either a Volvo or a SAAB. You've done your research and found out that the Volvo model you're considering has a better repair record than the SAAB, based on a thousand vehicles. Case closed—or so it seems.

But then you go to a cocktail party, and a guest tells you an absolute horror story, about how his Volvo broke down on a desolate road in the middle of the night. The actual sample size has just increased from 1,000 to 1,001, and the new information should thus have less than 0.001 weight in your final judgment.[1] But which will have more impact: the abstract information or the real human story?

Storytelling and powerful imagery tend to focus attention on the real issues. Human beings remember stories better because we have a "concreteness bias." To understand the future, you cannot merely talk about it. As a business leader, you cannot merely churn through buckets of statistics (although scenarios certainly can be presented this way for those who find the numbers more compelling). To really internalize the future, you cannot just speculate in the abstract about it. If you are like most people, you need to live in it before it becomes meaningful. In a sense, scenario planners use one bias (our penchant for concrete and vivid information) to overcome another bias (our limited ability to imagine multiple futures).

In the following discussion, I'll look at how the use of scenarios made the future more concrete for a pharmaceutical company, using a composite of several client projects. I'll then examine a systematic process for generating such scenarios.

But first, let's step into the future.

Here's Your Morning Paper

Imagine you are a manager at a major pharmaceutical firm. You wake up one morning at the start of 2007 in one of two very different worlds.[2]

The Last Frontier

As you get out of bed in January 2007, the sun shines brightly. Stepping into the shower, you check your latest news and e-mails on the antifogging, flat-panel screen that fills one wall of the shower stall, flanked by a set of sensors that automatically adjust water temperature. You glance at the subject lines and headlines—just long enough to see that stocks are up again in a bull market that has been virtually unbroken since the technology correction of 2001 and the short recession that followed. You've seen enough. So you give a brief voice command to switch the wall to a soothing image of a waterfall in a Brazilian rain forest and, in the rising birdsong, try to forget for a moment that you're in the 21st century. You can catch up on the news later.

In the kitchen the latest edition of your customized news publication is downloaded instantly onto your paper-thin tablet computer. You grab it off the table, telling the house to shut off all nonessential systems. You toss the paper onto the seat of your fuel-cell-powered automobile as the garage door opens automatically. As you place your hands on the steering wheel, hidden sensors measure your cholesterol and other factors noninvasively and beam the information off to your insurance company. You've agreed to this monitoring routine to obtain a slightly lower premium rate, since it is as effortless and comforting as the warning lights on the dashboard. You never even notice the system until you receive an e-mail from your physician about the need for an office visit.

Your car neatly files into the automated highway, which is about ten minutes from your home. As you make margin notes on some office memos while zipping along at seventy miles an hour, you have flashbacks to the bad old days when you made this trip manually every day, with frequent and endless traffic jams. Your road navigator alerts you to a slight slowdown ahead and recommends a detour. You decide to take it since you need to make a stop anyway for your monthly tank of gas. As the robot arm triggered by your smart card opens and fills your tank, you look up with satisfaction at the price on the pump. In exchange for giving up some personal and demographic data to the gasoline company, you receive a lower rate. As your navigation system guides you to your first meeting of the day, a soothing voice from the flat-panel tablet reads the headlines, which include the following stories:

SUCCESSFUL THERAPY FOR ALZHEIMER'S DISEASE DISCOVERED

ROCKVILLE, MD—Researchers have found a highly effective palliative therapy for Alzheimer's disease, according to an article in today's issue of *The New England Journal of Medicine.* The breakthrough is a welcome relief to the millions of people who suffer from Alzheimer's disease, a group that has been growing rapidly with the increasing elderly population. "We have turned the corner in the fight against one of our most debilitating illnesses, which has stripped so many of our citizens of their golden years," said Dr. Alfred Noe, one of the lead researchers who developed the therapy, in a press conference at the Ronald Reagan Center for Alzheimer Research. "I think all of us can look forward to growing older with a little more peace of mind."

The breakthrough has followed similar successes in treating Parkinson's disease, hemophilia, sickle cell anemia, multiple sclerosis, and even the common cold. These dramatic medical breakthroughs build upon the decoding of the genetic Rosetta stone uncovered through the Human Genome Project. Advances in functional genomics, proteomics, genetic engineering, and stem cell research have created exciting new medical therapies.

The voice begins a second story:

UPSTART CAPTURES 30 PERCENT OF U.S. HEALTH INSURANCE MARKET

REDMOND, WA—HealthSmart, an upstart health insurance company, has raced past established rivals based on its powerful use of medical information. In just over two years, the company has harnessed the new power of customer information and technology to drive down rates and increase benefits to its members. It has captured nearly a third of the U.S. market in the process. The company uses smart card technology to monitor patient information and convey medical and genetic information throughout the system. HealthSmart has used sophisticated models to analyze the information and identify past or potential medical problems. It also was a pioneer in methods of delivering health care, using "virtual medicine" to monitor patients remotely through tele-visits that handle routine issues. Teams of physicians at regional centers see only more critical cases.

HealthSmart's progress was aided greatly by new regulations removing tax exemption from medical benefits, eroding the value of employee health care plans. As more customers turned to the free market to purchase their insurance, HealthSmart proved to be a very effective marketer of its services. While many of the established players were uncomfortable with this kind of consumer marketing, HealthSmart moved aggressively into all channels, particularly electronic marketing. "We have created a new kind of company for a new health care environment," said HealthSmart founder William Teags, at a press conference announcing the milestone. "We are very pleased that our customers have responded so enthusiastically to this new approach."

As you finish with the headlines, the electronic newspaper shuts down. The sunlight glints on the roadway as the computer guides the car to your destination. You ask for a music download to your player. As jazz riffs fill the small space, you think about your strategy for the future. This promises to be a good year for your pharmaceutical firm, and your options have appreciated greatly in this boom time. But you also recognize that in such a prosperous, high-potential industry, many competitors will be racing to move in. What will a company like HealthSmart do to your margins now that it has increasing clout in the market? How can you protect your gains and ensure your position in the future? How can you keep ahead in medical technology? How well did you prepare five years ago to capitalize on this scenario?

This world is the dream in which medical technology is rapidly advancing, markets are thriving and information is flowing relatively freely. It certainly presents challenges for your company, but this world also offers tremendous opportunities.

Then again, you might wake up in a very different future.

Health Care Held Hostage

It is a cold, cloudy day in January 2007 as you walk out to the curb to retrieve your newspaper from the melting snow. You'll receive a tailored news update on your PC at work, but you still like the feel of the newspaper in your hands, and you have plenty of company. The combination of a cup of coffee and newspaper in the morning is a deeply ingrained habit. You pop breakfast into the convection oven, and as the children argue around you, you scan through the day's headlines:

HEALTHSOFT EXECUTIVE JAILED FOR PRIVACY VIOLATIONS

PALO ALTO, CA—A high-flying company that led in gathering and using health information was brought to the ground when federal regulators arrested the CEO for violations of new stringent privacy laws.

In a suit filed in federal court, the government alleges that Healthsoft had been sharing medical history information with biopharmaceutical firms. A company spokesperson contested the charge, claiming that they had obtained adequate releases from individual patients. But already the company's stock has lost half its value, and it is unlikely that the company will survive, regardless of the outcome of the suit, as legal injunctions loom. The resulting uncertainty drove down share prices of not just health care intermediaries but also the large pharma companies that have benefited greatly from the new information streams.

This is the first major legal test of tough new health care privacy restrictions enacted a year ago, a package of new laws designed to limit sharing of patient information and tracking visits through information systems and payment tools such as smart cards. While the ACLU has celebrated the action as a long-overdue defense of individual privacy rights, industry leaders contend that the tough regulations will ultimately lead to higher prices, hurting consumers. The privacy concerns were a serious blow to companies such as Healthsoft, which emerged to move from reactive disease treatment to more proactive disease management.

"This is the last nail in the coffin of disease management," said Dr. Rudolph Imagio, one of the pioneers of this new approach to health care. "In protecting patient information so rigorously, we are raising costs and decreasing the quality of health care. This hurts everyone."

MILLION RETIREE MARCH ON WASHINGTON

WASHINGTON, DC—The U.S. Capitol steps and Mall were filled with a sea of gray heads and wheelchairs. The faces of thousands of virtual participants were projected onto three-story-high banks of flat-panel displays in the largest rally of senior citizens in the nation's history. The Million Retiree March—which organizers claim surpassed the goal of one million participants if online "marchers" are included—was a graphic demonstration of the power of a growing and increasingly vocal senior population.

Organizers of the event were demanding increases in health care coverage and urging regulators to shore up the declining reserves of Social Security. Congressional leaders cautioned that in the current economic downturn, and with a declining population of workers to fund these initiatives, it may be difficult to meet these demands through the public sector. Legislators vowed, however, to push more aggressively for concessions from the private sector to ensure that health care options remain widely available for the nation's seniors. The sea of angry waving canes made a strong political impression.

As you drive into the office and look for a parking space, you are concerned. You represent the private sector, and these demands for more concessions will come right out of your dwindling margins. Overzealous privacy protection will limit your ability to use technology to improve efficiency and service.

Even without these new shocks, the research-based pharmaceutical industry faces a crisis. A handful of breakthrough pharmaceutical products still command some premium pricing, but fast followers offering discounts quickly erode margins. After investing millions in genomics, firms have yet to see payoffs from these investments. Huge government-backed programs to ensure access to medicines are putting further pressure on margins, using its leverage of controlling 40 percent of all health spending through Medicare, Medicaid, and other government programs. As more baby boomers move to retirement age, these pressures are only going to increase.

This is a very discouraging view, as you drive to the office. How can you find a silver lining in this cloudy environment? Where will future profits come from? How well did you prepare for this scenario five years ago?

The Need for Scenarios

These two scenarios require very different strategies and capabilities for success. It is highly uncertain which one might come to pass, but by thinking through both of them (and others), the manager can begin to develop the capabilities and reflexes to succeed, whatever future unfolds.

Why is it important to anticipate multiple futures? Examples of companies that have been blindsided by the future are abundant. Encyclopaedia Britannica thought it was in the book business until it woke up to find it was really in the knowledge and information business, which had gone digital. In 1989 Britannica was booming, with $627 million in sales of its $1,300 sets of encyclopedias. But by 1994 its sales had dropped 53 percent. Other encyclopedia companies (such as Encarta and Crozier) were developing CD-ROM alternatives, which made content more exciting, less expensive, and easier to use. Britannica failed to take this future seriously. It was locked into the wrong future. By 1996 sales had fallen by 70 percent. The CEO resigned, the sales force was disbanded, and the company itself was sold for its brand and content. Britannica became yet one more victim of tunnel vision and overconfidence. It had very intelligent strategic planners. It had talented, even visionary technologists. Yet it became trapped in an approach to planning for the future that didn't fit with the new demands imposed by external change and complexity. Instead of embracing the uncertainties of the future, it extrapolated the trends of the past while taking false comfort from the success that its increasingly outdated business models were still enjoying. As most companies do, it focused on the known and was reluctant to step outside its comfort zone to attack unknowns, even though that's where the opportunities were waiting.

Going to the Mountaintop

Imagine you are planning to climb a mountain. A traditional corporate planner would draw you a detailed map up the mountainside, describing

How Scenario Planning Differs from Other Approaches

How is scenario planning different from contingency planning, sensitivity analysis, and computer simulation? Contingency planning examines one key uncertainty at a time, whereas scenario planning examines the joint impact of various uncertainties. Similarly, sensitivity analysis examines the impact of changing one variable a tiny bit, while keeping all others constant; scenario planning changes multiple variables at a time, without trying to keep others constant. It tries to capture the new states that will develop after major shocks or significant deviations occur in key variables. Scenario planning looks at the extremes to gain insights on the possibilities in between.

Although complex simulation models can examine changes in multiple variables, they do not necessarily lead to clearer insights. The future often contains elements that are not easily included in formal models, such as changes in regulations, value shifts, and innovations. Scenario planning attempts to capture the richness and full range of possibilities, and to recognize the potential new states that result from them. Scenario planning also uses narratives that are easier to grasp and use than great volumes of data or formal models. Complex models can serve as inputs for or adjuncts to scenario planning, as I'll discuss below, but you need to cut through the detail to see the bigger picture. Scenario planning is about seeing the forest as opposed to seeing every tree, about being roughly right rather than precisely wrong.

every dip and elevation in the fixed and predetermined terrain. This tool would be very valuable, but it would also be incomplete. First, a two-dimensional map is not the territory but an incomplete and distorted abstraction. Second, it ignores variable elements such as weather, landslides, animals, and other hikers. What happens if a sudden avalanche occurs or a snowstorm moves in while you are hiking to the summit? In addition to drawing your map, you will probably want to think through some of these possibilities. On the other hand, if you think about all the limitless possibilities, you'll never begin your ascent.

Scenario planning helps you out of this dilemma. It simplifies the overwhelming data to a limited number of possible states or scenarios. Each scenario tells a story of how the various elements might interact under varying assumptions. Each scenario is evaluated for its internal consistency and plausibility. For example, a scenario that envisions high visibility and heavy snowdrifts is an implausible combination. Although the boundaries of a scenario may at times be fuzzy, a detailed and realistic narrative may direct your attention to aspects you would otherwise overlook. A vivid snowdrift scenario (with low visibility) may highlight the need for skin protection, goggles, food supplies, radio, shelter, and so on. Thinking through the scenarios will give you insights into the assets and capabilities you will need to make it up the mountainside.

Constructing Scenarios

How do you go about constructing scenarios? I'll examine below how the pharmaceutical company manager developed various scenarios, including the "Last Frontier" and "Health Care Held Hostage" visions described at the beginning of this chapter. This methodology is not a recipe for constructing scenarios but rather a framework that offers a starting point. The framework is designed to draw out the imagination of a large group of people in an organization. It disciplines this imagination and jump-starts discussions. But if you do not enter creatively into the process—and even set aside the framework itself when necessary—you are not engaged in true scenario planning.

The core of scenario planning is to determine what you know and what you don't know. You know that the mountain has a certain elevation, that the path proceeds according to the map, and that you can hike a certain number of miles in a day. These fairly certain things—the things you know—are the basic givens or trends of the scenario. What you don't know are the exact weather patterns, the interaction among the other hikers on the trail, and the changes in the terrain since it was last mapped. What you don't know are the key uncertainties.

These trends and uncertainties are the warp and weft of the loom on which the scenarios are woven, as illustrated in Exhibit 3-1. The trends are laid down like the warp that runs lengthwise down the loom. The uncertainties are the weft (or filling yarn) that runs across this same set of trends. The scenarios are the colorful patterns that emerge as the uncertainties are added into the trends. For the scenarios to be strong, the trends and uncertainties need to be tightly woven together. For the scenarios to be useful, the trends and uncertainties need to be brought together in a way that clear patterns begin to emerge. This process takes both science and art—meticulously stringing the loom and then creatively designing the scenarios.

Back to the Future

Now, let's return to our story of the manager at the pharmaceutical company, but wind the clock back seven years to January 2000. Imagine you have

Exhibit 3-1: Weaving the Patterns of Scenarios

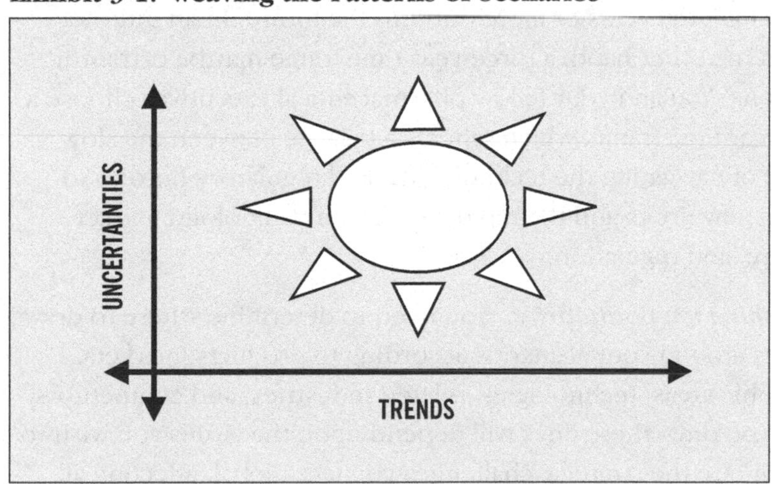

just celebrated the start of the new millennium and have breathed a sigh of relief that Y2K was a minor issue. With the future so emphatically at your doorstep, the company calls you into a scenario-planning meeting to look at the business going forward. In the process of this session, you and your colleagues envision the future and come up with the two scenarios "The Last Frontier" and "Health Care Held Hostage" as well as other possibilities. How do you generate these scenarios? Let's take a closer look at the process.

Stringing the Loom

The first step that you and your fellow pharmaceutical company managers take is to define the scope of the scenarios and the important questions that need to be answered. How many years out should the scenarios cover? What geographic regions and businesses should be considered? Who are the important stakeholders in shaping the future? Exploring these issues sets the boundaries for developing scenarios.

A variety of factors will define the scope of the scenarios:

- *Determining Time Frame:* The time frame should be influenced by the rate of technological change, the product life cycles, the planning horizons of your rivals, the stability of the political, social, and regulatory environment, the past volatility and uncertainty in the industry, and the time required to develop important new capabilities. In general, the shorter the cycles in the industry, the shorter term the scenarios should be. In a more stable industry, the scenarios may look ten years or more out into the future. In an Internet firm, on the other hand, a three-year time frame may be extraordinarily long. You and your fellow pharmaceutical executives choose a seven-year time frame, which reflects a balance between the slow process of navigating the technological and regulatory hurdles to develop new drugs and the rapid changes in technology, market structure, and regulation.

- *Establishing the Boundaries:* You need to determine where to draw the lines around your scenarios according to products, markets, geographic areas, technologies, related industries, and competitors. Where you draw these lines will depend upon the issues you wish to focus on. Are the strategic challenges you face global, affecting all your products and markets? Or are they focused on a particular part of the world or part of the business? For the pharmaceutical firm, you and the other managers chose to focus on health care services and products within the United States but viewed in a global context. While research is global, health care systems vary widely across nations.

- *Identifying the Stakeholders to Be Considered:* Who will have an interest in these issues? Whom will they affect? Who could influence them? These stakeholders usually include customers, suppliers, competitors, employees, shareholders, and the government. But there may be other players, such as the courts, the media, or lobbying organizations, and it is important to explore how their roles, interests, and power positions are shifting over time. What players will shape the future of your business and its environment? These are the people you need to identify and bring into the planning process. For your pharmaceutical firm, they include doctors, patients, hospitals, insurers, and regulators. The decisions of all these stakeholders will shape the health care environment of the future. Leaving any one group out will result in lopsided and possibly misleading scenarios.

In determining the scope of the scenarios, a variety of questions may be useful to consider:

- How are your competitors framing these issues?
- Does your organization have a natural bias? (For example, does it tend to think too short term and need to look farther out? Is it overly United States–centric in its views?)
- If you look back five to fifteen years, how valuable would it have been then to have peeked at the future of your industry? How much change has occurred, and how well did your organization anticipate and deal with it?
- Are new products, technologies, or competitors emerging in your industry? Are they contracting industry cycles? Are they expanding industry boundaries? Are new business models emerging? How can you include them in your analysis?

Defining Important Questions and Gathering Information

Once you determine the scope and the stakeholders, you need to begin gathering information, the raw material for the scenarios. You first need to formulate some guiding questions and define issues of strategic importance. Suppose you could ask the mythical all-knowing Oracle of Delphi any three questions about the external future—what would they be? What information would help you evaluate present strategies and develop viable alternatives for the future? Looking at the past, what do you wish you had known then that you know now? What questions should you have asked then (but didn't)? What have been the primary sources of volatility and uncertainty in your industry (social, political, economic, or technological)?

The whole management team and other groups of stakeholders may participate in the process of defining these questions. Their unstructured concerns and anxieties are often good starting points for scenario planning. At this stage, the process is still divergent in nature, aimed at generating key questions that are then used to gather information.

You and the other pharmaceutical managers use a broad process for gathering information. You interview or gather articles from industry visionaries. You interview your own managers. Finally, you gather information from and about insurance leaders, regulators, hospitals, doctors, and patients.

These interviews can be as focused or as extensive as necessary. They can involve broad, formal surveys, or they can incorporate the input from surveys that have already been conducted. They also can be based upon open-ended interviews. In general, you should conduct interviews with several key managers and several experts outside your organization. Also, make sure to include customers, suppliers, regulators, and perhaps even competitors (both traditional and new).

Identifying the Dominant External Forces

Through these interviews, you and your fellow pharmaceutical managers gather information about the dominant external forces that are driving change. As you sift through your assembled knowledge base, you begin to look for patterns. You specifically examine the forces that are shaping the future environment in health care: economic, political, societal, technological, industrial, and others. For the U.S. health care industry, you come up with a list of many forces driving change:

SOME DRIVING FORCES IN HEALTH CARE

Societal

- Focus on women's and children's health care needs
- Level of consumer activism in health care
- Extent of patient/consumer empowerment

Technological

- Genomics research and rational drug discovery and development, resulting in more efficacious and/or truly innovative products
- Robotics playing a significant role in health care delivery, access, and cost-effectiveness
- E-business influence on health information capture and dissemination

Economic

- Significant growth of the global economy
- Role of price controls and increased price transparency
- Environmental regulation becoming more restrictive

Political

- Privacy legislation restricting the use of individual health information/history
- Health care costs shifting to individuals and decreasing government/payer reimbursement
- Republican or Democratic government in Washington, D.C.?

In looking at these forces and issues, be sure they are truly primary sources of change in the industry. Perhaps some are symptoms of deeper drivers, such as increasing price transparency. Are the forces you identified affecting other industries as well? Are the forces global, national, or regional?

Determining the Important Trends and Key Uncertainties

By collecting all this information and identifying these forces, your fellow pharmaceutical managers are beginning to get a better sense of what they know about the future. But you now need to step back and consider what you don't know. Not all of these forces are the same. How likely are the underlying drivers to move in a certain direction? The parts that are very predictable are the trends. The parts that are very unpredictable are the key uncertainties. The trends can be presented as definitive statements, while the uncertainties are presented as questions. That information technology will be more widely distributed is a trend, but whether society will allow health care information to be captured or whether privacy issues will undermine that process is an uncertainty. As discussed above, separating the trends from the uncertainties is crucial to developing scenarios.

By sifting through the initial list of forces and issues, the pharmaceutical managers end up with the following trends and uncertainties:

Important Trends

T_1 Access to information will dramatically increase globally.

T_2 Health care costs will shift to individuals and away from government/payer reimbursement.

T_3 Industry consolidation will continue to alter industry players and dynamics.

T_4 Consumers will have more influence on decisions regarding health care service selections; the demand for high(er)-quality care, preventive care, homeopathic/alternative medical solutions, and so on will increase.

T_5 There will be continued movement toward market convergence (regional trading blocs, free trade, common currency), more free market activity, and greater harmonization in the health care regulatory environment.

T_6 Pricing of health care products and services will become increasingly transparent.

T_7 Innovative technologies, such as miniaturization, genomic research, stem cell research, and combinatorial chemistry will continue to be developed and supported with investment, with the expectation that they will produce true innovation.

Key Uncertainties

U_1 Will new medical technologies deliver truly innovative products and services?

U_2 Will society allow health care information to be captured and used to improve health care delivery? (e-health care)

U_3 How will the global economy change (in terms of unemployment, inflation, natural resources availability, capital availability)?

U_4 To what extent will government play a role in determining health care benefits and spending (centralized planning versus privatization)?

U_5 Will regulation restricting the pharmaceutical industry and health care delivery, including intellectual property rights and environmental issues, intensify?

U_6 How universal will access to health care be in the United States seven years from now?

U_7 How involved will consumers be in health management?

If you have doubts about whether a certain force is a trend or an uncertainty, consider the evidence that supports it. Can it be defended? Can it be plotted as a trend over time? What could weaken or reverse the force in the future? Do people broadly agree that it is a trend within the time frame considered? If not, it's an uncertainty.

Once you have surfaced the key uncertainties, it is useful to project a range of possible outcomes for each uncertainty. For example, if one key uncertainty is future GNP growth, the future level could be specified as being anywhere between –1 percent growth and 6 percent growth. This range, which can be thought of as a subjective confidence range, should generally be wider the farther you look into the future.

It is important to explain why these key uncertainties matter most, and to what extent they interrelate. For example, a correlation matrix could be constructed showing the extent to which each uncertainty is correlated with every other key uncertainty. Such a matrix also allows for a consistency test about people's underlying beliefs, since certain correlation patterns are statistically improbable.[3] It can also help to identify which uncertainties are central (tied to all others) and which are peripheral and isolated.

You and the other pharmaceutical managers rank the trends and uncertainties and graph the results to identify the forces that seem most critical across the entire group. Through this process, you identify the two most important uncertainties to consider in developing the initial scenarios. The top two uncertainties selected are:

- *The role of new technologies in innovation:* Will they lead to breakthroughs that will transform medicine within the next seven years, or will they prove to be overhyped and fail to live up to their promise?
- *The capture and use of health information (e-health care):* Will it flourish within the next seven years, allowing tremendous efficiencies and customization, or will it be thwarted by concerns about privacy?

Developing Detailed Scenarios

You then use these top two uncertainties to define a set of four initial scenario themes. The scenarios are defined by the boundary outcomes for each uncertainty, creating a two-by-two matrix. In this case, you create the matrix shown in Exhibit 3-2, based on the progress of technology versus use of information (e-health care).

- *Scenario A: Health Care Held Hostage:* This is the rather bleak future described in the second scenario presented at the opening of the chapter. Privacy concerns are limiting the use of health care information, and improvements in technology have been only incremental. In addition, the global economy is experiencing economic malaise, and there is strict regulation and pricing control of health care and pharmaceuticals. Finally, care is polarized based on wealth.
- *Scenario B: Intel Inside . . . You:* In this scenario, the technology generates tremendous breakthroughs. Genomic research has greatly increased R&D efficiency and effectiveness. Significant progress also is being made in gene therapy, prophylactic vaccines, diagnostics, and preventive therapies. Basic coverage is widely available, but patient information is not accessible. Privacy concerns have limited the use of information to better target and improve health care. In addition, global GDP is growing at a healthy 2 to 3 percent annually.

Exhibit 3-2: Scenario Matrix

U_2: E–HEALTH CARE? \ U_1: NEW MEDICAL TECHNOLOGIES?	Incremental Improvement from New Medical Technologies	Breakthrough Improvement from New Medical Technologies
Gradual Improvement in Capture / Use of Health Care Information via Internet	Scenario A: Health Care Held Hostage	Scenario B: Intel Inside . . . You
Quantum Change in Capture / Use of Health Care Information via Internet	Scenario C: Consumers Take Control	Scenario D: The Last Frontier

Source: *Decision Strategies International, Inc.*

- *Scenario C: Consumers Take Control:* While medical breakthroughs have been much slower than anticipated, an information-driven renaissance is improving the quality and rational use of care. Genetic profiling and disease susceptibility have been linked, and genetic testing is widely available. This gives customers much more control over their information and their own health care. Both physicians and consumers assume greater risk management responsibilities. Again, there is global GDP growth of 2 to 3 percent annually.

- *Scenario D: The Last Frontier:* This is the most optimistic scenario, described first in the chapter opening. Research has made quantum breakthroughs, and privacy issues are resolved so that information can be used to drive the efficiency and effectiveness of care. The pharmaceutical industry is in a state of rapid change, but tremendous opportunities emerge from its rapid growth. GDP among top countries is expanding at 3 percent annually and spending on health care in the United States is up by more than 5 percent, even with significant reductions in the cost of care.

These four scenarios may seem like an overly simplistic way to represent rather complex situations, and they are. The two-by-two matrix is only a starting point, like a machine translation of a foreign language: you may be able to get the gist of the story, but it will not appear in all its richness until you have cleaned it up and focused it. Part of its richness will come from incorporating the other trends and uncertainties into these core scenarios. They do not merely wash out in this process—they are kept and woven into the more detailed stories and blueprints that are created for each scenario. But for managers, having a fundamental framework is useful as a starting point, and it also helps to prioritize the most important uncertainties going forward. Some of this further richness is shown in Exhibit 3-3, which indicates how all the uncertainties are played out in the scenarios. Although the emphasis

Exhibit 3-3: Scenario Blueprint

Uncertainty	Scenario A: Health Care Held Hostage	Scenario B: Intel Inside . . . You	Scenario C: Consumers Take Control	Scenario D: The Last Frontier
U_1: Role of new technologies in innovation	Incremental	Breakthrough	Incremental	Breakthrough
U_2: Capture and use of health information	Incremental	Incremental	Breakthrough	Breakthrough
U_3: Health of the global economy	Recession	Strong growth	Modest	Boom
U_4: Role of government in health care	Significant; Centralized	Modest; Centralized	Modest; Decentralized	Free market; Privatized
U_5: Intensity of industry regulation	High	High	Low; Self-regulation	Low; Self-regulation
U_6: Level of access to health care	Limited access; Bankrupt payers	Limited access	Majority access	Universal access
U_7: Level of consumer involvement	Low	Low	High	High

Source: *Decision Strategies International, Inc.*

will differ, all the trends are present in some form in each of the four scenarios.

Once the blueprints for the scenarios are developed, then you need to go back and assess the internal consistency and plausibility of each one. How well does the scenario hang together? Are there fundamental inconsistencies in how the uncertainties are played out? Are the trends mutually compatible with one another, as well as with the outcomes assumed in the blueprint? Also, you need to consider the actions of major stakeholders. Are they placed in positions they do not like and could change? If so, add this possibility into the scenario. For example, even with privacy protections, there might be a customer backlash against the use of information, and this could fundamentally alter the scenarios that assume information will be widely available for use. Sometimes managers conduct role-playing exercises to identify these reactions. Are there predictable rules or patterns among the various factors within the system?

As a result of these questions, you can eliminate combinations that are neither credible nor possible and create new scenarios until you have achieved internal consistency. Then you need to go back and make sure these new scenarios bracket a wide range of possible future outcomes. In addition, you can further test the viability of the scenarios by asking for feedback from customers, suppliers, strategic partners, regulators, consultants, academics, or others whose opinions you respect. The purpose of scenario planning is to create a framework within which "deep dialog" can occur,[4] where members of the organization engage in discussions of important issues, so as to engender deeper strategic insight. The scenarios should capture the essence of the strategic conversation as it evolves within the organization and beyond.[5] Based on discussions with various stakeholder groups, you can identify topics for further study that would provide stronger support for your scenarios or that might lead to revisions.

The final scenarios might be presented in booklet form or a set of slides and given to others to enhance their decision making under conditions of uncertainty. In principle, scenarios can be used in a variety of ways, from helping to challenge the managers' mental models and key assumptions about the industry to improving risk analysis in specific projects. Above all, they should be used to test the robustness of the existing strategies and prepare the organization to cope effectively with the full range of uncertainties that lie ahead. Each strategy entails a certain level of commitment (willingness to stick out one's neck) and a certain degree of flexibility (the ability to change course in view of new information). Scenario planning can help calibrate both the nature and the extent of the commitment that a firm should make in pursuing a particular set of technologies, products, and markets.[6]

Animating the Scenarios

These scenarios are not static but unfold according to certain paths. A lot of money will be made or lost on the way to your five- or ten-year snapshot of the future. There are also many potential pitfalls and detours along the way. An influence diagram can be used to look at how the driving forces unfold over time within each scenario. Such a diagram portrays the dynamic logic of the scenario. It can be very useful in identifying the critical points along the path to the scenario that will determine whether and how it unfolds.

Consider the "Last Frontier" influence diagram shown in Exhibit 3-4. You'll remember that "The Last Frontier" is the most optimistic scenario, in which there is a strong global economy, breakthrough technologies for health care, and sophisticated use of patient information. As shown, the strong global economy leads to a thriving middle class with more disposable income to spend on health care. A restructuring in the insurance system leads to more bundled insurance. Meanwhile, effective privacy protection is allowing greater efficiencies through shared use of customer data. Breakthroughs in platform technologies reduce the costs of R&D and increase diagnostic, preventive, and curative therapies. These in turn lead to higher levels of health care spending, more customized solutions, and improved performance.

The influence diagram can be a place to test the sensitivity of various parts of the chain. What happens if the insurance system does not move to self-pay and benefits are not taxed, as assumed on the right-hand side? Then you have a consumer with greater ability and willingness to pay, but these funds do not have a way to flow through the system because of the buffer of employer-sponsored care programs. On the other hand, if the medical breakthroughs and privacy protections shown on the left-hand side do not materialize, pharmaceutical and other health care companies

Exhibit 3-4: The Last Frontier Influence Map

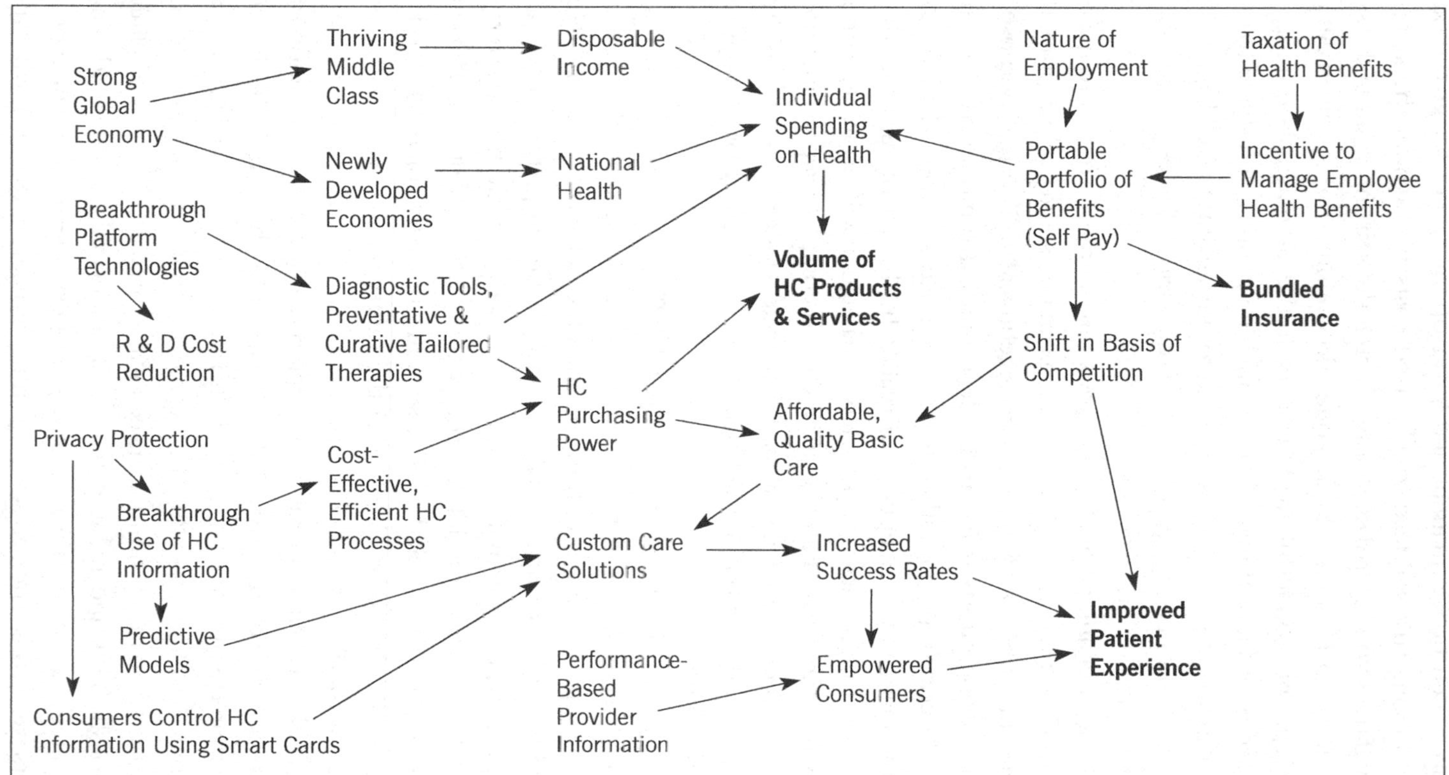

Source: *Decision Strategies International, Inc.*

will face much tighter margins and fewer opportunities for growth and consolidation. This will lead to increased costs throughout the system. Finally, if the strong global economy, which is the starting point of the scenario, does not materialize, the money flowing into the system is cut off at the tap. The wonderful breakthroughs in the lab may fall on unreceptive doctors and consumers who are pinching pennies and trying to take care of essentials. Developing and exploring an influence diagram for each scenario offers insights into how the various forces in the model interrelate and unfold over time.

As a further animation, the scenarios can be transformed into quantitative models. System dynamic modeling can be used to help capture the complex interactions of the scenario algebraically.[7] The real purpose of such modeling efforts is not to produce predictive models (like econometric forecasting) but rather to help surface the mental maps that underlie managers' perceptions of reality. In the act of surfacing these maps, two things may happen. First, managers will appreciate more deeply that their own mental maps are not a complete representation of the environment. Second, new maps may take root as the scenarios draw new connections among key constructs while weakening or perhaps severing old ones.

These formal computer-based models offer a way to crank through truckloads of data and explore a wide range of inputs and outcomes. They can thus offer a way to think through the details of a scenario. How important is the growing global economy to the big picture? What happens to the whole system if the expected growth rate falls by a quarter? By a half? The dynamic model can compute numerous options. The only caveat is not to be fooled by the seeming precision of these models. These are still broad-brush views of the future, even if you have added rather exact-looking numbers to the process.

A further dynamic needs to be explored as well: the oscillation of a system from one extreme to another. For example, historically health care in the United States moved aggressively into surgical, invasive procedures and long hospital stays. But then came a consumer backlash, moving toward more natural, nonpharmaceutical remedies, out-patient clinics, and holistic medicine. In biotechnology, farmers initially embraced genetically altered crops as a way of reducing pesticide use, but many consumers were concerned about tampering with nature to create what they referred to as "Frankenfoods." In the financial services industry, it is conceivable that once high-tech Internet banking takes off, a backlash may occur in the form of a desire for more high-touch, personalized banking of the kind offered by credit unions. The obvious path might look like a straight line, but it may actually be a more dynamic system that swings from one extreme to another. Indeed, even chaos can be introduced into the models.

These oscillating systems are very important to think through. Looking at scenarios at the extremes can usually help you get ready for these fluctuations. Back in the 1970s and 1980s a biotech company that developed creative scenarios would have anticipated the possible "green" backlash. A pharmaceutical firm thinking through political scenarios might have anticipated the backlash against use of expensive AIDS drugs in Africa or societal opposition to human cloning. The possibility of these sudden shifts in consumer attitudes, changes in regulations, or other factors makes scenario planning so valuable. It also underscores why you should seek outside opinions, and why you should explore scenarios that—when looked at from the present—appear to offer very radical views of the future. History has taught us that economic and political conditions often change radically.

A Paradigm Shift

To be of use, scenarios must challenge managerial beliefs. A scenario that merely confirms conventional wisdom is of little use. On the other hand, the scenarios have to be credible. A scenario that challenges deep beliefs while having little apparent chance of actual occurrence might simply be dismissed as "off the wall." The dilemma is that the future is often "off the wall." Hence a balance must be struck between what the future may really bring and what the organization is ready to contemplate or must consider for its survival. It's best to start with an intellectually honest and wide-ranging set of views and then rein in the scenarios—reluctantly and carefully—to accommodate the organization's legitimate political or emotional concerns. How do you know whether you're breaking out of the old paradigm? Watch people's reactions. Do they exhibit denial, confusion, discomfort, or outright anger? Do the scenarios stimulate vigorous debate and deep discussion? If so, you are probably challenging their fundamental beliefs in a healthy way.

Scenario planning differs from many other planning techniques in that its goal is often a paradigm shift. It paints concrete and vivid narratives of the future that hinge on key uncertainties whose outcome will shape the future environment. The act of jointly developing stories about the future, in a disciplined but imaginative way, enhances both the learning about and the acceptance of these futures—in contrast to developing a bare-bones set of bullet points.[8]

At the end of your January 2000 planning meeting, you have seen several possible futures for your pharmaceutical company. You have lived in the wonders of "The Last Frontier" and felt the bonds of an industry "held hostage" by technological and information constraints. Now what? How do you take this information and use it to prepare for the future? What competencies of the company will be valuable in this new environment? What new capacities does it need to build? How do you make sure you and your company are ready to wake up in January 2007 and succeed? Once you have thought through the trip up the mountain, in fair weather and foul, the next question is, How can you best prepare for the ascent? What gear do you need to bring along? The following chapters explore how to develop strategies for multiple scenarios.

Preserving Uncertainty

Something about humans makes it difficult for us to deal with even three or four possible views of the future at once. In the midst of all that uncertainty, all we know for sure is that not all these possible futures will be the actual one. We see the multiple scenarios as competing. We want and need to know which will be the winner. After going through the scenario-planning process, generating robust, alternative views of the world ahead, we want to move as quickly as possible to closure, to nail down the one *right* vision for the future. Like the television show *Survivor,* we want to sift through candidates and vote them one by one off the island to determine a single million-dollar winner. But life is not so simple.

Seeking certainty is hubris, says J. Edward Russo, a chaired professor at Cornell University and a pioneer in the study of decision making. "Scenarios should preserve uncertainty," he says. "When managers choose one future from among a set of scenarios, they are falling back into their old patterns of trying to nail down one view of the future."

Russo recalls the story of a major pharmaceutical firm that learned the hard way that placing all one's chips on one version of the future can be a dangerous bet. In 1993 the Clinton administration was aggressively pressing its proposal to change the health care system in the United States. The leaders of the company, with change so clearly imminent, decided they needed to move ahead of the curve. They assumed that some version of the Clinton health care proposal would become America's new public policy. Then they proactively took adaptive steps, such as substantially reducing their workforce. Just eighteen months later, the unthinkable happened: the Clinton plan was derailed. And the company, which had hitched its future to the reform, was caught on the wrong track behind a stalled engine.

"They put all their eggs in one basket," Russo explains. "They had to hire back some of the same people. They lost tens of millions of dollars in training and relocation costs. They missed their sales forecast by more than at any time in their history, almost certainly because of the low morale all the changes caused. It was nothing but a big bet, a bet that turned out to be wrong.

"This story is all too typical of what you get when you have 'decisive' senior managers," he continues. "They took clear strong action. The trouble is they took it on the basis of one scenario. They bet that they could predict the future, and they lost. Where were scenario B and scenario C? You can view this firm's senior managers as decisive, as assertive, as risk takers; or you can see them as arrogant for believing that they had the ability to predict the future. What gave them the power of foresight that others don't have, besides their lofty, invulnerable position at the top of the corporate pyramid where no one can effectively challenge them?"

This presumption of clairvoyance was less risky in an age when the environment was more forgiving. But now "the rate of change is increasing," Russo says. "That means two things: First, qualitatively, we are dealing with discontinuous events—we are not dealing so much with trends as with surprises. Second, the cycle of decisions has shrunk because of competition. You get less time to make the same important decisions before a nimble competitor will eat your lunch."

The dilemma facing managers today is that there is more information available than ever. Many of them believe that this information should make it possible to pinpoint the future with the accuracy of a global positioning system. Not a chance. First, the information is often overwhelming. Second, even if it all could be harnessed, there would still be great gaps that could radically alter the future.

Nonetheless, we continue to view uncertainty as the enemy, as a set of open doors that must be closed before we can move to the future. "As we develop our professional skill, most of our training and experience tells us that uncertainty is the enemy of planning," Russo says. "The obvious goal is to reduce uncertainty. However, the cost of reducing uncertainty in the traditional way is often unacceptably high—namely substantial delay. You just can't wait to make the decision until everything is known and uncertainty is zero."

But managers convince themselves that they can reduce uncertainty and avoid the anxiety it causes. "They often do things to reduce uncertainty that are delusional," Russo says. "They pretend the uncertainty is not there when in fact it is substantial. Senior managers ask for more facts, believing, with some justification, that more information will reduce the discomforting uncertainty. To add to the delusion, bosses are often told what they want to hear."

Russo, who earned two degrees in mathematics, once was hoping to find a straightforward mathematical formula to describe complex human decisions and activities such as scenario planning. But as he studied the issue, he became convinced that it just wasn't possible—and left behind mathematics to pursue behavioral science. Some things still cannot be boiled down into a simple mathematical equation.

So how do you keep the business from becoming a stew of touchy-feely mush? Statistically based management tools were created to add rigor to business analysis, to eliminate the wiggle room, and to enable managers to keep an eye on trends in a complicated business. When subordinates come back with vague projections for the future, it is often a sign of analytic weakness. When they express doubt and uncertainty, it often reflects a lack of information. Boiling down past performance and future prospects to a set of numbers was crucial. But as uncertainty in the environment increases, projecting trends based on past information makes less sense. The trends, as Russo says, are replaced with surprises. Anticipating the surprises and preparing for them becomes more important. In this environment precise numbers are actually less rigorous.

If the rigor is not in the numbers, where is it? The challenge is to use a rigorous *process* for anticipating and preparing for possible futures without reducing them to simplistic views or formulas. The challenge is to hold on to the doubt at the same time you develop plans that work across several different futures. It is not to search and destroy the uncertainty but to recognize that, in actuality, uncertainty can't be reduced to zero, so it must be *preserved.* "There are times when numbers conceal more than they reveal," Russo says. "The desire for numerical precision may be misplaced. It may give a false sense of precision. You need other kinds of rigor than numerical. Uncertainty should be reduced as far as it can be—and no further."

Chapter 4

Preparing for the Unknown

"The explorer . . . is looking, not for thrills, but for facts about the unknown. Often his search is a race with time against starvation. To him, an adventure is merely a bit of bad planning, brought to light by the test of trial. . . . Serious work in exploration calls for as definite and rigorous professional preparation as does success in any other serious work in life."

—ROALD AMUNDSEN, POLAR EXPLORER[1]

Imagine you are an early explorer setting sail into the true unknown. You consider three possible scenarios before you leave. The first is that you will arrive in an Arctic wasteland with drifting snow and sub-zero temperatures. But given your limited knowledge of the world, you determine that it may also be possible that this new world is one of intense Saharan heat. Third, you suppose you might find yourself working your way through the winding passes of treacherous mountains. What do you bring with you on your journey: sled dogs, camels, or pack mules? It depends on where you end up, but the problem is, you have no way of knowing at the time you set sail where that will be.

You could make a bet on one of the scenarios and pack only desert gear, for example, but then you would be totally unprepared if you ended up in the Arctic. If, instead, you carefully considered the different scenarios before your departure and prepared to some degree for all of them, you would be ready for all three extreme scenarios and anything in between.

The first things you pack are items that would be useful in all of the possible terrains. You will need food and fresh water wherever you go, although there may be local sources of both. You'll need cooking equipment and the basic household items necessary to sustain your life. You'll need a ship and navigational tools to get to your destination.

After you pack this first set of all-purpose items, you have to identify supplies that are specific to one of the three scenarios. You'll need sleds and snowsuits in the first scenario, sand gear in the second, and climbing gear in the third. But you have only limited resources to procure supplies and a limited amount of space in your ship, so you need to pack wisely. First you want to include items that can be flexibly deployed, such as lightweight material that can be used either for hot-weather clothing or as an outer shell for cold-weather gear. You might create sleds with runners that can move across both snow and sand and can be converted into wagons for the mountains.

Finally, some items are useful in only one of the scenarios: the goose-down sleeping bags and parka fill, for example, would be superfluous in the heat of the desert. For these items, you need to consider as much as possible the likelihood that each scenario will come to pass. You know you can't bet on a single scenario, but you may be able to assign a subjective probability. For example, you could research stories of travelers who headed in the same general direction. Even limited knowledge of global climate and other information might offer some insights into what lies ahead of you. You would pack more or less of the supplies related to one scenario based on your weighting of that scenario.

The Race for the Pole

The situation facing you as a manager is even more complex than a competition against nature. You are not only headed into uncertain terrain but are racing against competitors as well. When British explorer Robert Falcon Scott and Norwegian explorer Roald Amundsen were racing to the South Pole in 1911, they knew roughly which direction they were heading into, but the specifics of the unexplored terrain were unknown and the weather was highly unpredictable. In a race of this kind, you not only have to beat out the elements, you also have to beat out the competition. You need some resources and capabilities just to survive as well as others that will truly differentiate your efforts from your rivals'.

In the case of the race for the South Pole, differences in resources and capabilities contributed to Amundsen's success. He reached the pole first and brought his party back safely, while Scott perished with his men on the return trip.[2] One of the differentiating resources and capabilities was the mode of transportation. While Scott used unreliable motorized sledges, horses and man-hauling, Amundsen used dogsleds and skis, which were more efficient and better adapted to the environment.

Another factor that differentiated between success and failure was Amundsen's ability to create well-stocked and well-marked supply depots positioned close to the pole. He had stocked ten times as much food per person as Scott. This margin made a tremendous difference: Scott's party perished on the return trip just eleven miles short of a depot with one ton of supplies. Amundsen also used a strategy of marking depots with numbered flags at half-mile intervals perpendicular to his path. In the very uncertain environment of the return trip, in which his team was hampered by storms and poor navigational equipment, finding these needles in a haystack greatly increased his margin for error. It gave him a ten-mile barrier of small flags across his path, so even if he missed the depot itself, he was almost certain to run into one of the flags (as he did on at least one occasion in a dense fog).

Amundsen and his men also demonstrated a capacity for continuous learning, while Scott's party never became very proficient in using skis, dogsleds, or Eskimo clothing. Although Scott knew about these methods and had opportunities to study them—especially after the weaknesses of the British approach using ponies and man-hauling had been amply demonstrated—the British team never mastered these skills. In contrast, Amundsen had spent a lifetime as a careful student of the indigenous peoples in the Arctic, learning how to handle dogs and survive in polar regions. He took copious notes and voraciously read the accounts of previous explorers looking for fresh insights into strategies and terrain. And even as they waited at their base camp, Amundsen's men set up workshops and redesigned sleds, skis, and boots to reduce weight and improve performance based on their experiences out on the ice while laying in supplies.

In large part, the differences in resources and capabilities of the two polar parties contributed to their relative success and Amundsen's survival. Similarly, having resources and capabilities that are tailored to the environment and differentiated from those of rivals is what leads to success in business. But given the uncertainty of the future, how can companies develop the capabilities and resources they need to succeed?

Expanding the Resource-Based View

The question of which resources and capabilities will be most valuable on the journey has been a central focus of the "resource-based view" of corporate strategy.[3] This school considers the successful firm as a bundle of somewhat unique resources and capabilities. If these core capabilities are scarce, durable, defensible, or hard to imitate, they can form the basis for sustainable competitive advantage and surplus profit. The resource-based view was initially inwardly focused, aimed at identifying those core competencies of the firm that give it advantages over rivals. Looking forward from this inward approach, managers would ask how these same capabilities might be leveraged in other applications. For example, Honda took its experience in small engine design and leveraged it from motorcycles to small cars to snow blowers.[4] And Marriott is leveraging its hospitality and property management capabilities into retirement and nursing homes.

But the inward focus is just half the picture. As the external environment changes, so does the competitive advantage that these capabilities confer. Honda's small engine capabilities became much more valuable as the oil crisis of the 1970s created a strong demand for small fuel-efficient cars. But it became less valuable as easing oil prices opened the way to a proliferation of large trucks, minivans, and SUVs. By looking outward and forward, a company not only can identify ways to leverage its existing resources and capabilities but also can better see what new capabilities it needs to develop further. This process helps identify which capabilities might be discarded and how changes in the environment create opportunities to apply resources and capabilities in new ways.

Key Success Factors: What It Takes to Win

The resources and capabilities that set firms apart in their overall performance in a given environment are *Key Success Factors* (KSFs). The notion of KSFs is based on the intuitively appealing idea that certain activities, resources, or capabilities are much more important to success than others in a particular industry, and that senior managers should focus on those that are key.[5] Key Success Factors answer the questions, What will it take for a leading company to continue to lead? What will it take for a start-up company to succeed in this marketplace?

Some of these resources and capabilities are merely "table stakes," those needed to stay in the game, as illustrated in Exhibit 4-1. These are important, but they don't differentiate a company from its rivals. In banking, for example, automatic teller machines are needed to serve customers, but they don't provide an advantage over rival banks because they all use ATMs. Table stakes are necessary but not sufficient for success. In contrast, Key Success Factors are those resources and capabilities that differentiate a company from its rivals. Companies need to have table stakes to stay in the game and Key Success Factors to win.

In golf, for example, the main Key Success Factor is not the length of a player's tee shot but rather how well the player can putt (at least on the pro tour). Skill in putting is a KSF, while skill in driving is a table stake, as the expression "drive for show and putt for dough" captures so well. If

Exhibit 4-1: Key Success Factors and Table Stakes

	COMPANY	RIVALS
KEY SUCCESS FACTORS (Not all rivals master these equally)	Capability	
	Resource	
	Capability	
	Resource	
TABLE STAKES (Rivals also have these)	Capability	Capability
	Resource	Resource
	Capability	Capability
	Resource	Resource

you can't make a tee shot, you are out of the game, but ability to putt is what sets golf pros apart from the rest of the competition.

While the distinctions between table stakes and Key Success Factors, as well as those between assets, resources, and capabilities are important conceptually, here I focus primarily on KSFs since they are directly concerned with *what it takes to win* in a given scenario.

Exhibit 4-2 shows highlights of a list of potential Key Success Factors that was developed for credit unions. KSFs were identified in the areas of management, technology, marketing, operations, and member service. While some of these KSFs may be relevant to your industry, this list is only illustrative. Also, whether a factor is a Key Success Factor or merely a table stake for you depends upon your relative capabilities in relation to your rivals; again, this will vary by industry and by firm.

Some KSFs may be current strengths, while others may need to be developed. For example, the ability to engage in data mining was not a traditional strength of most credit unions. This is a capability they now have to develop. To develop each of these KSFs, managers have to engage in activities, acquire or develop a particular set of skills, and assemble necessary resources. As an illustration, consider the KSF related to building data-mining capabilities. It requires the activity of data acquisition and member analysis, skills in data base administration, and the resources of a server, database system, and workstations. (A more complete picture of the activities, skills, and resources is provided in Exhibit 4-3.) Each KSF entails a complex *system* of interrelated components that reach deep and wide across the organization. As managers begin to assess and build these KSFs, this more detailed analysis is critical.

Shifting Key Success Factors

Key Success Factors are different in different environments. In most parts of the world, gold is much more valuable than water, but if you are alone in the hot desert and are dying of thirst, gold is nearly worthless. Clearly, the value of a given asset or capability depends upon the environment.

The KSFs I have talked about are a snapshot at a given point in time. When the competitive environment remains relatively stable, successful companies are usually well adapted to it. It is when there is a shift in the environment that the organization's current capabilities and resources

Exhibit 4-2: Possible Key Success Factors for Credit Unions

Management and Board
• Caliber and quality of board and senior staff • Having a shared strategic vision among senior staff, board, and sponsor • Creating and maintaining strategic relationships with vendors and other partners • . . .
Technology
• Complete integration of data-processing systems with other systems (e.g., CRM, MCIF, ATM) • Wireless and Internet access for all transactions and communications • Developing data-mining capabilities to detect trends and new patterns in member preferences • . . .
Marketing
• Ability to recognize and respond to changing market conditions (re customers and competitors) • Having a strong and consistent branding strategy in everything done • Ability to cross-sell products and services based on deep knowledge of member needs • . . .
Operations
• Efficient operations and low cost of processing transactions compared to industry average • Regulatory compliance and timely reporting to all relevant authorities • Having a well-trained and motivated workforce through hiring, selection, and education • . . .
Member Service
• Developing and maintaining a reputation for excellence in member service • Creating and maintaining a member-centric culture in which the customer comes first • Developing appropriate metrics and reward systems for customer excellence • . . .

Source: *Credit Union Executives Society and Decision Strategies International, Inc.*

Exhibit 4-3: Illustration of Activities, Skills, and Resources Contributing to a KSF

KSF: Develop Data Mining Capabilities to Detect Trends and New Patterns in Member Preferences		
ACTIVITIES	**SKILLS**	**RESOURCES**
Set Goals and Objectives	Strategic Planning	Management / Board
Data Acquisition / Cross-organizational Validation	Data Base Administration Cross-functional Cooperation Defining Business Rules	ETL (Extract Translation Loading) Expertise Data Base / System Server Capital
Member Analysis • Modeling • Segmentation	Interpersonal, Technical, Analytical, Financial, Operational, Marketing / Sales Presentation	Management & Staff Vendor / Partner Robust Workstations for In-House Work Capital / Investment
Product Analysis • Pricing • Fees	Interpersonal, Technical, Analytical, Financial, Operational, Marketing / Sales Presentation Rate Shopping Knowledge of Competition	Management & Staff Vendors / Partners
Tracking of Results	Analysis & Reporting	Technical and Marketing Staff and Management

Source: *Credit Union Executives Society and Decision Strategies International, Inc.*

may be mismatched with the future KSFs. A Bedouin with a camel and tent is well adapted to life in the desert but would be ill prepared for a move to the Arctic. Now capabilities that once were sources of success may no longer be Key Success Factors; in fact, they may be liabilities or failure factors. Consequently, as the environment shifts, organizations may need a new set of capabilities to be successful.

The challenge of uncertainty is that you cannot know for sure what capabilities will be most important for the future. Should a pharmaceutical firm move aggressively into genomics and biotech, or should it continue its traditional drug-development capabilities? Should a bank launch a major online initiative, or should it sink its resources into developing its branches? Should a newspaper pour millions of dollars into a new publishing plant, or should it put more resources into developing wireless news services? There is no way of answering these questions a priori since the value of these investments will depend on what environment unfolds.

Many industries have seen their Key Success Factors shift radically over time. During the 1960s the top key success factors in the automobile industry were (1) efficient mass production using an automated assembly line, (2) labor cost control through complex negotiations with unions, and (3) an efficient and exclusive dealership network. After the energy crises of the 1970s and the subsequent globalization of the car industry, the key success factors shifted toward fuel efficiency, high-quality manufacturing, brand development, supply chain management (to allow for more flexible production of different models), and strategic alliances to obtain global reach. Similarly, the steel industry saw its key success factors shift from economies of scale (remember the dominance of U.S. Steel) to short delivery cycles, flexible manufacturing (via minimills), and marketing. Shifts in scenarios for the external environment are a key driver of change in the key success factors needed to win. In the U.S. pharmaceutical industry, the quality of a company's sales and marketing activities has been a greater contributor to profitability than the quality of drug discovery over the past decade, but this may change with the rise of biotechnology and genomics. Similarly, a series of external changes in the infant formula business has radically transformed the key success factors in that industry (see box).

While we can usually recognize shifts in Key Success Factors in retro-

Changing Key Success Factors: A Shifting Formula for Success

U.S. infant formula makers have seen a variety of changes in regulation, industry structure, and customer demand that reshaped the industry. In the mid-1960s, driven by rising use of formula, the industry enjoyed secure and stable markets. A few companies, led by Ross Products (a division of Abbott Laboratories) and Mead Johnson Nutritionals (part of Bristol-Myers Squibb), controlled over 80 percent of the American infant nutritional market. Because infant formula is viewed by the Food and Drug Administration (FDA) as a medical food, strong ties to hospitals along with cozy relationships with pediatricians were the keys to high and stable margins. In the 1980s, however, the situation began to change. The Infant Formula Act was enacted in 1980 to assure high standards for all infant formulas. The act assured consumers that all formulas were safe and consequently weakened claims of product differentiation. Then the Women, Infants, and Children (WIC) program was launched by the U.S. government, providing low-cost access to infant formula for many families. WIC soon accounted for over 50 percent of domestic sales. Eventually, companies had to compete on price (generally winner-takes-all bids, state by state) to qualify for the government's program.

In addition to legislative changes, there were also social changes. The increasingly powerful La Leche League extolled the virtues of breast milk over infant formula and cow's milk, reducing demand for formula. There were also shifts in the competitive landscape, as international food and pharmaceutical giant Nestlé S.A. of Switzerland entered the U.S. market in 1988 by purchasing the Carnation company. Nestlé decided to target parents directly in its marketing, bypassing pediatricians, who had gradually lost power due to fundamental changes in the U.S. health care sector. Nestlé's direct marketing approach was in part possible because the United States was not a signatory to the World Health Organization's (WHO's) guidelines for marketing and selling infant formula (following abuses in emerging markets). The incumbents needed to develop a new set of capabilities to succeed in this transformed market.

The Key Success Factors of the infant formula business changed dramatically in a short period of time. The leading companies had competed by offering a differentiated product (with high margins) to pediatricians and hospitals in a domestic market, but then had to offer a low-cost formula directly to customers and compete against global players. The forces that brought about this change were both external (such as globalization, health care restructuring, and governmental regulation) as well as endogenous to the industry (low-cost formulations, lobbying, charges of collusion, and new entrants). The ability of the traditional players to succeed depends on these shifts in the environment and competition, as well as the resources and capabilities they bring to the table or can develop.

spect, the challenge is to anticipate them and prepare for their possibility before they emerge. A company will pay a high price for holding on to a buggy whip in an automotive age. But the company also pays a price for moving too quickly in the wrong direction, such as the pioneers who developed interactive television in the early 1990s only to find the world had moved to the Internet.

Scenarios can offer insights into the KSFs that might be valuable in the future. In the health care scenarios discussed in Chapter 3, if the technologically repressed world of "Health Care Held Hostage" emerges, operational capabilities that allow a company to be more efficient will become far more valuable. If, on the other hand, the high-tech "Last Frontier" scenario emerges, capabilities to create and manage advanced information technology and knowledge-management systems will be the new dimensions of competition. Looking more deeply at scenarios offers insights into what KSFs might be most valuable in the future and, even more important, which KSFs will be valuable *across* multiple scenarios.

Segments and Synergies

Before considering how to develop flexible capabilities across scenarios, I must address another issue in assessing what it takes to win. You have to consider not only the possibilities for the environment but also the specific playing fields that you will choose to compete in. Profits from uncertainty come from targeting distinct business segments, and the choice of these segments will determine what it takes to win. In this section, I will consider how segmenting your business affects KSFs.

Scenarios address the potential weather conditions into which a business is heading, but another important factor is the terrain in which the business chooses to compete. Scenarios might be thought of as the weather conditions, while the segments are the features of the terrain. The combination of both creates the overall competitive context and hence determines the resources and capabilities that will be needed to succeed.

Research indicates that profitability varies far more across segments within an industry than across industries.[6] The focus in KSF analysis, therefore, should be on key business segments rather than on an entire industry. Certain resources and capabilities will be valuable only in some segments of the market. For example, a personal computer maker who competes in the business market will need different resources and capabilities than a computer maker competing in just the home market.

As a simple illustration, consider the different characteristics of key market segments in the early days of the personal computer industry:

- *Big business:* Large quantities purchased, central purchasing, limited price sensitivity, less need for user friendliness, high need for networking capabilities, computing power important.
- *Small business:* Smaller quantities purchased, individual buying decision, more price sensitivity, more need for user friendliness, low need for networking capabilities.
- *Home:* One unit purchased, individual buying decision, high price sensitivity, high need for user friendliness, low need for networking capabilities.
- *Education, university:* Large quantities purchased, central purchasing, more price sensitivity, less need for user friendliness, high need for networking capabilities, computing power and sophisticated software important.
- *Education, elementary:* Large quantities purchased, central purchasing, more price sensitivity, high need for user friendliness, high need for networking capabilities.
- *Workstations:* Small quantities purchased, individual or group buying decisions, less price sensitivity, less need for user friendliness, high

need for networking capabilities (via servers), computing power and speed very important.

The very different sets of customer needs, technologies, channels, and rivals encountered in each market segment suggest different Key Success Factors. Some of these resources and capabilities overlap, but others are distinctive to a particular segment. For example, the big business segment requires a strong corporate sales force, while the consumer segment requires strong consumer marketing capabilities, but both require similar manufacturing capabilities. Choosing to compete in a given segment is a de facto commitment to develop the Key Success Factors needed to win there. Given limits on the company's resources and focus, managers need to choose their battles wisely. For example, after the rise of the personal computer, Apple decided to get out of the large business segment, concentrating on education, home, and small business (particularly graphic design and video production).

Frames for Reconceptualizing Segments

Within an organization, segments are often fixed in its mindset and structure (with different divisions serving different segments). It is easy to accept these segments as reality, losing sight of the fact that they are just a frame of mind based on conventional wisdom. For example, while Coca-Cola and Pepsi were engaged in the cola wars, outsiders began transforming the beverage market by adding iced teas, sports drinks, and bottled water. The cola giants had to expand their view of the market (and their capabilities) to include these new segments. In uncertain markets, more than ever, it is not just the business that is changing but also the customers it serves.

The forces driving such consumer changes—from an aging population to a focus on ethnic interests to changes in disposable income—properly belong in the scenarios. They constitute the external context in which firms are competing. But the possibility that these forces (in combination with perhaps others) may create entire new market segments—such as diet drinks, eco-safaris, and space tourism—should be reflected in the strategic segmentation framework.

The best way to create new segments or redefine existing segments is to explore the segmentation task through multiple lenses. Business segmentation has a long history, starting with product segmentation in the 1950s, market segmentation in the 1960s, and product/market segments in the 1970s and 1980s.[7] In *product* segmentation, the focus is on the varying requirements and strategies from a manufacturing viewpoint. In *market* segmentation, the focus is on the different needs and characteristics of each customer group. In *strategic* segmentation, the aim is to highlight and delineate the important but essentially different battlefields that the firm is or might be competing in.

Segments can be organized around a variety of frames, from traditional to unconventional (see box). These may include such strategic factors as technologies used, customer needs satisfied, marketing channels, growth rates, innovation, forces of competition, entry and exit barriers, pricing practices, distribution channels, value chains, customer profiles, government regulation and protection, and so on.

To give an example of different ways of segmenting, consider the insurance industry. A traditional (and common) frame is to segment by product (life insurance, health, property and casualty, and so on) or region (United States, Europe, Asia). A more enduring scheme (since products come and go) is to focus on customer needs satisfied, from protection needs to wealth accumulation to advice. A deeper and perhaps more strategic segmentation is to consider what causes insurance products to fail. One cause is adverse selection, which occurs for instance when homeowners with a low risk of flooding don't insure their homes and only the high-risk customers remain. Another factor is moral hazard or the risk of fraud (such as faking a loss of jewelry or setting fire to one's home). Segmenting on the basis of adverse selection and other causes of failure could lead to new insights and strategies, even if these segments are unusual. For example, some financial services companies such as Providian have become successful by targeting segments that had traditionally been considered poor risks. By creating special products for these segments, they managed the risks and provided an appropriate return. (Providian, however, did not fare well during the recession of 2001, which indicates a failure to consider multiple scenarios.)

The business segmentation task can be approached from the top down or from the bottom up. It can be performed intuitively or systematically. Approaches can range from asking managers to think about ways they might resegment their business to using formal multidimensional

Potential Ways to Segment the Market

- By product or service
- By customer profile
- By delivery channel
- By geographic region
- By type of competitor
- By growth or profitability
- By degree of regulation
- By value chain

scaling and cluster analyses to statistically define relevant segments.[8] In sum, various tools can be used to distill the relevant bases of segmentation and to identify the major segments.

Creating Segments That Are Relevant across Scenarios

The best segmentation maps apply across scenarios. Creating them requires a deeper analysis of the playing field to rethink the existing approach and define segments that make sense across all scenarios. For example, a newspaper company created an initial segmentation scheme focused on channels for communicating information (such as telephone, radio, TV, print, and PC). But then it became apparent that in one of its scenarios—one focused on digital convergence—these distinctions no longer applied. This observation provided the necessary impetus to segment the playing field in even more fundamental ways—such as print versus electronic or one-way versus interactive communications—that would be meaningful across all the scenarios.

While the segmentation scheme itself should be invariant across scenarios, the size of each segment and the nature of the competition may be very different under different scenarios. The actions the company needs to take to win in each segment may also be very different depending on the scenario. For example, a segment targeting cyberconsumers will be much larger and filled with many more rivals in a scenario of rapid Internet diffusion than in a scenario that entails a slow spread of technology.

A sound strategic segmentation framework must meet at least three conditions:

1. The segmentation scheme itself must be applicable across all scenarios.
2. It should be broader than the firm's current product scope, markets served, and technologies employed.

3. The segments identified within the scheme must be limited in number (four to eight) and truly differ strategically in terms of their competitive structure.

In practice, companies have the most difficulty doing the above when facing converging markets or entirely new ones.

Converging Markets

Sometimes the forces driving the scenarios themselves offer fundamental ways to reshape segments, as suggested above in the newspaper example. Technological shifts reconfigured segments of the information industry. In the 1980s, broadly defined, it contained separate markets for office equipment, telecommunications, distribution, computers, consumer electronics, information vendors, and media and publishing, as shown in Exhibit 4-4.[9] Over the next two decades, these separate continents drifted together, moving toward a single fused market for information, as shown in Exhibit 4-5. Markets that were once distinct became blurred. The financial services industry is presently undergoing a similar blurring of boundaries, as is health care.

In such cases, companies often have to develop resources and capabilities in areas where they have not had traditional strengths. A computer company might need telecommunications or consumer electronics capabilities to succeed. It also means that companies are competing against a new set of rivals. Consumer electronics and entertainment companies such as Sony that have moved into computing or cable operators such as Comcast are bumping into telecommunications. Some of the Key Success Factors that once provided a distinguishing advantage in the original market may be mere table stakes in the new combined market. For example, a computer company with some communications capabilities may have been a stand-out in competition with other computer companies but could be a laggard in competition with telecom firms.

Regulatory changes or shifts in complementary industries can also lead to powerful shifts in market definitions and Key Success Factors. Pharmaceutical firms have had to address the emergence of the health maintenance organization (HMO), which inserted a new set of powerful players between the large pharmaceutical firms and the doctors making prescriptions. To compete for the customers that are part of HMOs, com-

Exhibit 4-4: Information Industry in 1980: Separate Worlds

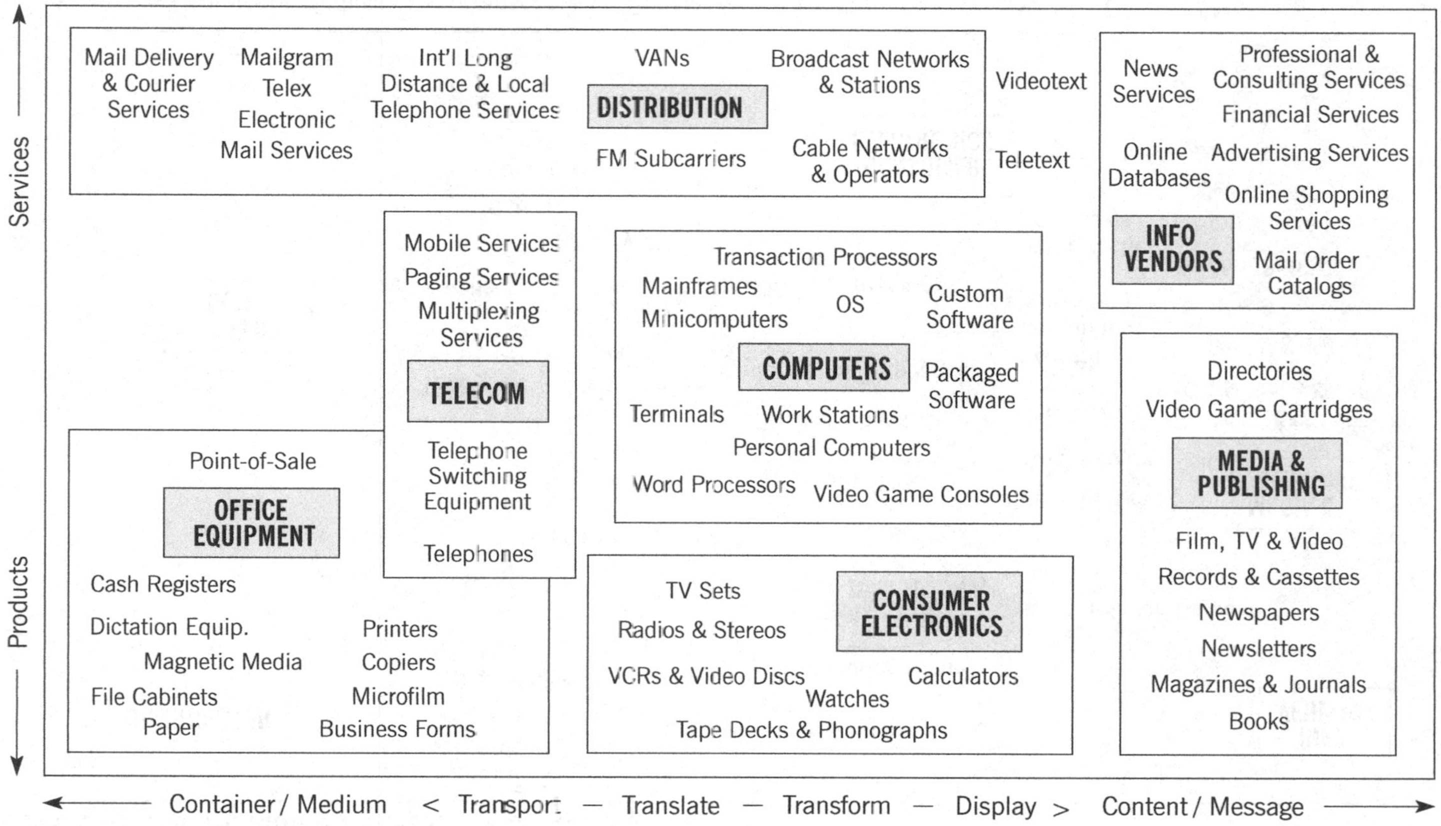

Source: *John Sculley, Apple Computers*

Exhibit 4-5: Information Industry in 2000: Convergence

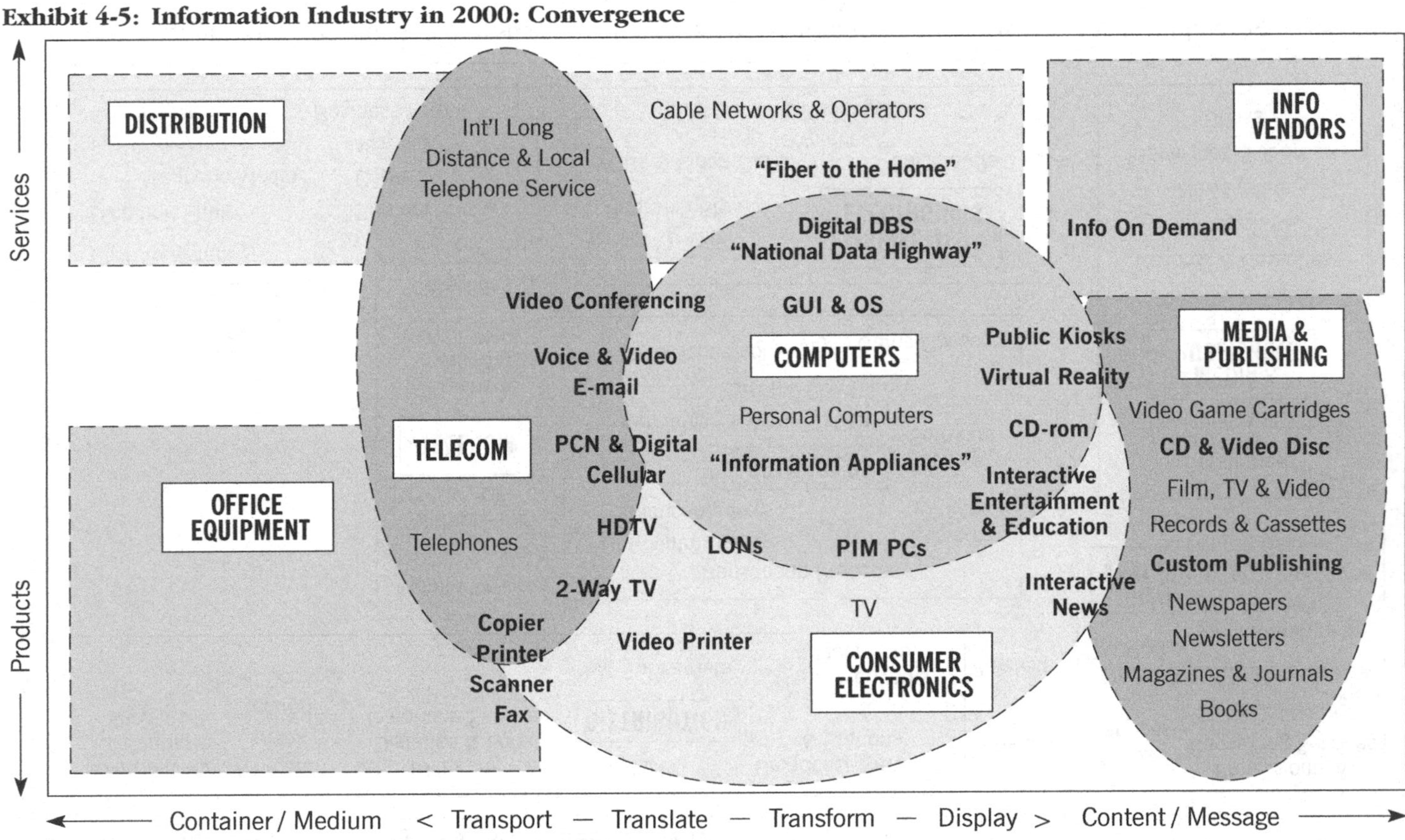

panies need a different set of resources and capabilities from those under traditional insurance plans.

There are great challenges in adding capabilities to meet these converging markets. AT&T found this out when it sought to draw in the computing capabilities of NCR. The company ultimately was spun off again, at great cost to AT&T. Similarly, Pepsi found that its business formula became too watered down when it sought to absorb several fast-food franchises, and it ultimately sold them off. And as will be discussed in Chapter 5, Monsanto and other chemical companies expended great efforts and resources to develop life sciences capabilities that proved controversial and hence less valuable than initially imagined. Companies need to consider acquisition and alliance strategies to add these new capabilities for success. But the caveat is that many acquisitions and alliances fail to deliver on their promises and that the premium that the acquirer paid often becomes a loss.

Assessing Segments That Don't Exist

One of the serious challenges of segmentation in an environment of rapid change is anticipating new segments that might emerge. What did the strategic segments look like for Internet users in the early 1990s? What were the characteristics of the home computer user segment in the early 1980s? What did the market for fax machines look like in the early 1970s?

In the 1980s Knight-Ridder moved aggressively into a new technology called videotext that some thought might replace the physical newspaper. It was designed to deliver news to customers' television monitors via cable rather than traditional newsprint. After investing $50 million and nearly three years in its Viewtron system, Knight-Ridder pulled the plug in 1986. As James Batten, then president of Knight-Ridder Newspapers, commented at the time, "Sometimes pioneers get rewarded with arrows in the back."[10]

At the same time, major newspapers such as Knight-Ridder, like most of the rest of the world, were slow to see the potential of the Internet until the market was well developed. Even when the technology trajectory is clear, the interaction of consumers with the technology is far from certain. This uncertainty about the market creates uncertainty about the resources and capabilities needed to win. The Key Success Factors that are needed to satisfy consumers who have embraced videotext are quite different from those that are needed to succeed in a market that has moved onto the Internet.

There are a variety of strategies for identifying strategic segments for a new technology before customers in these segments even know they exist (see box). While these approaches are critical in launching new technology, they also can be used to creatively approach the challenge of identifying broad and enduring strategic segments. New ways of segmenting may initially seem awkward. Like new shoes, you have to get used to them. But getting stuck in an outdated view of your business will hurt more than the occasional blister associated with new shoes. Too many generals have ended up fighting the previous war—and losing. As John Sculley was fond of saying when heading Apple Computer, If you think like your competitors, you are not thinking. So try to develop fresh strategic views of your business.

In addition to looking at the new capabilities needed to meet existing or transformed segments, companies also need to look outside their traditional industry for applications of their existing capabilities. What are the emerging markets, and where can the firm's capabilities be applied? For example, by identifying the need for glass in telecommunications, Corning redeployed its expertise in glass manufacturing to fiber optics. And the Marriott hotel chain is applying its hospitality, lodging, and real estate management capabilities to the growing market segment of assisted living and retirement homes.

Strategies for Preparing for Multiple Futures

Given that Key Success Factors differ across scenarios and segments, how can you identify the resources and capabilities that you will need to develop for the future? Companies cannot turn on a dime. By their nature, strategic capabilities are deeply embedded and cannot be bought or sold on the open market. (Those that can be tend to be less valuable and are almost always in the realm of table stakes rather than discriminating Key Success Factors.) Differentiating resources and capabilities are typically built over many years, are deeply rooted in the culture and processes of the organization, and take time to change or redeploy. To develop the resources and capabilities that you will need three, five, or ten years into the future, you may have to start building or strengthening

Creating Markets from Scratch: Insights from George Day

How can managers assess the potential of markets that don't exist? Marketing professor George Day of the Wharton School, author of *Market-Driven Strategy* and *The Market-Driven Organization,* offers a variety of strategies, including:[11]

- **Learning from lead users** The early adopters of any given technology can offer important insights into the diffusion patterns of the technology and how it might be used. While these early users may be quite different from the market that will ultimately emerge, they can offer a valuable practical understanding of the needs of the future segments.

- **Learning about latent needs** Rather than focusing on the technology, focus on the needs that the technology can meet. What are the customers' underlying needs? These needs can be assessed by monitoring customer complaints, listening to customer stories, or observing customer behavior. For example, when Kimberly-Clark listened carefully to stories of parents, it realized that parents viewed diapers as clothing. Based on this insight, it developed training pants that looked and functioned like underpants. In assessing the market for fax machines in the 1970s, Xerox looked at the extent and frequency of urgent written messages, their time sensitivity, and the form and size of the message (number of pages, use of graphics, and so on). It contrasted the potential of fax capability with existing solutions such as mail, telephone, telegrams, and express delivery. Using this process, it estimated a latent demand for fax-type features at about 1 million units per year. Although it still significantly underestimated the market potential for fax machines, this careful analysis of latent needs made Xerox far more optimistic about the potential market than its peers. (Unfortunately, to meet this need Xerox chose a PC-based system rather than the stand-alone fax that became the standard. This shows that even if one accurately anticipates *what* a potential future scenario might be, it is also important to anticipate *how* to get there.)[12]

- **Anticipating inflections** The diffusion of emerging technologies is marked by inflection points where the market takes off and aggressive competition begins. Getting too far ahead of this curve can lead to an aggressive push into a market that has yet to develop. Getting too far behind the curve can cause the company to be left in the dust. Among the ways managers can anticipate these inflection points are: tracking leading indicators, performing diffusion modeling, and using "information acceleration" to create studies that place consumers into a realistic future technological environment to see how they react.

them now. But given the uncertainty of the future, which ones should you focus on? As you set sail toward this uncertain future, what do you need to stow aboard your ship at the start of the journey?

Once you have identified scenarios and segments, you can determine the Key Success Factors needed to win in the different scenarios and strategic segments. To illustrate, consider the highly simplified KSF matrix shown in Exhibit 4-6 for the two health care scenarios discussed in Chapter 3 crossed against just two different market segments—consumers and hospitals/doctors.

Exhibit 4-6: Simplified Key Success Factor Matrix

		"Last Frontier" Scenario	"Health Care Held Hostage" Scenario	Resilient across Scenarios
SEGMENTS	Consumer	Customer relationships Data mining Branding Genomics, Biotech Consumer marketing	Customer relationships Data mining Branding Consumer marketing Lobbying Privacy protection	*Customer relationships* *Data mining* *Branding* *Consumer marketing*
SEGMENTS	Hospital / Doctor	Customer relationships Data mining Branding Genomics, Biotech Direct sales force	Customer relationships Data mining Branding Direct sales force Lobbying Privacy protection	*Customer relationships* *Data mining* *Branding* *Direct sales force*
	Synergistic across Segments	*Customer relationships* *Data mining* *Branding* *Genomics, Biotech*	*Customer relationships* *Data mining* *Branding* *Lobbying* *Privacy protection*	*Customer relationships* *Data mining* *Branding*

Robust KSFs

Depending on how often they occur across segments and scenarios, KSFs fall into different categories:

- *Resilient across scenarios:* Some KSFs are shared across different scenarios for a specific segment. For example, "consumer marketing" is a KSF in the consumer segment of health care whether the "Last Frontier" or the "Health Care Held Hostage" scenario emerges. But this is not a KSF for the hospitals/doctors segment under either scenario. Instead, the direct sales force is a KSF in the hospitals/doctors segment regardless of what scenario emerges. The choice to invest in building or expanding these resources and capabilities depends upon the weight the company gives to a specific segment. For example, if managers give the hospitals/doctors segment more weight, they will invest more in the direct sales force than in consumer marketing capabilities.

- *Synergistic across segments:* Some of the KSFs are synergistic across all the segments of a given scenario. For example, genomics and biotech capabilities are vital to the "Last Frontier" scenario regardless of the segment. Strong lobbying and privacy protections are vital to the "Health Care Held Hostage" scenario no matter what segment is targeted. In this case, the weights that managers attach to the different scenarios can help guide investments in these KSFs. If managers assess that the "Last Frontier" scenario has a 75 percent likelihood of emerging while "Health Care Held Hostage" has a 25 percent likelihood, they should invest resources in the related KSFs accordingly.

- *Robust across scenarios and segments:* Finally, some of the KSFs will be robust across both scenarios and segments. No matter what scenario emerges or what segment the company targets, these resources and capabilities will differentiate it from its rivals. Whether the high-tech, information-rich environment of the "Last Frontier" scenario or the constrained environment of "Health Care Held Hostage" emerges, whether it focuses on consumer markets or hospitals/doctors, the company will need strong customer relationship capabilities, data mining, and branding. These are types of KSFs that can be built and invested in with relative confidence. They are the low-hanging fruit that will provide value across all the anticipated scenarios and segments. They constitute "no regret" decisions.

The approaches used to develop various KSFs depend upon synergy, resilience, and robustness. For those that are not robust, the commitment will depend upon the weights given to the scenarios or segments. In this case, managers should consider using an options approach to make a limited commitment up front that creates the opportunity for stronger commitments later on. For example, a pharmaceutical giant that makes a small, early-stage investment in a biotechnology company buys a strategic option for commercialization if the new technology proves successful. The creation and deployment of such strategic options are discussed in more detail in Chapter 6.

As KSFs continue to change, close monitoring of the scenarios and segments will offer insights into when or whether to exercise these strategic options. Chapter 7 will explore strategies for dynamic monitoring. These strategies can be used to identify when a particular scenario is becoming more likely to emerge, which means that the value of KSFs related to that scenario will be more valuable. This, in turn, will affect investments in the particular KSF over time.

This combination of approaches will ensure that the company can develop the resources and capabilities needed to succeed across a range of scenarios and segments—and do so in a way that balances organizational commitment and strategic risks. Note that this is done not by reducing uncertainty but by more fully understanding the implications of uncertainty and developing creative as well as flexible strategies to deal with it.

Setting Sail

Any detailed analysis of KSFs quickly evolves into a rather complex picture of the future, as shown by this simple example of just two health care segments and two scenarios. In an actual case, this process could yield a wide range of potential KSFs arrayed across multiple scenarios and segments. The resulting welter of potential directions does not lead to the kind of rallying cry that would compel an organization to follow its leaders to the ends of the Earth. Now that we have examined the KSFs and segments, you need to zoom out again to see the bigger picture and connect it with the organization. You need to use these insights into capabilities and segments to create a unique strategic vision that builds on your present assets, capabilities and culture. This is the focus of Chapter 5. How do you round out the big picture? What do you need to do today to win in the future? How do you need to change your resources, capabilities, and perhaps culture? How can you organize and motivate the organization to get there?

In working through this process with companies, the analysis of scenarios, segments, and KSFs sometimes seems to managers like a detour in getting to this big picture. Managers are often in a rush to get to this broader perspective. But the careful analysis of the future and segments helps ensure that the strategic vision is firmly grounded in the reality of the situation. This prevents it from drifting into vacuous statements or lofty ideals that are either not based in reality or are limited by the blinders of conventional wisdom and past experience. Once you understand your KSF matrix, you can then start to create an overarching vision that embodies your organization's best collective wisdom about where the world is headed and what your company needs to do to succeed. This grand synthesis is the focus of the next chapter.

Chapter 5

Building a Robust Strategic Vision

"Vision is the art of seeing things invisible."

—JONATHAN SWIFT

The story was compelling. In 1995 Monsanto CEO Robert Shapiro began to reposition the giant chemical firm as a "life sciences" company. As Shapiro explained, "We're talking about three of the largest industries in the world—agriculture, food, and health—that now operate as separate businesses. But there are a set of changes that will lead to their integration."[1] The chemical industry was undergoing what Shapiro characterized as "unprecedented discontinuity," and acting boldly in response was a life-or-death issue for companies. As he declared in a 1997 interview, "businesses grounded in the old model will become obsolete and die."[2]

The idea was that as a life sciences firm, Monsanto would manipulate plant and animal genes to develop superior seeds that would resist pests, using fewer pesticides. Monsanto spun off its specialty chemicals unit and invested heavily in agricultural biotechnology.[3] The company was galvanized around this vision. Rivals such as DuPont, Dow, Novartis, and Hoechst moved to the same vision. The industry was fundamentally reshaped. Farmers waited in line to buy one of Monsanto's first products, Roundup Ready corn, a strain of corn resistant to Monsanto's Roundup chemical weed killer, increasing sales of both the corn and the chemical. Wall Street valuations of these reborn life sciences companies soared.

But five years later the "life sciences" vision had gone to seed. Monsanto and other companies were retreating, stung by unexpectedly strong public opposition to so-called "Frankenfoods," concerns about concentration of power in the industry, and resulting investor skepticism. In December 2000 DuPont's board approved a plan to divest its pharmaceuticals business and refocus on chemicals. Monsanto and drug-maker Pharmacia & Upjohn merged to create Pharmacia and spun off Monsanto's agricultural-biotechnology business at the end of 2000. Monsanto became an autonomous subsidiary of Pharmacia.[4]

Beacons and Blinders: Telling a Certain Story in an Uncertain World

The story of life sciences represents both the power and pitfalls of a compelling strategic vision. Shapiro's vision galvanized his organization and attracted attention from Wall Street to what had been considered a commodity business. It propelled the organization forward in a new direction and reshaped the industry. Yet at least in the short run, it turned out to be a flawed vision. Monsanto and its peers placed a big bet on a future that has yet to come to pass. In essence, they bet on a single scenario for the future of the industry, despite the great uncertainty about the technology and its public acceptance.

The life sciences companies obviously recognized that there would be public concern and opposition. For example, when Calgene (later purchased by Monsanto) introduced its FlavrSavr tomato, a vegetable engineered to have a much longer shelf life than an ordinary tomato, it delayed its launch to obtain a lengthy FDA approval of its marker gene as a food additive. This helped to assure the public that it met the highest possible standards, avoid possible regulatory problems later, and create a higher barrier for competitors. Calgene also provided information to the media and to government regulators and Congress to address societal concerns about biotechnology.[5] But the life sciences industry, like the nuclear industry in the 1970s and Nestlé with infant formula in developing countries, perhaps underestimated the depth and impact of the opposition.

The Monsanto story highlights an inherent tension in creating a strategic vision for the future. A sense of certainty and clear direction are crucial to moving an organization forward, but the world is inherently uncertain. Visions can be very powerful—even if they are wrong. Leading organizational theorist Karl Weick tells the story of a troop of Swiss soldiers lost in the Alps who found their way back to camp by following a map they had found. When they arrived safely at base camp, their commander realized that they had been following a map of the Pyrenees. Just the fact that they had a map had given them the resolve to move forward and find their camp.[6] Strategy requires commitment to a course of action and belief among the troops in that action. But you shouldn't overcommit.

In developing a strategic vision for an inherently uncertain future, the delicate balance is to tell a compelling story while never losing sight of the uncertainty. As we saw in our discussion of scenarios, the future is not a straight arrow but a cone of uncertainty bound by possible scenarios, as shown in Exhibit 5-1. The breadth of this uncertainty increases the farther we move into the future. While Monsanto's investors and managers placed a bet on the scenario of life sciences flourishing, they actually lived in a world in which any number of alternative scenarios might have emerged, including the one in which public backlash left life sciences "wilting on the vine."

As powerful as stories are in propelling an organization forward, the danger is that those who created the stories begin to believe them blindly. They may pay lip service to the idea that there are uncertainties even as they ritualistically spell these risks out in great detail in their SEC filings. But the seductive power of the strategic vision often takes over, and it

Exhibit 5-1: A Certain Vision in an Uncertain World

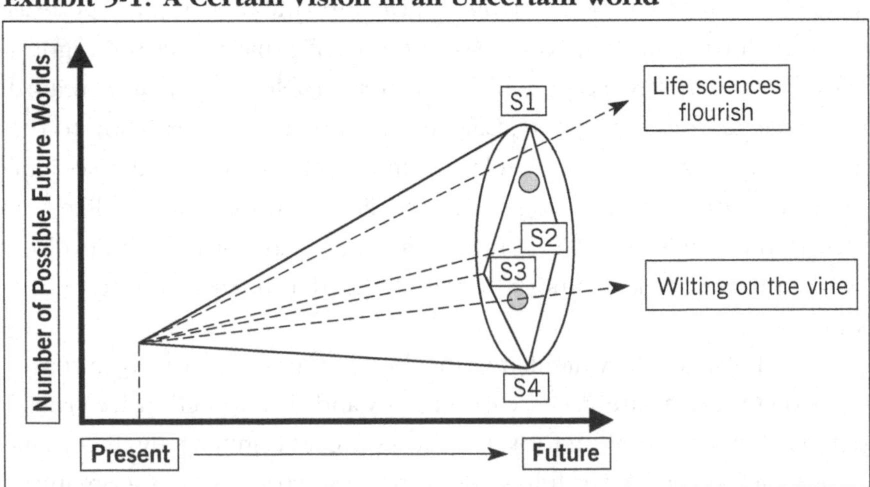

Exhibit 5-2: When a Story Becomes a Fairy Tale

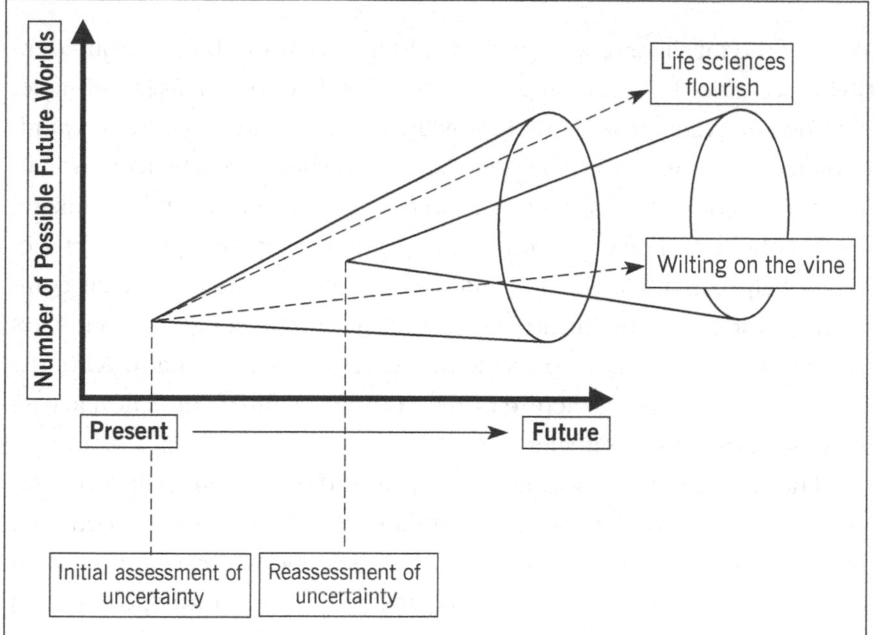

narrows the perceived "cone of uncertainty," underestimating the possibility that some scenarios will play out and overestimating the possibility of others. A careful and continuous reassessment of the "cone of uncertainty" over time may reveal that the straight-line vision falls outside the current realm of possible futures. As shown in Exhibit 5-2, the idea that life sciences would flourish now falls out of the realm of possibility, while "wilting on the vine" continues to be a stronger possibility. The once-compelling story has now become a fairy tale (a term Warren Buffett used to describe the dot-com boom in 2000).

Visions provide both beacons and blinders. The question in the case of Monsanto is: Did its vision slow its recognition of the changes in the outside environment or its reactions to these changes? Was the company prepared enough to meet the alternative future that actually it helped create? Or was it blindsided by an unusual turn of events that no one could have reasonably predicted? After all, business is about taking calculated risks in an inherently chaotic world, and so there are bound to be hits and misses.

The Need for a Robust Vision

Many of the managers I work with would like to move directly from identifying scenarios to developing action plans and options. This is a mistake. An unconnected set of initiatives will be much harder to understand, implement, and monitor. The organization will not have a beacon or map to follow. A compelling strategic vision can serve as a powerful organizing force within a firm and provides an ongoing test of strategy. Just as scenarios help sort through the welter of possible futures to create compelling stories of the future environment, the strategic vision sorts through the multitude of possible strategies for the company. A robust vision offers a coherent picture of the company's future direction across these scenarios and strategies.

The strategic vision speaks about where the company will compete, how it will compete, and what capabilities it will need to succeed (see box). It should not be confused with the amorphous corporate "mission statements" that have been criticized for producing more "poetry than product."[7] Effective strategic visions are designed with a clear understanding of the strategic challenges presented by potential emerging environments and the organization's own capabilities. John F. Kennedy's famous vision to put a man on the moon by the end of the 1960s provided a compelling direction, but it also was based on an underlying plan to achieve it. The vision was formed after careful consideration of military and geopolitical challenges posed by the Soviet launch of Sputnik as well as current and emerging capabilities in propulsion technology, materials, and computing. It was a stretch but not impossible, as it would have been if Kennedy had declared that the United States would put a man on Mars or achieve a lunar landing in a year or two. Cold war competition with the Soviet Union, and Kennedy's youthful leadership, provided a compelling motivation for the nation to get behind the idea. A good vision may appear deceptively simple, but to be successful it usually reflects a lot of underlying detail and analysis.

In an environment that was totally chaotic and unpredictable, it would be impossible to craft a coherent strategic vision at all. Any such attempt would merely be a crapshoot. In the extreme of total chaos, business leaders should seriously question whether to be playing in that environment at all. But fortunately most business environments have a mix of

Elements of an Effective Strategic Vision

A good strategic vision should include:

- A statement of what the organization wants to be and how it will get there
- Concrete goals and milestones (financial and otherwise)
- Core capabilities that need to be developed
- A description of how to change the organization
- A proposed market and product scope supporting the vision
- Robustness in the face of multiple scenarios
- Stretch to reach beyond the organization's current grasp
- Passion, in order to galvanize the organization
- Simplicity and clarity of purpose

An example of a strategic vision developed by a local newspaper company in the late 1990s:

> *"We will be the premier source of news, information, and advertising for and about the region and its residents, reaching two-thirds of the households in our eight-county geographic market on a daily basis with a variety of products and services—print, electronic, video and databases. We shall do this by excelling in . . ."*

fairly clear trends and fairly definable uncertainties, as well as some areas of outright ambiguity. This mix allows business leaders to take calculated risks, but they must do so with an understanding not only of the environment and necessary Key Success Factors (as discussed in Chapters 3 and 4) but also the organization's own capabilities. Just as John F. Kennedy had to understand the emerging capabilities in technology that would make a lunar landing possible, companies have to look for the matches between their own capabilities (and those they can develop easily) and the varying demands of different future scenarios.

Core Competencies: The Key to Robustness

When Monsanto decided that it needed to be a life sciences firm to compete in the future, the first thing it recognized was that it did not have the requisite capabilities to fulfill that vision. It could draw upon its well-developed capabilities in shepherding crop chemical products through the hurdles of government approval (a process that typically took an average of twelve years and cost over $100 million). As part of this process, it had also developed capabilities in commercializing and evaluating the potential of new products.[8] But these capabilities were not enough to become the kind of successful life sciences company that Shapiro's bold vision demanded.

Monsanto was primarily a chemical company, without deep expertise in genetic engineering and other fields that were needed to be a successful life sciences firm. So the company embarked on a radical restructuring to obtain the resources and capabilities it would need and to spin off those that no longer fit with its vision. This type of reconstructive surgery is both painful and highly risky. What if the new capabilities can't be grafted onto the existing organization? And what if the new capabilities and resources are not as valuable as they were anticipated to be? They are usually acquired at great cost, financially, strategically, and organizationally. And the clock is difficult to turn back, so a significant commitment is implied by such a strategy.

Capabilities are difficult to acquire or develop. This is why, for the most part, companies do not develop their strategies for the future from a blank slate based on the needed Key Success Factors. The outside-in vision of the Key Success Factors (discussed in Chapter 4) must be balanced against an inside-out assessment of the firm's capabilities: "What can we reasonably do, given our existing assets, resources, and capabilities? And what can't we do, given our culture and constraints? How do we need to reshape our current platform of assets and capabilities to meet the opportunities that lie ahead?" As dramatic as Monsanto's changes were, Shapiro did not completely reinvent the company. Monsanto held on to many of its existing capabilities, such as its customer relationships and marketing.

There is a long-standing debate in the strategy literature about whether structure follows strategy or vice versa.[9] Do you build the strategy around the company, or do you build the company around the strategy? Every company needs to resolve this chicken-and-egg question in its own way. Even those companies that choose to completely reshape their capabilities based on a new strategy have to know where they are starting from. Their assessment of these internal strengths is crucial to shaping and implementing strategy.

Core Competencies

If you currently have a successful business, it is probably because you already have some competencies that fit the Key Success Factors needed in your current environment. So let's first understand more about the nature of core competencies, because this understanding provides the platform on which to build a future vision.

Since hard assets usually can be readily obtained on the open market, the deeply embedded competencies tend to be the source of greater differentiation and advantage. Because core competencies are by definition deeply ingrained in an organization, they have staying power and are difficult for competitors to imitate (even when they can see them). For instance, most competitors understood Wal-Mart's logistics capabilities and other competencies, especially after articles and business school case studies described them in some detail.[10] Yet these capabilities proved very difficult for competitors to copy. Such deeply embedded competencies are often the basis of a company's past success and can be the foundation for its future.

Assessing Competencies

Because competencies are embedded, many managers have a hard time identifying those that lie at the core of their current business. In general, managers tend to be too generous in their lists of core competencies. True competencies are few and far between. While there are many variations and points along the spectrum, in their strictest definition competencies must pass stringent tests.[11] They must:

- Provide an advantage over competitors
- Be hard to replicate or imitate
- Be a source of value to customers and shareholders
- Potentially apply across multiple product lines
- Be complex and diffused across groups and employees

Two ways to identify core competencies, without being distracted by the many assets and skills on the surface that are not true competencies, is to think of the organization as either an onion or a tree.

The Firm as an Onion

Think of the firm as an onion made up of layers of functions, services, and production operations. Those that are in the core usually have to remain within the firm, but those that are more on the periphery can often be outsourced to other firms. Ask which activities determine the firm's essence or core and which are at the periphery. For one firm, for example, the outer layer may include product design, selling, or even marketing, whereas these same skills and capabilities might constitute the core of another firm. Honda's core consists of the design and manufacturing of engines, which underlie its strengths in passenger cars, motorcycles, lawn mowers, and race cars. Other car manufacturers have different cores. Chrysler, for example, subcontracts major portions of its engine design and manufacturing. For biotech firms, a core capability would be R&D, including how to access academic know-how and commercialize it through strategic alliances. Selling and marketing, in contrast, fall in the outer layer for those biotech firms that license their products to established pharmaceutical firms. Exhibit 5-3 illustrates how this onion would

Exhibit 5-3: The Firm as an Onion — A Newspaper

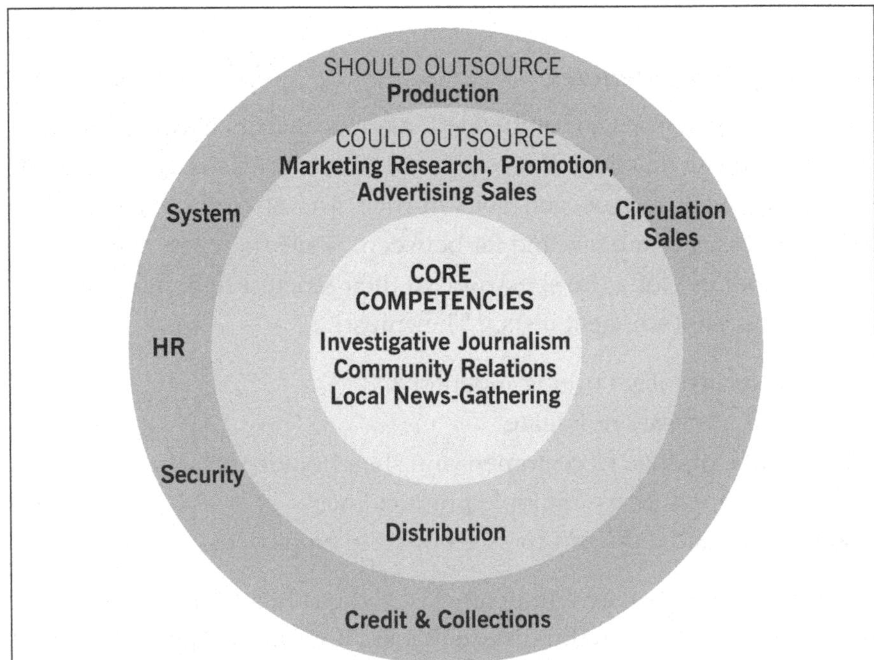

look for a newspaper company. Production, human resources, security, distribution, credit and collections, circulation and sales, and IT systems surround its true set of core competencies, which consist of investigative journalism, local news-gathering, and community relations.

The Firm as a Tree

An alternative way to explore core competencies is to think of the firm as a tree. In this metaphor used by Prahalad and Hamel,[12] the leaves and fruit represent the firm's end products and services. The branches constitute strategic business units (SBUs), which combine related products and services (such as midsize cars, heavy-duty lawn mowers, and 500 cc motorcycles). The trunk denotes core products, such as engines in Honda's case, which support each of the SBUs and end products. Lastly, the roots represent core competencies that enable the firm to sustain its existing branches and grow new ones. In Honda's case, this would be engine design and manufacturing, as well as attracting top-flight engineering talent from Tokyo University, Japan's premier academic institution.

Exhibit 5-4 illustrates this "tree" approach by showing the core competencies of a national stock exchange. Beneath its specific product and service offerings (leaves) are its core strengths (branches) in operations, technology, and clearing functions. These strengths, in turn, are derived from its core competencies (roots): historic leadership in capitalism, innovative culture, international know-how and reputation, new product development know-how, and long-term planning.

Unlike a core product, a core competence is not a stand-alone, sellable service or commodity. Examples of potential core competencies include high-quality manufacturing, good supplier relations, service excellence, innovation, short product development cycles, well-motivated employees, a marketing culture, and a strong service reputation. The challenge is to think of the firm not just in terms of its visible end products but also in terms of its invisible assets and the core competencies at its root.[13]

Gap Analysis

To understand the work that you need to do to develop your KSFs, you should conduct a gap analysis. Since the distinction between Key Success Factors and table stakes is based on your firm's capabilities relative to

Exhibit 5-4: The Firm as a Tree — Stock Exchange

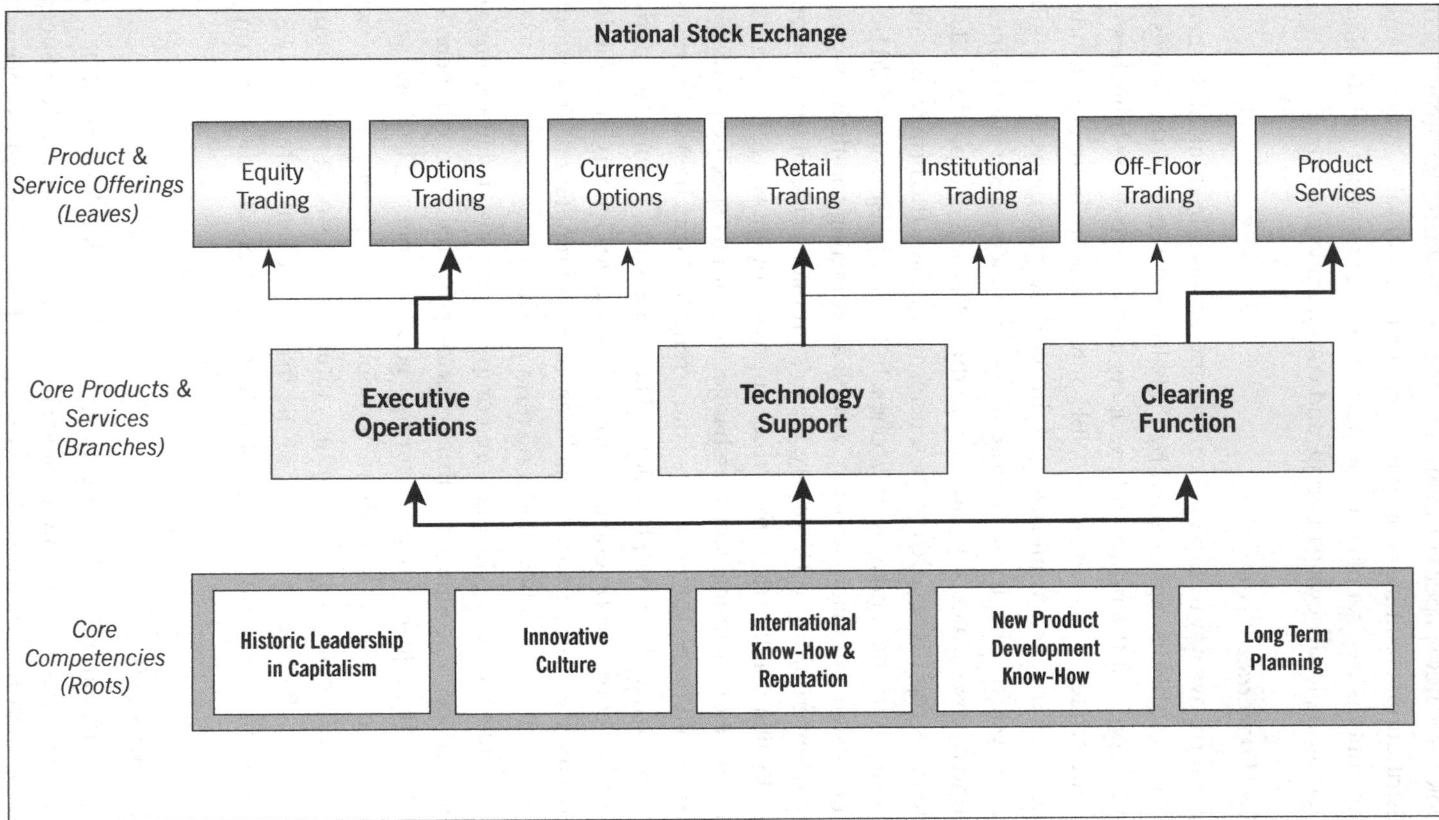

those of its rivals, an important task is benchmarking your strengths in these areas against rivals in your industry and across industries. This comparison identifies the gap between your current capabilities and the ones you have determined you need to develop to succeed. For example, a newspaper publisher looked at gaps in capabilities related to KSFs of interactivity and customer knowledge, as shown in Exhibit 5-5.

The typical newspaper company has little skills in interactive communications. Indeed, some have difficulty even in accepting credit cards by phone for new subscribers. But they can look to companies outside their industry—such as Autobytel, Dell, Microsoft, America Online, and Amazon—for examples of highly developed capabilities in interactive communications. The average newspaper also has little mastery of using detailed customer knowledge. Often they don't even own information on key subscribers since third parties may handle distribution. But newspaper firms could learn from companies such as USAA, American Express, and major airlines, which are very adept at collecting and using this knowledge. By looking outside its industry, the newspaper company might be able to develop capabilities that differentiate it from its peers. These capabilities can represent Key Success Factors for the company even though they may not be best-of-breed when measured across industries globally (as long as these competitors outside the industry don't ultimately decide to enter).

Exhibit 5-5: Assessing the Gap

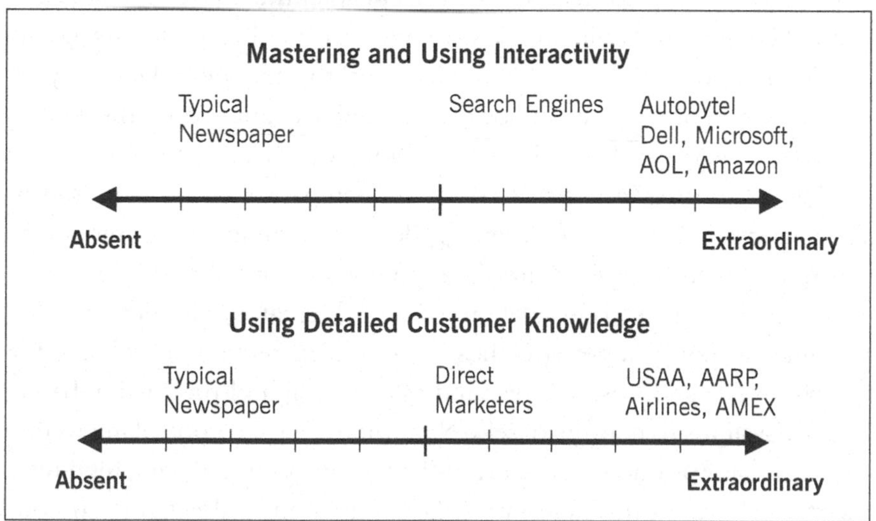

From Key Success Factors to Vision

A set of Key Success Factors, no matter how carefully developed, is not a rallying cry for an organization. Identifying the top five Key Success Factors doesn't tell you where to go. It looks at the trees rather than the forest. Organizations do not move forward by analysis alone. They move forward through a compelling strategic vision. The creative leap is to take these external and internal insights on scenarios, Key Success Factors, and core competencies to build a coherent vision, as shown in Exhibit 5-6.

In its early days, Apple did not merely offer a piece of equipment and a brand; it was pursuing the vision of a computer in every home. This strategic vision fit with its view of the emerging competitive environment and its own strengths. Without creative leaps, you have a nicely tailored set of scenarios and Key Success Factors, but these detailed lists do not add up to a coherent picture.

The trick is that a creative leap, while necessary, may discourage rigorous analysis and thus increase uncertainty. Monsanto could have looked at the same set of scenarios and its internal assets and decided to move more into its existing business or move in a completely different direction (exploiting materials science, for example, instead of biotechnology).

Planting the Seeds of the Future

For a more detailed example of how a company moves from exploring Key Success Factors to shaping a vision, consider the case of a major agricultural equipment company. This company decided several years ago to develop a set of scenarios about the future of the agricultural industry.[14]

In a world of rapid technological and global change, even the simple tractor has been transformed. Biotechnology, which led to the fundamental changes in the businesses of chemical companies such as Monsanto, also changed the process of farming. Global economic development creates new demands for food and for farm equipment tailored to different environments. The consolidation of farms creates the demand for machines to cover larger stretches of land. New technologies allow for "precision farming," using integrated information and production-based farming systems to maximize yield. New approaches to controlling weeds and pests allow for no-till or reduced-tillage approaches. Finally, high-tech smart machines permit automated farming without direct human con-

Exhibit 5-6: Strategic Vision Building

INPUT

- Key Success Factor (KSF) matrix
- Ranked KSFs
- Current core competencies
- Aspirations, mandates
- Competitors' vision

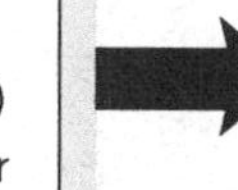

ANALYSIS & DIALOGUE

- Segment and scenario weights
- The gap between ranked KSFs and current core competencies:
    - Relative to rivals
    - Absolute (what it takes)
- Organizational capacity to deliver
- Fit with culture and history
- Level of senior management support and buy-in

OUTPUT

- A statement of what you want to be and how to get there
- Emphasizing concrete goals and timelines
- Highlighting core capabilities that need to be developed
- Describing how the company will develop the requisite capabilities
- Proposing a market and product scope in support of the vision
- Clarifying the organization's culture, values, philosophy

trol. These new machines include pilotless tractors, sprayers that identify plant or soil needs and apply appropriate solutions, and artificial intelligence or learning systems. But how quickly will farmers adopt these new approaches and technologies? How will global food demand and farming patterns affect the future?

To answer these questions, the company went through the process of developing scenarios (as discussed in Chapter 3), identifying segments in which it could compete, and identifying Key Success Factors for each scenario (both discussed in Chapter 4). To shape its scenarios, the managers identified two overriding key uncertainties: (1) economic changes that would affect both global food demand and investment ability of farmers, and (2) technological changes. After four full-fledged scenarios were developed from the starting matrix (see Exhibit 5-7), managers assessed the probability of each scenario, as shown in the parentheses.

- *Scenario A: 21st Century Dynasty:* In this scenario, a growing worldwide middle class causes food demand to outpace supply. China rises as a superpower. Farming prices change incrementally, and technologically advanced equipment is slow to catch on. The equipment industry is fairly stable except for the rise of a new global player. The economy runs into a cyclical downturn. Farm equipment industry volumes are down from turn-of-the-century levels in developed countries, and up in developing countries.

Exhibit 5-7: Scenarios for an Agricultural Equipment Company

Technological Changes?	Economic Changes?	Incremental	Radical
	Evolutionary	Scenario A: 21st Century Dynasty (15%)	Scenario B: The Drawbridge Is Up (10%)
	Revolutionary	Scenario C: Enviro-Tech (40%)	Scenario D: Opti-World (35%)

- *Scenario B: The Drawbridge Is Up:* In this scenario, the global economy has entered a downward spiral and protectionism is rampant. Alternative uses for crops such as ethanol have emerged, but margins in farming are shrinking, leading to accelerated consolidation of small farms. Biotechnology and smart equipment are slow to catch on. Farm equipment volumes overall are down in developed countries although they continue to rise in developing countries.

- *Scenario C: Enviro-Tech:* This scenario represents incremental economic change but radical technological change. With worldwide food supply meeting current demand, increasing attention is given to environmental preservation. Tough new laws are imposed on the use of pesticides and on sales of genetically altered crops. Organic foods have risen in popularity. Smart machines and other technological breakthroughs have gained widespread adoption. This advanced equipment is more expensive, but it more than makes up for its cost in performance improvements. Because no single company can meet the complex demands of these high-tech farmers, there has been a rise of intermediaries who can offer one-stop shopping.

- *Scenario D: Opti-World:* This scenario represents radical economic change and revolutionary technological change. A thriving global economy and falling trade barriers have led to rapid expansion of agricultural production in developing nations. Driven by the adoption of new farming technologies, the agricultural business has splintered into large megafarms and microfarms specializing in niche areas such as high-value genetically engineered crops. While overall volume of sales of agricultural equipment is down, the demand for high-value, customized equipment has increased significantly. Yields on farms in China and India increase manifold thanks to new technology, foreign investment, and global best practice.

In addition, the company's managers identified four key market segments they wished to serve based on the distribution channel, ranging from direct sales through dealers. The managers then assigned a weight to each segment based on its strategic importance (as indicated in the parentheses):

- Dealer-served market (70 percent)
- Distributor-served market (15 percent)

- Government mediated (10 percent)
- Direct sales (5 percent)

Each of the four scenarios and the four segments entails a distinct set of Key Success Factors. For example, adaptable/flexible manufacturing is key in the distributor-served market but is less important in the dealer-served market. A well-capitalized, low-overhead, dealer-served market is less important in the "Opti-World" scenario than in the other three. So each scenario-segment combination can be considered to determine the relevant KSFs needed. A simplified view of these scenario-segment combinations is shown in Exhibit 5-8, for just two scenarios and segments.

Then, for each cell (scenario-segment combination), the managers assessed whether a particular KSF would be important (using a simple score of 1=yes or 0=no). A simplified version of this table is shown in Exhibit 5-9 (with just four cells and a limited number of KSFs). Columns A, B, C, and D reflect the crossing of just two scenarios and two strategic segments (as in Exhibit 5-8). The KSF scores were then assessed based on the probability of each scenario and the importance of each segment to develop an aggregated score for each KSF.

Finally, the managers made an assessment of the size of the gap the company faced with respect to each KSF based on (1) how its own capa-

Exhibit 5-8: Scenarios and Segments

		Two Scenarios	
		21st C. Dynasty (.3)	**Opti-World (.7)**
Two Segments	**Dealer-Served Market (.83)**	Cell A (.25)	Cell B (.58)
	Distributor-Served Market (.17)	Cell C (.05)	Cell D (.12)

Note: Weights in parentheses are recalibrated from weights shown in Exhibit 5-7 to sum to 1. The cell weights are used to calculate the score in Exhibit 5-9.

Exhibit 5-9: Simplified KSF Matrix

KSF	A	B	C	D	SCORE	GAP
Ability to develop and manage a differentiated brand image	1	1	1	1	1	0.57
Ability to consult with farmers: providing technical / process / business knowledge and training	1	1	0	1	0.95	0.14
Ability to collect, analyze information such as agronomic, climatic, farm productivity	1	1	0	0	0.83	0.43
Ability to select, attract, and maintain business relationships with different members of the food value chain and governments	0	1	1	0	0.63	0.57
Shortened time to market for products, services, and solutions	0	1	0	0	0.58	0.29
Ability to manufacture in multiproduct plants	0	0	0	0	0	0.29

Note: The columns A, B, C, and D refer to different cells of the scenario-segment matrix and are weighted as shown in Exhibit 5-8. 1 = KSF matters; 0 = KSF is not discriminating

bilities stacked up against benchmarks of its rivals, and (2) the organizational *challenge* of developing these capabilities, as numerically summarized in Exhibit 5-9. This process led to a final ranking for the KSFs, weighted for scenarios and segments as well as for the size and difficulty of the leap to build these new KSFs. This process across all scenarios and segments led to an overall ranking of importance of the KSFs, as shown in Exhibit 5-10.

The ability to develop and manage a differentiated brand image proved to be a KSF that was resilient across scenarios and synergistic across the target segments. The ability to develop biotechnology solutions might at first glance have seemed a very significant capability to develop, because of the tremendous media attention this issue received at the time of this planning process (circa 1995). Yet by looking across scenarios and segments, the company was able to give it a more realistic weighting. In

Exhibit 5-10: KSF Ranking

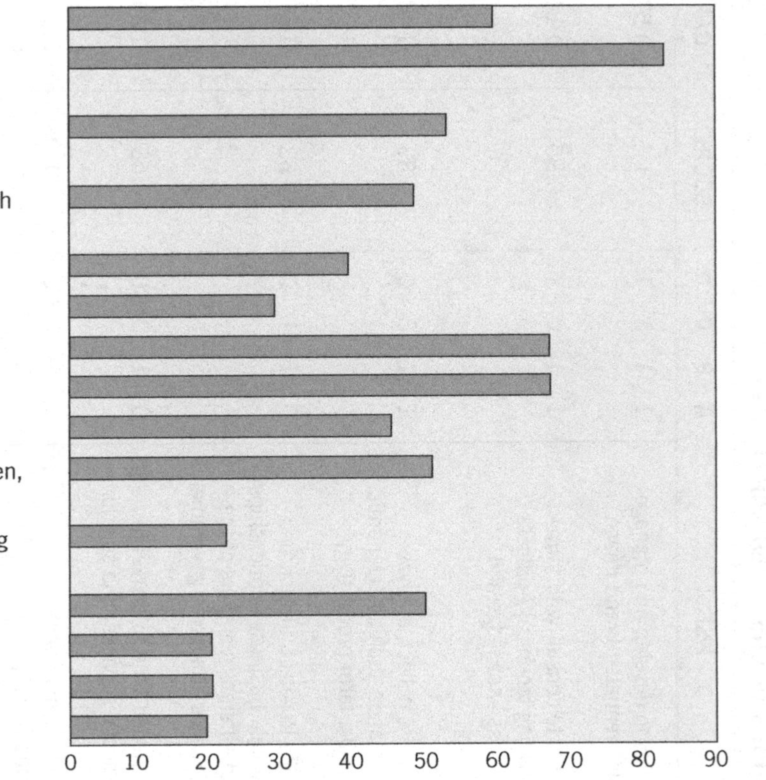

Note: This ranking of KSF is based on the full-blown analysis of four scenarios and four segments rather than the reduced two-by-two example shown in *Exhibit 5-9*.

contrast to Monsanto and other chemical companies noted at the opening of the chapter, this agricultural equipment company didn't place all its eggs in that basket. Instead, it invested heavily in those competencies needed across multiple segments and scenarios, and it invested more flexibly in those capabilities appropriate in just one scenario or segment.

Based on all this work, the company created a strategic vision to encompass the most important Key Success Factors for its future, while building on its current assets and competencies. In a nutshell, its vision was:

> To build and leverage our world-class brand by working with farmers to harness the value of agricultural information and develop innovative, integrated farming solutions using the latest technology. In five years, we shall have transformed ourselves from an equipment manufacturer to a total solution provider specializing in global farming, knowledge management, and technology. To do this, we must develop world-class expertise in . . .

Approaches to Shaping the Strategic Vision

While the strategic vision needs to explicitly or implicitly take into account the external environment as well as the internal capabilities of the firm and competitors, there are many ways it can be created and implemented. Should the vision be developed at the top or bubble up from the organization? Shell chairman Sir Peter Baxendale refused to be the "finger of God" for his $100 billion enterprise. He did not see his job as "telling them what to do but to give them a process and resources." Some companies use a "finger of God" approach with good results, while others focus on process, and still others create an environment in which the organization can self-organize. The primary approaches for developing and implementing a strategic vision in an uncertain environment are:

- *Iron filings (centralized):* The vision is developed centrally and serves as a magnet that pulls the iron filings of the organization all in line. This approach has the benefit of clarity and consistency, but even if the vision is shaped from the top, leaders need to ensure broad involvement. It is important that radical and offbeat voices are represented in the inputs to the vision, so that all major uncertainties and trends are included. It is also important that the vision is carefully and consistently communicated so that the organization aligns around it and periodically tests it against reality.

- *Formation flying (self-organized by process):* By setting up a set of simple rules, like the ones that describe the flight of geese in formation, the company can create processes that allow it to develop its strategic vision. In this case, leaders need to ensure that these processes are consistent with identifying and addressing uncertainty. Shell's strongly ingrained processes for scenario planning, for example, ensure that the entire organization lives with the uncertainty and adapts well to the changing environment. The strategies are formulated first at the division and country level, and are then aligned centrally as well (see Chapter 8).
- *Slime mold (self-organized by environment):* In this approach, leaders of the organization create the petri dish in which the strategic vision grows. They control the nutrients and the temperature in which the organization can self-organize. Studies of slime molds have found that they act relatively independently in conditions of abundance, but when food and other resources are scarce, these simple organisms begin to work together to form self-organizing systems. They create a collective intelligence.[15] By controlling the environment, leaders of the organization create the conditions for self-organizing vision. While this approach gives the organization great flexibility and adaptability, it also can quickly devolve into chaos. Leaders need to create a context that accurately reflects potential futures for the firm, effectively allowing the outside environment to flow into the organization. For example, to encourage managers to address a scenario of resource scarcity, senior executives might create an environment of limited resources in one part of the firm. Different parts of the organization could be encouraged to experiment with distinct scenarios. The success or failure of experiments in these different petri dishes could shape the strategy for the organization. Leaders of the organization need to have sharply attuned insights to distinguish a dish full of penicillin from a dish of useless green mold. They need to be careful not to walk by the innovations that could shape the future of the industry, as Xerox did with the innovations in its own petri dish at its Palo Alto Research Center (PARC) (see Chapter 6).

Conclusion: Growth Strategies

The analogy of farming offers a framework for understanding the interrelationships among the scenarios, Key Success Factors, competencies, and strategic vision. The scenarios are like the general weather conditions that would affect the growing season. The Key Success Factors identify the types of crops that would thrive in each possible set of weather conditions. The farmers furthermore have to consider the competencies they have in growing different types of crops. In choosing the planting strategy, the farmers also need to consider *where* to plant (soil segments and so on). Some crops will thrive in certain areas of the land (with rich soil and much sunlight), so the strategies need to be tailored to both the segments and the crops that the farmers have the capabilities to grow. Like farming, the choices involved in growing a successful set of strategies are interrelated.

In addition to the firm's own competencies, the risk attitude of senior management will also affect its strategic vision. An organization that has a propensity to take larger risks will have a broader set of strategic options to choose from and may make a more decisive commitment to a particular strategy. A company that chooses to hedge its bets will take a much more conservative approach. Since we are dealing with probabilities and uncertainties, there is no single, general answer to what the risk posture should be. Business is about taking calculated risks, but too often managers are unaware of the true risk they are taking, and consequently they don't manage those risks very well.

The strategic vision may also change over time. Periods of crop rotation will be needed as soil is depleted, and changes in the external environment will require a shift in strategy. The farmer is constantly reassessing the strategy and adjusting the approach as the strategic vision plays out over time. At the point where the field is prepared but the crop is not yet planted, the farmer still has the option to change the crop. The farmer might have to write off the investment in seed or may have been able to postpone that investment as well. Once the crop is in the ground, the farmer is committed to it, and the costs of reversal are much higher. How such options are created and valued is the focus of Chapter 6, while the process of dynamic monitoring to reassess the strategic vision will be considered in Chapter 7.

Chapter 6

Creating Flexible Options

"A wise man will make more opportunities than he finds."

SIR FRANCIS BACON, ENGLISH PHILOSOPHER

Ever since 1999, when he made the leap from the security of a corporate career with GE and Lockheed Martin, Scott Snyder had been on the wildest ride of his life. He had left behind a vice presidency at Lockheed Martin where he was in charge of a business unit for a $1 billion telecom group. After moving up to Pennsylvania from Virginia in 1998 and experiencing firsthand the hassle of selecting his own utilities, Snyder came up with the idea of a free online service that would help consumers select from burgeoning utilities options. In the process he could collect a referral fee from the suppliers if a consumer actually switched. Snyder and his partner Tom Borger founded OmniChoice.com to implement this idea of consumer empowerment.

OmniChoice seemed destined to have a heady future. As a young online firm in the late 1990s, investors were throwing money at it. The biggest complaint of the venture capitalists was that the firm wasn't spending money *fast* enough. At the same time, established utilities were figuring out how to play in the newly deregulated environment, and they took a keen interest in this start-up, which was designed to be a neutral point of contact for confused consumers. Exelon, the deregulated business created by PECO Energy, poured $10 million into OmniChoice.com within five months of its founding. The company ramped up from zero to fifty-five employees within a year and went through a fast transition from the founders' basements into spacious new offices in King of Prussia, just outside Philadelphia.

Shortly thereafter, however, the company found itself caught in the whirling maelstrom of the dot-com bubble and the shifting riptides of deregulation. Much of this uncertainty was unanticipated, and it took many companies off guard. In this turbulent environment, OmniChoice needed to be able to understand the new market realities quickly and find flexible new options so it could adjust.

The environment was actually far more uncertain than it initially appeared, and the company was jolted when the polarity suddenly reversed. "All of the trends started to invert on us," Snyder recalls. The overall e-commerce investment climate shifted from focusing on consumers (b-to-c) to business applications (b-to-b). The new competitors in telecom and other utilities markets began dying off. And then the Internet rout spread, and companies began erasing the dot-com behind their names and painting over the *e-* in front. Perhaps the greatest surprise was the reaction of customers. It turned out that many visitors to OmniChoice would work through the decision tools but were reluctant to actually purchase from a relatively unknown company. In hindsight, Snyder admits that he and his partner may have put too many eggs in the basket of this one scenario, but they did better than most of their competitors, who had gone belly up or were barely alive in the fall of 2001, when I met with Snyder.

One of the things OmniChoice did right was to prepare a plan B. As they were developing their technology for the consumer business, the managers spent extra time and money creating a generic platform that was more flexible. They deliberately created embedded options. When the consumer market dried up, this platform allowed them to shift their effort to a business-to-business model, selling software to utility companies that could use it themselves to guide their own customers in choosing among different plans. OmniChoice had also tried to hire flexible employees who could thrive with a variety of challenges.

But there was a limit to how flexible they could be. Some of the employees didn't want to change, and the skills needed for consumer marketing were very different from those needed for corporate sales. Now they had to sell much higher up in the organization, and the sales cycle also was much longer. The company downsized, cutting more than forty of its fifty-five employees. "When we reset our vision at the beginning of the year toward selling software, a lot of people were bewildered and lost," Snyder says. "You can see the wall, and the question is: Can we turn the ship fast enough?"

How do you know when you are on the wrong path? In the early days, OmniChoice was so busy building the business, there wasn't as much time for careful planning and monitoring. Now Snyder and his partner set up clear milestones for completing deals. Of course, the environment makes it difficult to stick to simple milestones. OmniChoice had set a milestone of closing two major software deals in September 2001, but when that date arrived, it had closed only one and had verbal commitments from two others. "You have to be somewhat flexible but without fooling yourself," Snyder says.

This patience paid off. By the end of 2001, OmniChoice had closed two major software deals in the wireless and broadband space and received additional financing. The company was on a path to be profitable by mid-2002.

Snyder also has gained a deeper appreciation of the value of an outside advisory board. Some advisers early on had expressed concerns about the b-to-c focus and the likely reluctance of consumers to trust an unknown company with their utilities. The managers in the business are often too close and too invested in decisions to pull the plug as quickly as they need to. As cheerleaders, they need to believe in their own vision while also being objective. Every day they may face a new set of decisions that can mean life or death to the fledgling venture.

The devil is often in the details when trying to manage options. While OmniChoice created flexible software platforms, it didn't build enough flexibility into the five-year lease on its sprawling first-floor offices in the Philadelphia suburbs that it signed just before the downturn in their industry in September 2000. The downsizing left many of the blue-carpeted offices empty, and the PCs sitting idle. In a tough real estate market, it was very hard to renegotiate or sublet, but the company was eventually able to negotiate a reduced lease and move into smaller quarters.

The irony is that in the much more upbeat environment in which the lease was signed, the landlord probably would have agreed to a mild escape clause. But in that heady environment, in which all lines were trending up, Snyder never thought to ask. "We looked at one bullish scenario of the business," he recalls. "Scenario planning might have led to incremental space or an out clause in the lease, but we didn't ask. It was one of thousands of decisions we made." And it was one they lived with, month after month.

One advantage of a slower environment is that the managers now have more time to carefully consider various scenarios and options. It has been an unbelievable education for the thirty-six-year-old entrepreneur. "It is very dynamic, and you can't be rattled by changes," he warns. "You are thrown a curve ball every day, a key decision that affects the future of the company. You need to have a strong stomach. You need to be able to think at both a strategic and a tactical level and toggle back and forth pretty quickly."

Photos and drawings of some of Snyder's four children encircle his desk. Two of his children were born during the time he was building the business. Does he ever regret having taken the leap out of the certainty of his old life? "I did give up quite a bit," he observes. "I'm fortunate to have the strong support of my wife. I don't regret it one second. I've never awakened every day with more excitement about what I'm doing."

Commitment and Flexibility

Scott Snyder and his partners in OmniChoice created flexible options by building a generic architecture for their software. It gave them the ability to move forward with their original business-to-consumer strategy while keeping open the option of moving into business-to-business if conditions shifted, as they did. This ace in the hole kept them alive after most of their rivals had shuttered their operations. On the other hand, their failure to create options for their office lease trapped them into one view of the world—continuous strong growth—so they didn't have the necessary flexibility when conditions changed.

In both cases, the resources needed to create these options were small relative to the risks that the overall investments entailed. The creation of more generic software incurred some small expense and delay in launching the new program architecture, and the lease option might have been had for the asking.

The challenge in business is balancing commitment and flexibility. Business is sometimes won by placing big bets, by making a strong commitment. As the old saying goes, you cannot cross a canyon in two steps. And yet commitment is dangerous: you often end up in the chasm. Spanish conquistador Hernán Cortés successfully made his assault on the Aztec capital in Mexico by pursuing a life-or-death strategy. He beached his ships so there could be no quick retreat. His soldiers were thus forced to make a total commitment to the battle, and they succeeded. On the other hand, Spain lost most of its Armada and global supremacy in 1588 by committing its large and inflexible fleet in an attack on Britain.[1] During the personal computer revolution, Digital Equipment Corporation and to some extent IBM lost their preeminent positions because of their strong commitment to mainframes.

The perils of commitment, as well as the lack thereof, are easily assessed by Monday-morning quarterbacks. But managers must deal with these trade-offs while they are on the playing field. The challenge managers face is much more like the one presented to European wireless providers by the auctions for licenses for 3G (third-generation wireless): Should they pour millions of dollars into this untested technology, potentially gambling the future of their companies? Or should they hold on to their cash and wait on the sidelines, potentially risking being left out of the future of their industry? In a few years, they might be seen either as prescient pioneers or as foolish gamblers who put their company's futures on the line for a pipe dream that never materialized. The heated bidding for licenses rose to a total of $125 billion—and left European telecom companies staggering under a collective $200 billion in debt.[2] Similarly, Motorola and other smart companies bet billions on satellite-based telecommunications services such as Iridium, only to watch these technologies with such promising trajectories spiral back to Earth. The industry is suffering from significant overcapacity and a shakeout is taking place.

A Bias for Action

OmniChoice CEO Tom Borger stresses that scenario planning and the creation of flexible options should not be used as an excuse for inaction. Business leaders still need to make tough decisions quickly. "This is not an academic exercise of keeping all the balls in the air or considering infinite possibilities," he said. "You are looking at the landscape and make the best decision based on the alternatives. This is all driving toward action today and planning for action as things in the landscape are changing. It is important to stress that it is not perfection we are after, but the pursuit of perfection."

Exploring scenarios early on can help managers deal with changes in the environment without going into "crisis mode," Borger notes. "We knew going into the business that there was a lot we didn't know. We made a decision to hire people who were flexible and prepared for a number of different directions for generating revenue. Our first action item was to develop an e-commerce business. That helped us get out of the gate. The landscape changed very quickly, but we had already developed a plan to sell the software directly to providers. We didn't anticipate we'd need to move so fast, but we were prepared to move in that direction as our environment changed."

With the dot-com collapse, OmniChoice saw the group of competitors thinned from ten to just two other firms. Many of the companies that failed were well funded and seemed to have promising futures. But many of the flameouts, urged on by zealous investors, were overcommitted to the consumer e-business path and didn't have the capabilities and flexibility to move in new directions. "Everyone got caught up in the same sort of frenzy," Borger says. "Instead, we focused on building a core technology, which none of our competitors did. It took a significant investment in time and money, but gave us a real point of differentiation, additional depth, and a platform that would allow us to adapt our business to a changing marketplace. If you don't go through scenario planning, you may get stuck in the delusional worldview you started with and then you start to rationalize the facts."

Borger compares the process of generating scenarios to doing architectural work for a building or developing a "creative brief" in advertising. "A lot of people want to get right into the process of developing the ad," says Borger, who helped create outstanding advertising campaigns for Children's Tylenol as an executive at Johnson & Johnson. "Where a lot of ads break down is that people don't spend enough time planning up front."

Borger stresses that the goal of this "foundation work" is to make it easier to move decisively when conditions change. "If you haven't built the foundation, you are going to waste far more time doing something in crisis mode," he says. "When you sense things are going in a different direction, you need to move as decisively as you moved initially. When you start to see things looking like the scenarios you've outlined, jump."

How can companies keep options open without making too strong a commitment? How can they create flexible options that properly balance commitment and flexibility?

From Strategic Vision to Flexible Options

In Chapter 5, we examined the process of developing a strategic vision. The vision paints a broad picture for getting from point A to point B (where we would want to be in the future). But now we need to consider a systematic process for planning to get us from here to there. The question you address here is: How do you want to travel? Do you want to proceed in small experiments in many directions, or do you prefer to mass your forces in one great assault? Many routes may lie before you, none of which have been traversed before, and they may entail various levels of uncertainty. Given the Key Success Factors needed in your possible scenarios and given your own capabilities, how should you plan?

This chapter presents a systematic approach to exploring strategic options, given the scenarios and strategic vision generated in the preceding chapters. Note that the scenarios embrace the external uncertainty while the vision part of the process balances commitment and flexibility in terms of overall direction. This options phase refines this balancing act in the context of specific business initiatives that will bring the vision into reality. The first step in developing these strategic options is to generate a wide range of alternatives. Next, we have to assess their consequences in view of the external uncertainty, as well as reactions from customers and competitors. Finally, we need to screen or rank these options using appropriate criteria in line with the vision.

If a company had perfect knowledge and unlimited resources, it would simply pursue all the strategies in its vision that offer a positive return. But knowledge is imperfect, so the returns from various initiatives are uncertain. Resources are also limited, so managers need to make trade-offs among investments. Making limited investments in future options allows companies to conserve resources and at the same time fill in gaps in their knowledge before making a stronger commitment. The resource constraints and uncertainty problem are in general best addressed through an options approach to investment, in which small initial invest-

Exhibit 6-1: Certainty and Commitment

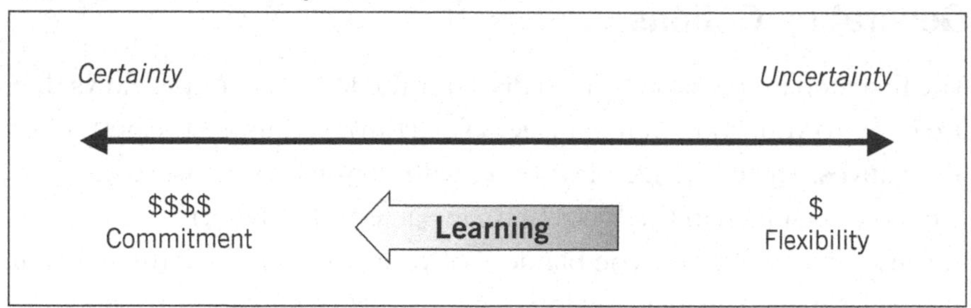

ments create opportunities for more commitment down the road. As new knowledge is gained with the passage of time, learning and adjustment can take place. As illustrated in Exhibit 6-1, investments should be more flexible when uncertainty is greater; and as uncertainty decreases—through feedback and learning—larger commitments can be made or the investment can be scaled down.

Almost any investment can be made more flexible than first imagined. When a company hires a new employee, a trial period can be included or a contingent exit option negotiated. But often we fail to build in such flexibility because either we are too sure about how the future will unfold or we lack the imagination to create additional flexibility. The real-options perspective seeks to increase future maneuverability and put an economic value on this gain in flexibility. When constructing a new plant, managers should build in opportunities to defer, expand, contract, terminate, or otherwise modify the project as the future unfolds, so as to take full advantage of potential favorable developments while limiting the negative effects of adverse ones. Profit equals revenue minus cost. Profiting from uncertainty at its core entails creating options that let you increase revenue and decrease cost as you learn more about how the future turns out.

The greater the uncertainty inherent in your decision, the greater the value of such managerial flexibility. Only the rare decision offers no possibilities to capture any value of real options. Ask yourself: At what points in time (in the evolution of a project) might you be able to alter the flow of revenues, costs, and other outcomes? Can you defer or accelerate portions of the project? What actions could you take to capitalize on better-than-expected outcomes? How might you mitigate the effects of worse-than-expected results?

Generating Options

The first step in this process is to discover the full range of pathways that are open to you. Too often managers select from an impoverished set of alternatives. The challenge of working with options is not just to evaluate them (where much of the focus of financial tools has been) but to generate and then craft them. The blinders of your past frames or the belief in a single scenario can lock you into a narrow set of rigid options. If OmniChoice had been focused solely on the business-to-consumer market, which presented a very rosy picture at the time, it wouldn't have seen the need to create a business-to-business platform down the road. But it was able to consider these two possibilities simultaneously and creatively develop strategies for both.

While it takes some time and attention to evaluate options once they are generated, organizations generally do not suffer from the problem of generating too large and rich an array of options. Most often, they suffer from a paucity of creative options. It is not possible here to review the rich set of techniques for effective brainstorming, creativity, or options generation;[3] these approaches can significantly expand your pool of possible options. Instead, we examine here the direct relationship between uncertainty and options generation. The same scenarios that helped you develop a strategic vision can also be used more explicitly to generate and value options:

- *Take a phone call from God:* Suppose you receive a phone call from God, who tells you point-blank that scenario A is going to happen. All the uncertainty is gone, and you can actively think about options. If, for example, you've found out, like Noah, that it will rain for forty days and forty nights, you now need to creatively generate options for this flood scenario. In the process, you might just come up with the idea of building an ark. But if you saw the flood as a very remote possibility, you might never conceive of the ark option. By going through all of the scenarios and turning them into 100 percent certainties (for example, by assigning small groups in the organization to live with each scenario as a certainty), you will generate many more options than might be developed if the scenarios are examined as an uncertain set. For an even broader options-generation exercise, you might go back and explore each of the original uncertainties that contributed to the scenarios and postulate extreme outcomes for each. What if you knew that the demand for 3G wireless service would increase by 100 percent per year? What if you knew that there would be a glut of energy in five years? What would you do? The goal at this point is not to evaluate the likelihood of these events taking place, nor to reevaluate your overall vision. The goal is merely to generate as many options as possible.

- *Preserve uncertainty:* While few managers do get a call from God, many act as if they have. They narrow their focus down to a single scenario and fail to preserve the true complexity and uncertainty of the situation. They find themselves with a beautiful ark when they should have been preparing for a drought as well. As you examine a set of different options, you need to ensure that you don't get locked in to a single view too soon. In addition to building an ark, you should also consider leasing one or sharing it with another party. The final choice will of course depend on the odds of a severe flood and the cost of each option. Zooming in and out of each scenario will help create the right array of options, with varying degrees of commitment or flexibility explicitly considered.
- *Look for outside help:* To get creative ideas, you may have to look beyond the limited perspective of your organization or industry to the broader system. Union Oil Company, in its search for a way to pinpoint leaks across hundreds of miles of gas pipelines in the desert, engaged some unlikely allies: vultures. The company injected ethyl mercaptan into its gas lines, an odorous substance that is only mildly noticed by humans but produces a smell of rotting flesh that is highly attractive to turkey vultures. Wherever these birds swooped down along the pipeline for scavenging, a fix-it squad followed quickly.[4] Hovering vultures and other players that initially may appear to be completely outside the problem at hand can be brought into the picture and utilized in creating a strategic option. How can you draw in other players and perspectives to create additional options? What are all the drivers of a given scenario and all the players in the broader ecosystem that might influence its development?
- *Let the outliers be heard:* The same voices that need to be heard to generate effective scenarios also need to be invited into the options-generation process. Some companies do this through venture fairs, at

which promising new ideas can connect with champions. Other companies create separate centers for generating original thinking, such as the famed Bell Labs. At Xerox's Palo Alto Research Center (PARC), director John Seely Brown recruited a group of young people to brainstorm with the staff scientists about what the workplace would be like in the year 2010. The BrainStore, an "idea factory" in Biel, Switzerland, also turns to young consultants when they need new options. Their BrainNet is a 1,500-person global network consisting mainly of young people aged thirteen to twenty; the BrainStore often mixes those young people with members of its client teams during creative workshops.[5] But as the Xerox PARC experience suggests, the rest of the organization has to pay attention to these think tanks.

- *Take off the blinders of your current business:* Even when options are generated, existing corporate frames may block their recognition and assimilation. Xerox PARC has an impressive record of generating new ideas but a humbling record of transferring these inventions back to its parent corporation. Xerox failed to capitalize on PARC's invention of the graphical user interface, whereas Steve Jobs quickly recognized its potential. It became the inspiration that drove the early growth of Apple computers. The use of scenarios to explore uncertainties and threats can be a powerful force in stripping away these corporate blinders. If managers at Xerox had examined a forceful scenario involving the rise of the personal computer, they might have taken their own technology more seriously. Ironically, Xerox's own core business was the result of the rejection of a new technology for photocopying by IBM and others. In 1958, when IBM considered adding the Haloid-Xerox 914 copier, its primary concern was whether the existing electric typewriter sales force could handle the new product. The focus was on spreading the selling cost of this division over two product lines, rather than viewing it as an entirely new business for IBM. Since copiers did not look attractive within this rather narrow frame, the opportunity was rejected.[6]

These and other approaches can help you develop a rich set of options that are not initially apparent. For example, consider how a health care organization creatively enlarged its set of options for increasing donations to blood banks (see box).

Blood from a Stone

A team of executives at a health care organization was concerned about falling donations to area blood banks. What could be done to increase the availability of donated blood for transfusions? Initially, they wanted to use education, multimedia advertising, or telethons to raise public awareness. But then the executives in the Wharton School's Critical Thinking program creatively generated a broader set of options. They used analogies to other areas, such as the loss of subscriptions at a newspaper, fishing, and voter registration. They came up with a variety of other solutions that were not apparent at first. The new options included:

- Taking donations at new areas or events (airports, convention centers, sporting events)
- Offering a sliding scale or variable draw so donors can give smaller amounts
- Giving more formal recognition to donors than stickers (pins, T-shirts)
- Issuing better and more frequent reminders, including public listings
- Pursuing international import options and relaxing standards
- Creating incentives for giving, such as a "finder's fee," frequent flier miles, or a wellness program
- Using blood from prisoners, military, or the recently deceased
- Capturing waste blood or harvesting blood during surgery
- Using bloodless surgical techniques or reducing blood loss
- Increasing awareness through a "Got Milk?"–style campaign using celebrities
- Changing laws to provide a tax benefit or to make it a legal obligation, like military draft registration
- Investing in artificial blood and new emerging plasma technologies

Preserving Flexibility

In general, the more strategic options you can generate the better, because this means you have more potential strategies for addressing future uncertainty. The next step after generating these options is to look for ways to preserve your flexibility. The minute you make a commitment to head down one of those pathways, you begin to decrease your flexibility.

The challenge is how to pursue specific strategic options while preserving as much flexibility as possible.

Flexibility can often be embedded in options, and such flexibility creates value. The classic financial option allows you to invest a small sum with the option to invest more in the future or to pull the plug and suffer a modest loss. Your commitment is small at first, but the potential payoff of exercising the option can be very high. The financial call option is a powerful metaphor for approaching strategic options in business that are highly uncertain.

There are two potential sources of flexibility in strategic options. The first is intrinsic flexibility, stemming from the reversibility and adjustability of the options themselves. Can the commitment be reversed? Can it be scaled up or down with learning or as the external environment becomes more certain? Flexibility can also be increased through a second source, external to the specific project. This additional flexibility might come from financial strategies involving hedges or from increased organizational agility.

The first approach focuses on increasing the intrinsic flexibility of the project, technology, or organizational setting itself. How can the project be designed in such a way that downstream flexibility is increased? Among the approaches:

- *Increase the degree of reversibility:* The right to change one's mind is one of the key sources of flexibility. Can the decision to pursue a particular option be completely reversed with little impact? OmniChoice's decision to create a business-to-consumer software package was designed to be reversible if the original application didn't pan out. A plant that can be redeployed for another purpose offers a way to reverse its strategy. The question for each strategic option is: What are the sunk costs, and is there a way to design them so they are more easily reversed? How easily can the assets or strategic investments be redeployed to other uses? The reversibility of an investment can be thought of as the value of the investment in its second-best use relative to the initial cost of the investment. The higher this ratio, the less committed you are to the investment.

- *Staged investments:* While reversibility is concerned with the ease of undoing the investment, staging is concerned with pacing your investments over time. Do you have to make one massive commitment to pursuing this option, or can you proceed in small steps? The strategy of postponement in manufacturing is an example of staging investments. Fashion ski-wear manufacturer SportObermeyer, facing highly uncertain demand for different styles, created generic shells, and then added distinctive finishes such as colored zippers as close as possible to the time and place of purchase. Hewlett-Packard also used this approach in manufacturing printers for global markets. By making its products modular, separating the power supply and packaging (which vary greatly from country to country) from the rest of the machine, it could build standardized printers and then add the power supply and instructions in the local country. This means a given printer might be sent to China or France or the United States based on market demand, with the power system still tailored to the local standard. This approach did increase the production cost of the inkjet printers by delaying customization until the machines arrived at the warehouses, but Hewlett-Packard ultimately saved $3 million a month by more effectively matching supply to highly uncertain demand.[7]

In 1998 a power company demonstrated the value of flexibility and staged investments when it made the counterintuitive decision to build electric-generating plants that were not economical to run. These plants were powered by jet engines modified to run on natural gas. They were so expensive to operate that the electricity cost 50 to 70 percent more than the most efficient plants—in other words, more than it could be sold for, except for a few days throughout the year when demand truly peaked. The decision to build the plants seemed to fly in the face of reasoned financial analysis, which would instead try to get the best use out of assets by working them to capacity and invest in plants where the cost of generation would be well below the average price of electricity.

But the company did not build the plants to run them through the year. It built them to create an option to generate power during peak demand when high prices justified high generation costs. The uncertainty of electricity prices and the relatively low investment to acquire the inefficient generators made the option to run these plants valuable enough to justify, even though they sat idle throughout most of the year.

The wisdom of creating these options was confirmed when energy costs spiked in the summer of 1999. As energy prices skyrocketed, jumping from $40 per megawatt-hour to an unprecedented $7,000, the company quickly fired up its "peaking plants" and was able to make substantial profits on its investments when some of its rivals were forced to drop out of trading energy. The company was handsomely repaid for creating an option that could readily be used to profit from uncertainty.

While the strategic options themselves can be shaped to preserve flexibility, possibilities for creating flexibility may exist outside of the initiative as well. The first possibility is using financial techniques such as contingent contracts to hedge investments. A related strategy is risk sharing. A third approach is to create organizational agility through early detection and fluid decision making. (This external approach will be considered in more detail in Chapters 7 and 8, where I will explore strategies for dynamic monitoring and implementation.) I recommend that for any project or initiative, managers (1) creatively look for many more options, (2) seek to increase their flexibility, and (3) develop an organizational capacity to exploit this flexibility in a quick and smart manner.

Assessment of Consequences

Once you have developed an attractive set of options, your next challenge is to analyze how these options might play out over time. The first part of this analysis is to look at the stages of exercising the options and the key decision points along the way. The second part is to examine the potential reactions to each of these steps on the part of customers, competitors, and other stakeholders. If you build a new plant, what will they do in response? These reactions add significantly to the complexity of assessing the consequences of strategic options, but this complexity can be played out through competitive simulations.

Map Your Strategic Options Using a Decision Tree

The stages of exercising an option are best represented through a decision tree. Suppose, for example, that you must decide whether to build a $10 million plant, but you don't know whether your project will have enough demand to justify the expense. Using traditional financial analysis, you determine that if demand is low, you will incur sizable losses. Further, these losses will barely outweigh the potential gains if demand is high, and thus in terms of expected returns, the option to build looks unattractive, as shown at the top of Exhibit 6-2.

Exhibit 6-2: Options Thinking

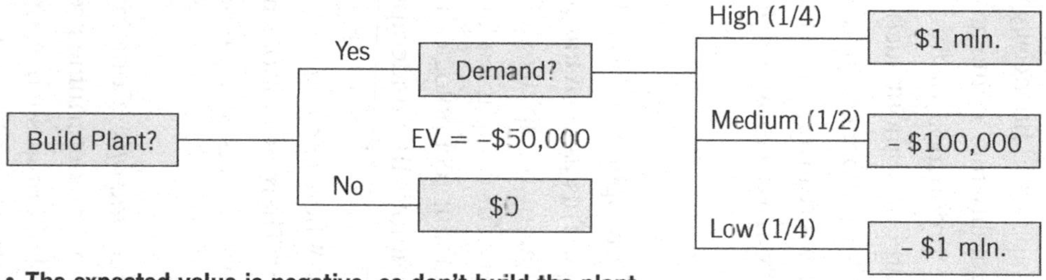

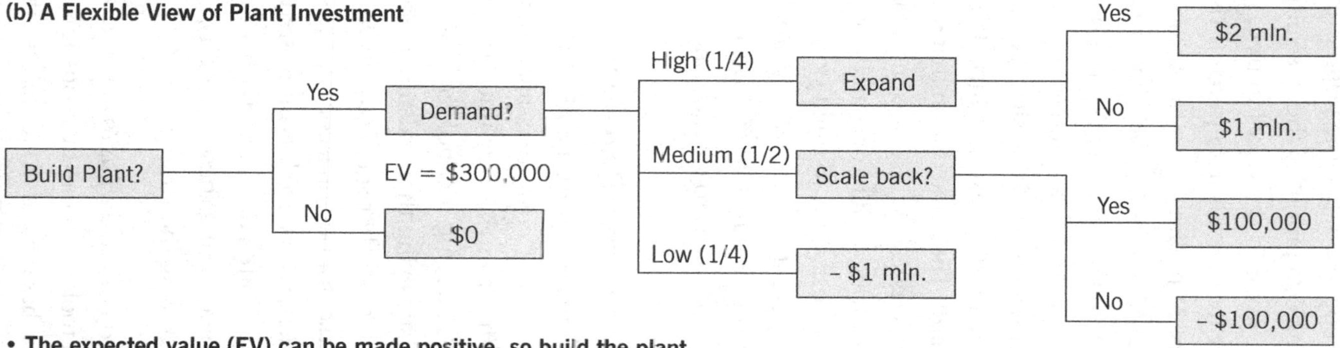

From a real-options perspective, however, you would adopt a more flexible approach, test the waters, and then expand (running more shifts or adding equipment) if there is sufficient demand. In this way, by adding another node to the decision tree, you've created more flexibility. While the first tree entails a 25 percent risk of losing $1 million for a possible payoff of $1 million, the more flexible second approach offers a potential payoff of $2 million for the same downside risk of $1 million. If demand is high, you have the option to ramp up and make a larger return on your investment. And if demand is medium, you can scale back.

Further, you might design the plant with flexible machinery that could be converted to make product B, in case demand for product A fails to materialize. The same option that originally appeared financially risky may now make good economic sense. Such flexibility may come at a price: a manufacturing facility designed for flexible production or future expansion may cost more to build or operate than one without such flexibility. But the potential value to be gained from flexible options may make the investment worthwhile. So once you have creatively structured your options, the key is to lay each one out clearly in a decision tree format.

Assess Customer Reactions

One of the great uncertainties in assessing any option, as noted above, is the reaction of customers and competitors. This assessment is particularly difficult in the very uncertain environment of rapidly shifting markets or emerging technologies. Many successful companies fall into the trap of surveying their existing customers about technologies that really sell best to another set of customers. For example, IBM underappreciated the market for personal computers since it was too close to its mainframe customers, who were less interested in PCs. When a product is unfamiliar, customers often don't know what they want. There are various marketing tools for assessing these reactions, even for products that are new to the world. Among the strategies:

- *Use conjoint analysis to assess consumer trade-offs:* Conjoint analysis, a tool that measures consumer trade-offs to determine preferences, has been used to design successful offerings such as Courtyard by Marriott and E-ZPass automated toll collection. This and other tools provide a more precise view of what product and service attributes are important to consumers and also what they are willing to pay for them—usually before the product itself has been created.[8]

- *Use information acceleration:* For products that are new-to-the-world, with which consumers have no experience, companies can use an "information accelerator," an approach pioneered at MIT, to put consumers in a simulated future environment to see how they react. A recent study at the Wharton School on "auto-drive cars" (cars that are self-piloting on special roadways) showed subjects fictitious newspaper articles, *Consumer Reports* reviews, television commercials, and personal recommendations before asking them to complete a conjoint survey weighing factors such as safety, speed, and cost. These approaches can offer insights into potential consumer reactions, even though the product itself does not yet exist.

  In 1995 Mercer Consulting used information acceleration to study consumer reaction to video-on-demand and broadband networks at a time when the Internet itself was foreign to most consumers. Although the study found, as expected, that there was demand for video-on-demand services and that consumers would pay up to $45 a month for them, this was not enough to justify an investment of as much as $1,600 per household to upgrade the telephone and cable networks to full two-way broadband capability. The research also predicted that consumer online services would be a $5 billion market by 1999 with 30 to 40 percent household penetration. Both predictions have been born out by subsequent events.[9]

We explored other approaches for assessing "segments that do not yet exist" (such as looking at latent needs) in Chapter 4. These approaches can also be used to assess the impact of customer reactions on specific strategic options.

Use Competitive Simulations

While the reaction of customers determines the total value generated by a given option, the reaction of competitors determines how that value will be divided. In assessing the consequences of options, managers need to carefully assess the impact of the reactions of rivals. To do this right, you must engage in game theory, which quickly gets complex.[10] Fortunately, competitive simulations, using computer-based models, can elucidate the complexities and provide insights into players' reactions and their overall impact on your share of the pie.

For example, a major oil company that was contemplating a shift in its strategy in the U.S. market decided against the move after playing out a competitive simulation. The company was considering the option of expanding its presence by creating many self-service pumps at convenience stores and other locations. This would offer twenty-four-hour access in many more locations without adding staff. Using a sophisticated computer-based simulation, the company assessed both customer and competitive response in ten key markets using dynamic modeling and customer surveys. The results showed that the initiative would be very successful—adding $315 million in profits in the test market—but only if the company's competitors sat idly by and watched it happen. When the reactions of competitors were added to the simulation, the model indicated that a "pump war" would ensue and the company would lose $133 million compared to not pursuing the strategy.[11]

In industry after industry, price wars and other competitive reactions undermine what initially appear to be brilliant strategies. The use of simulations, either the very formal processes used by the oil company or less formal war rooms and role playing, can provide valuable insights into competitive responses to your strategic options.

Consider Other Stakeholders

Besides customers and rivals, other interested parties may influence your payoff. These parties may include government agencies (at federal, state, and local levels), nongovernmental agencies (such as lobbyists, or trade groups and other special interests), suppliers, strategic partners, and society at large through media, the courts, and so on. For example, when Royal Dutch/Shell had to decide how to dismantle its Brent Spar oil platform in the middle of the North Sea, it underestimated the powerful reaction of Greenpeace, which orchestrated boycotts of Shell products in Germany and caused major political havoc. Shell had conducted careful environmental impact studies, using outside experts, about the relative merits of its three main options: (1) dismantling the platform at sea and ferrying the pieces to shore; (2) dragging the entire platform into a harbor and then disassembling it; and (3) sinking the giant contraption into the depths of the ocean.

Shell, as well as the British government of John Major, favored the third option since the risk of spilling oil was lowest if the mammoth structure, which included an oil depot, was kept intact and stationary. The high seas way off the coast of England made the other two options very risky. Moreover, several marine biologists had argued that the oil platform, once it was at rest on the bottom of the ocean, would form a natural reef for fish and other marine life. But trying to sink an oil platform into the ocean didn't make for good public relations, especially since it also turned out to be the cheapest of the three options. Not surprisingly, Greenpeace saw in Brent Spar a powerful cause célèbre through which it could attack the oil industry, and the British government at large about its perceived lack of a proper environmental policy. The boycott worked beautifully for Greenpeace—Shell had to reverse its decision, and the platform was eventually disassembled at sea, brought to shore in pieces, and finally reused to expand the harbor area in a small Norwegian oil village.

Pool Internal and External Wisdom

To fully explore the impact of stakeholders, you may wish to use strategies for collecting group judgments without falling victim to groupthink. A tried-and-true approach is the Delphi method, in which a group of experts is asked for an initial forecast for, say, the price of oil six months out. Using the Delphi method, these initial forecasts are then distributed anonymously to the same experts for a second round, along with supporting arguments. The experts are asked to adjust their forecasts based on this information (with or without interim discussion). This continues through subsequent rounds until the forecasts stabilize (that is, when no further change is seen in people's estimates).[12] In the spirit of scenario planning, make sure your estimates include confidence ranges in addition to point estimates. Preserving and calibrating uncertainty is key.

Ranking Your Options

Now that you have identified a set of strategic options and assessed the consequences of these options, you are in a position to evaluate them and decide which ones to pursue. How attractive are the various options to you? The evaluation of strategic options might involve the following criteria:

- *Investment:* What resources must be invested in this project?
- *Return horizon:* When will the company receive the benefits from the project?
- *Risk:* What risks surround this option (in view of the scenarios)?
- *Likelihood of success:* How likely is it that you'll succeed if you pursue this option?
- *Fit with culture:* How well does the project fit with the company's culture?
- *Strategic fit:* Does this option advance the overall vision or strategy?

Approaches to evaluating options range from constructing detailed financial models to using more simplified sets of decision principles and rules.[13] The detailed models usually add a level of rigor and precision to the analysis but may also at times give only the illusion of precision, producing a precise answer to the wrong question. Sometimes the greatest value of a move may be its "strategic" value or its "public relations" benefit, which may be very hard to quantify.

Let's explore some of the tools that are available to support the evaluation of options:

- *NPV and real-options analysis:* Net present value (NPV) and options analysis can be very valuable tools in assessing the potential costs and returns of specific options. NPV assesses the value of a strategic alternative by projecting out the expected cash flow and then discounting this incremental cash stream for time and systematic risk (see Appendix B). This approach, in theory, applies to any kind of investment, but in practice it works best for yes-or-no decisions with clearly identifiable costs and revenues. The problem with NPV analysis in uncertain environments is that it tends to overly discount for risk. In contrast, real-options analysis recognizes that a flexible approach to uncertainty has tremendous value if the company has options to capitalize on changes in the environment. While NPV typically penalizes uncertainty, options analysis places a value on it. Investments are viewed as creating a portfolio of options where the commitment of additional resources is subject to attaining defined milestones and resolving key uncertainties. As discussed earlier, these options are investments that give the investor the right but not the obligation to make further downstream investments.[14]

- *Multiattribute utility models:* These models can help to weigh attributes across a complex set of strategic options, without trying to reduce everything to dollars and cents. For example, each option might be scored in terms of its expected return, its overall risk, its strategic fit, and the level of organizational challenge it poses. The overall risk can be assessed by examining the option under multiple scenarios. And strategic fit can be judged in terms of how effectively the option advances the organization's strategic vision. For example, in the mid-1980s, Royal Dutch/Shell had to make a decision where to build the first pilot plant for converting oil to gas while staying ahead of the competition. Fifteen countries were potential locations. Shell planners used a multiattribute model to rank each option and score them based on the above four criteria. They found that Malaysia, for example, was not financially the most attractive in terms of risk but offered a good strategic fit. Shell desired at that time not to invest more in Europe but to focus instead on the Far East, since more growth opportunities were envisioned there. They chose Malaysia.

- *Project-level simulation:* For those specific projects that still have high levels of uncertainty, a simulation may be needed that ties the project-level parameters (such as cost, demand, and price) to the macro-level scenarios that address global and regional parameters (such as economic, political, social, and technological factors). As shown in Exhibit 6-3, this translation may require some intermediate layers that address the industry-level and the firm-level consequences of these macro scenarios. This creates a nested hierarchy of scenarios from the macro level, to business level, to project level as shown in the exhibit. For example, a global recession scenario will need to be translated into corresponding industry conditions, depending on how fast and dramatically suppliers and competitors react to changing economic conditions. Once those industry implications are understood, the link to the specific market segment (i.e., customer and channels) and other determinants of project success should be made by local

Exhibit 6-3: Levels of Scenario Analysis

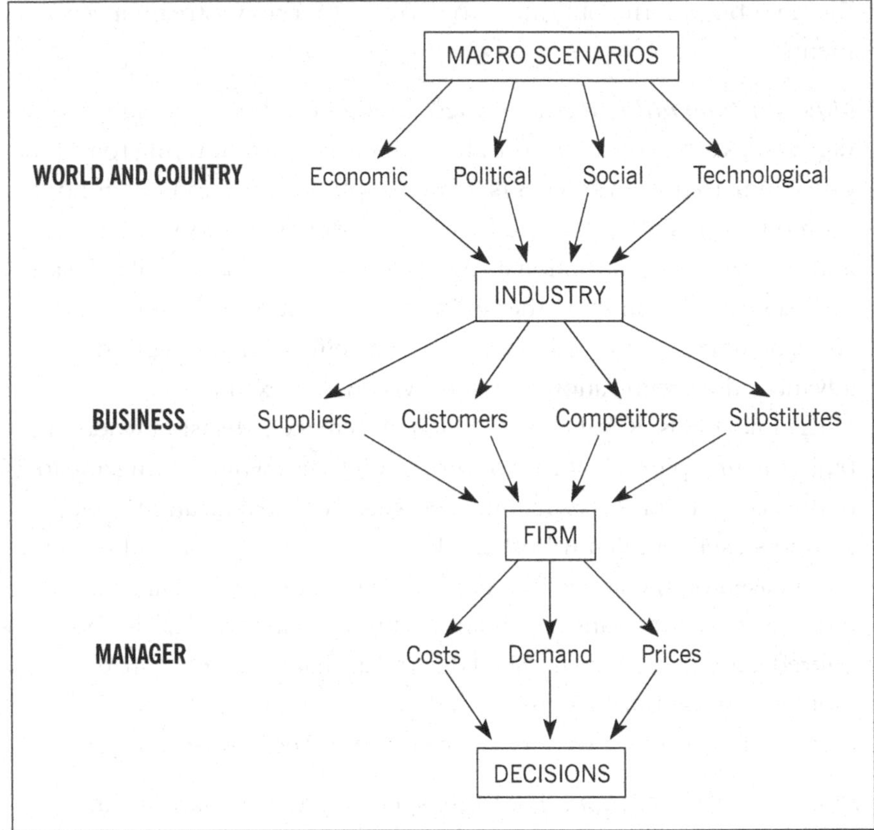

managers. The challenge is to translate the qualitative macro scenarios into numerical estimates (both point estimates and uncertainty ranges) for parameters that directly affect the success of a specific project. Often some computer modeling and simulation may be required to accomplish this.[15]

Adopt a Portfolio View

Smart investors know that having a well-diversified portfolio is the greatest protection against random risks. The risks inherent in any one holding are at least partially offset by the (different) risks of another holding. By creating a "portfolio" of options, you can afford yourself the same protection. The risk in any one option may be partly hedged by the risks of other options, making the portfolio as a whole less risky than the sum of its parts.

Too often people look at options in isolation. But seasoned decision makers will naturally see connections between two projects that others regard as separate. Ask yourself whether you can find pairs of alternatives such that when conditions hinder the success of one option, they promote the success of another. For example, when new cars aren't selling well, the used car market and auto parts industry are usually performing superbly.

Portfolio thinking should be brought to bear on the financial risks associated with many major projects. Looking at the risk of an individual investment (be it a stock or a new project) in isolation from all other investments already made or contemplated may lead you to a poor decision. In the early 1990s the U.S. division of NatWest Bank, for example, lost over $200 million in its middle-market lending portfolio, in part because managers didn't appreciate that macroeconomic factors would affect their real estate, cable, and energy loans in very similar ways.[16]

Microsoft is a prime example of an established firm that used a portfolio of options to maintain flexibility in the face of uncertain technologies. Its much-celebrated "turn on a dime" response when confronted with Netscape's Internet browser is just one instance of its pattern of purposive agility. Microsoft was already placing multiple bets as early as 1988.[17] While Microsoft was continuing to develop its own operating system, it was working with IBM and OS/2 and with SCO on a Unix platform. Furthermore, it was introducing various application software packages, including Excel and Word, for both Windows and Apple's Macintosh. In essence, Microsoft had developed a strong hand of cards to play in a variety of worlds that might emerge. In hindsight, its portfolio of options was commensurate with the uncertainties surrounding hardware and software development at the time.

Conclusion: Animating the Picture

The above approaches for creating and assessing options can form the foundation for much more precise and sophisticated analysis. Many companies have developed complex tools for evaluating options, but the key is to ask the right strategic questions at the outset so that more thorough analysis can be applied to the right problems. If the pool of options is too narrow, many creative possibilities will be overlooked and the result will be suboptimal. If the consequences are not thoroughly considered, the strategic implications of the options will be misestimated. After these strategic issues have been addressed, then a rigorous option evaluation becomes more meaningful and adds a crucial measure of discipline to the process.

An options approach looks at a storyboard for the future, examining frame by frame how it might unfold and impact subsequent decisions. Unfortunately, the world that managers inhabit is not a sequence of carefully considered still frames but a fast-moving motion picture. The decision trees and milestones identified during the process of creating strategic options can keep managers focused on key decision points. But managers then need to follow through by dynamically monitoring and adjusting the strategy in real time as needed. This continuous dynamic monitoring is the focus of the next chapter, since up-front planning and analysis are only a part of the overall challenge. With high uncertainty, reality will still fall outside the bounds of your analysis at times, and this is when you need to be perceptive and agile.

Chapter 7

Dynamic Monitoring and Adjustment

"People sometimes stumble over the truth, but usually they pick themselves up and hurry about their business."

—WINSTON CHURCHILL

Jeff Yass is looking at his watch. In a half hour, U.S. Federal Reserve Chairman Alan Greenspan is expected to announce a cut in the interest rate. The volatility in the market that follows such an announcement offers opportunities for Yass and his colleagues.

"We have no special information. We don't have economists. We don't look at GDP numbers. We see what everyone else sees but try to react to it more efficiently," says Yass, a founder of Susquehanna International Group, one of the largest options trading firms in the world.

"The market presents a constantly changing situation," says Yass, who relies on the collective market wisdom more than his own judgment or the perspectives of individual experts. The market he is looking at today is the Fed Fund Futures, which is running 82 percent in favor of a half-point cut in the prime rate of interest and 18 against. So if buying or selling is inconsistent with these expectations, Yass and other SIG traders hovering over banks of flat-paneled screens in a nearby trading room, will immediately capitalize on these opportunities. This requires vigilant monitoring.

"We approach trading purely in terms of probabilities," Yass says. "We take the market price and see what it implies in terms of odds. Informed trading avoids accepting market events at face value but rather interprets what the market is implying through those events and then capitalizes on any contrarian views."

Yass and his fellow principals at SIG met while in college at SUNY Binghamton. They spent much time studying probability, statistics, and game theory, as well as playing poker, and after graduation applied their accumulated wisdom in the arena of the global financial markets. In addition to theoretical knowledge, the markets also require quick decision making to capture the short-lived opportunities.

Yass has always been an unconventional thinker. He once asked David Sklansky, author of the card playing field guide *Getting the Best of It* (required reading for Susquehanna traders), about a strategy to use in seven-card stud poker. After Sklansky replied, Yass then asked him if the same would be true for "*eight*-card stud", a completely hypothetical example. "At that moment, I knew I was talking to a man who was going places," Sklansky wrote.[1]

Yass has gone places. Susquehanna, founded in 1987, has grown into a global trading and technology company with over 1,000 employees active in financial markets on five continents. The firm accounts for 3 percent of listed stock volume, 2 percent of Nasdaq and as much as 15 percent of listed equity options trading.

Susquehanna relies on top-flight technology coupled with a sophisticated quantitative research function to create and execute successful trading models. But they are convinced that even the most advanced infrastructure is worthless in the hands of an ill-prepared trader. In other words, no formula can ever replace informed human judgment, so trader education plays an integral role in Susquehanna's strategy. Susquehanna also takes a portfolio approach to trading and risk management. Traders covering different industry groups, geographic regions, and financial instruments share information to help the firm better see and respond to the ripple effect a single event can have on different markets. Susquehanna has been successful at establishing a large presence in many varied markets, from equities to bonds and from Philadelphia to Sydney. "Each new market requires adaptation to the local norms, but the core philosophy remains essential to their success," says Yass.

They are comfortable accepting risks while carefully limiting their exposure. They use embedded options to place many small bets and monitor the outcome in real time. "It is not just taking the initial risk, but rather establishing multiple positions and hedges that ultimately gives you a higher probability for winning with smaller fluctuations," Yass says.

As Yass watched on October 2, 2001, Greenspan drove down interest rates by another half a point to their lowest level since 1962. It was the ninth rate cut in a year, and the second since attacks on the World Trade Center had deepened the nation's economic decline. It was the expected move, what 82 percent of the Fed Fund Futures market had anticipated. The broader market responded to the announcement and in the uncertainty before and after, Yass and his colleagues found their opportunities. As that opportunity was played out, Yass had already moved on to the next one.

Yass and Susquehanna have built a profitable business on the basis of superior monitoring and adjustment in real time. This superior ability gives them an edge over rivals, even where there is a relatively even playing field of information. In other businesses that are not directly related to trading financial products, how can you build this kind of flexibility and monitoring into your decision making to profit from uncertainty? How can you recognize patterns in the environment that others have missed? How can you adjust your strategy to avoid the emerging risks and benefit from the new opportunities?

Embracing Uncertainty: Zooming Back Out

In this chapter I'll explore strategies for dynamic monitoring that can help your company better understand uncertainty and profit from it. What are the human and organizational obstacles to monitoring and making sense of new data? What are the new uncertainties you should track? At what point does a key uncertainty become more or less certain? How should you respond to such new information to reshape your strategic vision and strategic options?

The process of creating scenarios and shaping the strategic vision and strategic options might be thought of as moving from tremendous complexity and uncertainty to a simpler problem. In essence, you reduce the uncertainty to a set of scenarios and strategies, as illustrated in Exhibit 7-1. Based on these boundaries (as discussed in Chapters 4 and 5), you further focus upon a specific set of Key Success Factors and strategic vision. Then (as discussed in Chapter 6) you develop strategic options. While this bounding of uncertainty is important in creating a clear map for moving forward—preventing your organization from being paralyzed by the

Exhibit 7-1: Zooming In and Out to Master Uncertainty

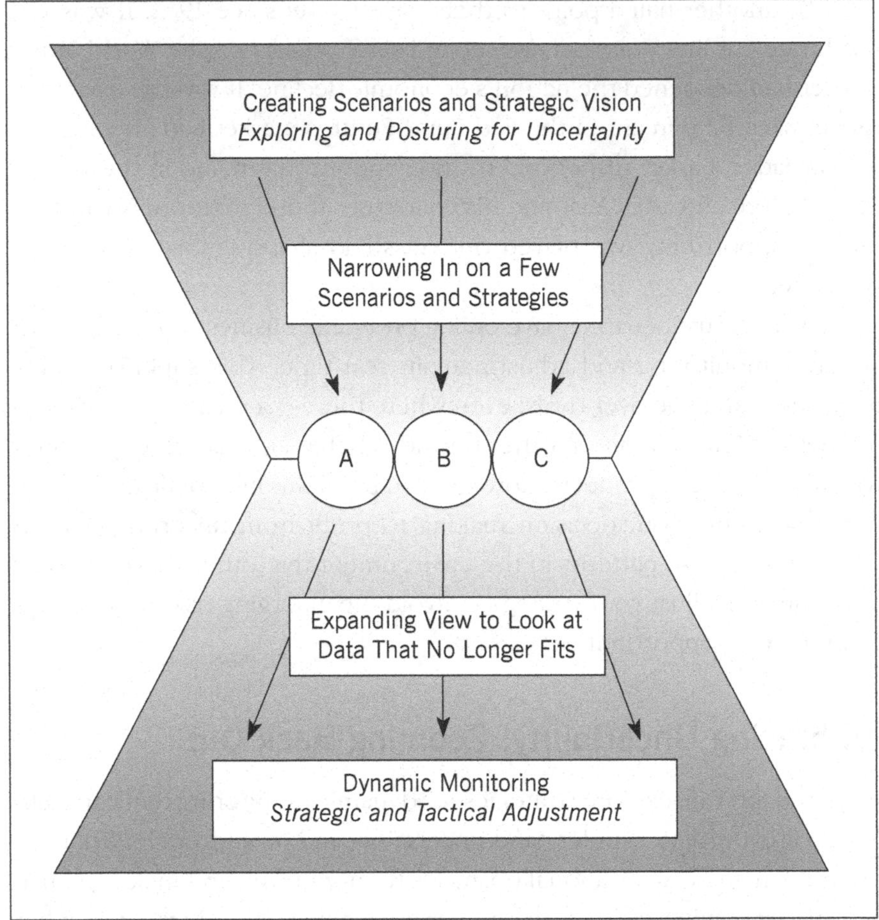

complexity of the environment—you have to be careful. You have to watch that you don't fall into the trap of accepting the stories you have concocted about the future as reality. So you need to devise a process for stepping back and looking at the full picture before zooming back in to focus on the fine details again.

Essentially, dynamic monitoring is a process of letting the chaos back into your world. Through it you keep a continual eye on the uncertainty at the edges of the stories you have created. You need to recognize when some stories no longer hold and when new ones are emerging. This requires a very different process from the one used to bound the uncertainty into a set of scenarios. The process might be thought of as freezing and then unfreezing the action. The scenarios are a painting of the world at a given time, exaggerating key features of it, almost like a caricature, but the world continues to move forward and change, so this image becomes out of date. Like a painter, you have to keep looking back at the model to make sure the painting reflects reality and at times redraw the picture to reflect the current situation.

The key is to develop a systematic process for monitoring the changing environment and making sense of it. First, you need to identify *what* to monitor and then you need to develop the tools and strategies for *how* to monitor. And throughout all of this, you must be aware of some common traps and illusions that we can all fall prey to.

The Difficulty of Monitoring and Sense Making

The first trap to keep in mind is that humans try to make too much sense within just one view of the world. As discussed in Appendix A, we become overconfident about a single view of the environment. Systematic monitoring through multiple lenses is vital because we are not good at seeing the world objectively. Our need to make sense distorts what we see.

On the morning of December 7, 1941, the captain of the destroyer USS *Ward* heard the sound of muffled explosions coming from Pearl Harbor on the mainland. The destroyer captain had just dropped depth charges on an enemy submarine moving into the harbor and had apparently sunk it. Yet when the captain heard the muffled explosions while sailing back to port, he turned to his lieutenant commander and said, "I guess they are blasting the new road from Pearl Harbor to Honolulu." Despite his encounter with a foreign submarine that morning, he made sense of the sounds from his peacetime mindset and thus failed to see the signs of the first hostilities between the United States and Japan. This mindset was so strong that the captain forced the sound of explosions into a peacetime context of road building rather than the more realistic wartime context of an enemy attack.[2]

History offers many examples of businesses that similarly failed to see the warning signs, even when they might have been clear, because they were so locked into their existing mindsets. For example, sailing ship manufacturers failed to see the potential promise of the steam engine, and most went bankrupt. Many companies reacted slowly to the electrification of factories in the 1900s. NCR maintained a fatal myth about being on the top of the shift to electronics. Large disk drive manufacturers failed to see the next wave of smaller drives.[3] Similarly, traditional pharmaceutical firms initially played a secondary role in biotechnology (through joint venturing and licensing), while new billion-dollar biopharmaceutical firms, such as Amgen, Biogen, Chiron, and Genentech, were emerging. Companies in the service sector have also failed to evolve effectively: few original telegraph companies (like Western Union) remain in the telecommunications industry. Of the hundred top U.S. industrial firms named by *Forbes* magazine in 1917, more than half had gone out of business or were greatly diminished fifty years later.[4]

Human Obstacles to Monitoring

Our strength as humans is our ability to find patterns in the complexity of the world. We are masters of making sense, weaving stories around disparate data points. Indeed, we are so good at it that we see patterns that aren't there and believe them more than we should (as illustrated by the image of the man/mouse in Chapter 2). From patterns in stock prices to hidden trends at the roulette table, we see order amid chaos, since we are hardwired to seek meaning. And once locked in to one view of the world, we often force-fit new information into our old models. In addition to this tendency to find patterns where none exist, our monitoring abilities are weakened by a variety of other human limitations. Consider a few illustrative examples:

- *Information is interdependent:* It is often hard for us to gather fresh information and to interpret that information properly because our sources of information have dependencies that we fail to recognize. This difficulty is illustrated by a humorous story about Native Americans on a remote reservation who asked their chief whether they faced a cold winter ahead. Unfortunately, the modern chief had lost the old ways of divining the weather, so to be on the safe side, he told the tribe it would be a cold winter indeed and that they should collect firewood. A short time later he decided to double-check his hunch by calling the National Weather Service. The meteorologist told the chief it looked like the winter would be quite cold, so the chief then told his people to gather even more firewood. The chief called the meteorologist back a while later to check on the forecast once again. "Are you really sure it will be a cold winter?" he asked. "Trust me, it will be a very, very cold winter," replied the meteorologist. "How do you know?" asked the chief. "Well," said the meteorologist, "the Indians are collecting firewood like crazy."

While this is a funny example, it is amazing how many organizations have similar types of self-reinforcing systems. People in the organization talk to one another and draw conclusions from the same information until there is no one left to challenge their shared view of the world. They are all dining together inside the *Titanic* and don't even see the possibility of an iceberg because no one is on the bridge looking. Similarly the rise of technology stocks at the end of the 1990s was driven by the rosy forecasts of analysts, who became increasingly optimistic as investors drove up stock prices, which further encouraged the analysts, resulting in a speculative bubble that eventually burst.

- *Real-world information is often incomplete:* We are often missing the feedback we need to assess if we are making the right decision. Always ask: "What am I not seeing that might matter?" For example, before the *Challenger* space shuttle explosion on January 28, 1986, technicians had noticed a pattern of serious wear on the O-rings from seven previous flights, and they raised concerns about possible failure at low temperatures. But when they plotted the temperatures at the time of the seven previous incidents, the technicians found they occurred across a range of temperatures, from the low fifties Fahrenheit to as warm as seventy-five. Managers at NASA and rocket booster manufacturer Morton Thiokol concluded that evidence to support a theory that low temperatures caused O-ring problems was "inconclusive." After the crash, when O-rings failed, they looked at a different set of data. Instead of focusing on the seven incidents of damage alone, they looked at failures across *all* flights. This showed that every one of the previous flights with no evidence of wear on the O-rings occurred at sixty-six degrees or above. This broader feedback raised much more emphatic questions about the safety of a shuttle launch at low temperatures. The initial data had been defined too narrowly.[5]

- *We look for confirming evidence:* In our age of information abundance, it does not take long to find evidence that supports one's view, even if it is erroneous. We can fool ourselves in ever more sophisticated ways and fall victim to a deep-seated human bias to look for evidence that confirms rather than disconfirms our views.[6] As I say jokingly to Ph.D. students, if you torture the data long enough, it will confess. When Apollo astronauts returned from the moon with samples of moon rocks, NASA finally felt it could put to rest competing theories about the origin of the moon. NASA sent each of the samples to leading theorists and gave them three months to study the rocks independently. Then it sponsored a conference for the scientists. The result, however, was that each lab was more convinced than ever that it had the right answer. Each one analyzed data to support its preconceived idea. As Thomas Kuhn observed, science advances not so much through new evidence but because the established guard that protects old beliefs eventually dies off in sufficient numbers.[7]

Organizational Obstacles to Monitoring

In addition to weaknesses in our basic psychological makeup, organizational limitations also pose challenges for making sense of new information. The internal workings of an organization often create obstacles to proper sense making, resulting in the following paradoxes:

1. Planning and budgeting are episodic activities, while external change is continuous.
2. The most reliable metrics are historical ones, whereas the more valuable indicators deal with the future.
3. Organizational processes are based on systemization and conformity, but new insights often come from outliers and inconsistencies.

Many companies perform variance analyses, but they mostly study the negative deviations from plan, when departments or functions fail to meet a target. They should study positive surprises at least as much, since these may point to unrealized potential. Any variance suggests that we really don't fully understand or control the world around us. The key issue is whether the departures from expectation are random or systematic. In the latter case, a learning opportunity is lurking.

Organizational forces often tend to sustain the status quo. A study of appliance sales at Macy's stores found that salespeople unconsciously sought to maintain the same ratio of sales of refrigerators to dishwashers despite changing demand. The patterns were so deeply ingrained that the salespeople seemed to adjust their strategies to maintain the status quo, in much the same way as a thermostat adjusts its heating or cooling output to maintain a steady temperature in a room.

A Framework for Monitoring

Any comprehensive framework for dynamic monitoring should address two key issues: what to monitor and how. Since you cannot look at everything, you need to focus on specific issues. Once you identify the indicators to look at, you need to develop strategies for monitoring those factors and responding effectively.

In the broadest sense, you should monitor the external world in view of your scenarios and segments (customers and rivals) as well as your internal progress in developing Key Success Factors, fine-tuning your strategies, and implementing your chosen options. The latter include all business options, such as launching a new product or signing up new partners, as well as organizational initiatives embarked upon such as training, culture change, compensation, or changes in organizational design and process.

Once your managers agree on *what* to monitor within each of these external and internal areas, you must examine *how* you will monitor. Monitoring ranges from leading to lagging indicators, from soft to hard measures, and from centralized to decentralized approaches. Monitoring deserves a book in its own right, so I restrict myself here to addressing the special challenges of navigating and managing uncertainty.

You might end up with a framework such as the one shown in Exhibit 7-2 (in simplified format). The actual framework would include a detailed list of factors under each of the headings related to key assumptions or milestones in the scenarios and business strategies.

Within each cell of this table, you should note whether the measures are quantitative or qualitative, and what degree of reliability each measure possesses. Then, taken as a whole, you should ascertain how comprehensive and timely the tableau of measures really is and whether it will help your organization make rapid adjustments when necessary, so as to fully profit from uncertainty.

Exhibit 7-2: A Simplified Framework for Monitoring

		HOW?		
		Lagging	Concurrent	Leading
WHAT?	EXTERNAL			
	Environment			
	Customers			
	Competitors			
	Partners			
	INTERNAL			
	Strategy (KSFs)			
	Options			
	Organizational			

What to Monitor

On the external side, you should especially develop—in addition to the usual measures about consumer behavior and competitive intelligence—signposts and early warning signals that tell you which way the world is evolving. Ideally, you included some of this work in the scenario-planning phase of the process. For example, as the pharmaceutical executive who wakes up in different futures in Chapter 3, you should know in which world you are waking up by tracking various key indicators. If the technology-savvy environment is materializing, you would see a flurry of new ventures emerging trying to harvest the promise of the genomics revolution, which would be in full swing in that scenario. In the monitoring phase, you might quantify this leading indicator by measuring how much early-stage funding and subsequent venture capital are flowing into new genomics start-ups.

Identify Early Warning Signs

For each scenario, a rich set of indicators should be devised that lets managers gauge which way the wind is blowing before it is evident to all. So leading indicators are especially valuable here, rather than historical measures that look in the rearview mirror.

Since market analysis and competitive intelligence are normally part of what firms monitor anyway, you have an opportunity here to link these existing data sources to the broader scenarios. In each scenario, you would expect to see varying patterns of consumer spending, channel preference, and so on, as well as distinct actions by competitors and/or strategic partners in response to the scenario.

The closer you can make this connection the better, since it will force you to understand the scenarios not just in a big-picture way but in terms of concrete behaviors and metrics that can be monitored on an ongoing basis. Credit unions, for example, are concerned about member loyalty and the tendency of banks to cherry-pick their most profitable customers. Specific metrics can be devised to gauge such cherry-picking, and different levels of competitive pressure can be associated with specific scenarios.

Another key uncertainty for many businesses is technology. Managers can track specific technologies by attending conferences, subscribing to relevant journals, and building relationships with key researchers or hiring an expert to help track developments. There may be key technology people inside the organization who could be assigned this task. In particular, you should look for key tipping points that indicate the system is going in one direction or another.[8]

Use Influence Diagrams to Identify Turning Points

In addition to monitoring certain trends, you can identify key milestones or turning points, forks in the road that will lead to one scenario or another. It is important to understand in advance where these forks are, so you know what road you are traveling on.

By creating an influence diagram, such as the one shown in Exhibit 7-3 (and discussed in Chapter 1), you can better assess where these turning points are. By thinking through how the scenarios might unfold, you can identify key milestones and turning points. When certain conditions are met, a particular scenario is more likely. The dynamic evolution of the scenarios can be expected to follow particular pathways. An influence diagram can help to develop a scenario as well as to track it.

As an example, consider the diagram in Exhibit 7-3, for one of the health care scenarios discussed in Chapter 3. The scenario starts with a weak global economy that restricts spending on health. It is also driven by a lack of breakthrough technologies, strong privacy protection, and

Exhibit 7-3: An Influence Diagram for a Health Care Scenario

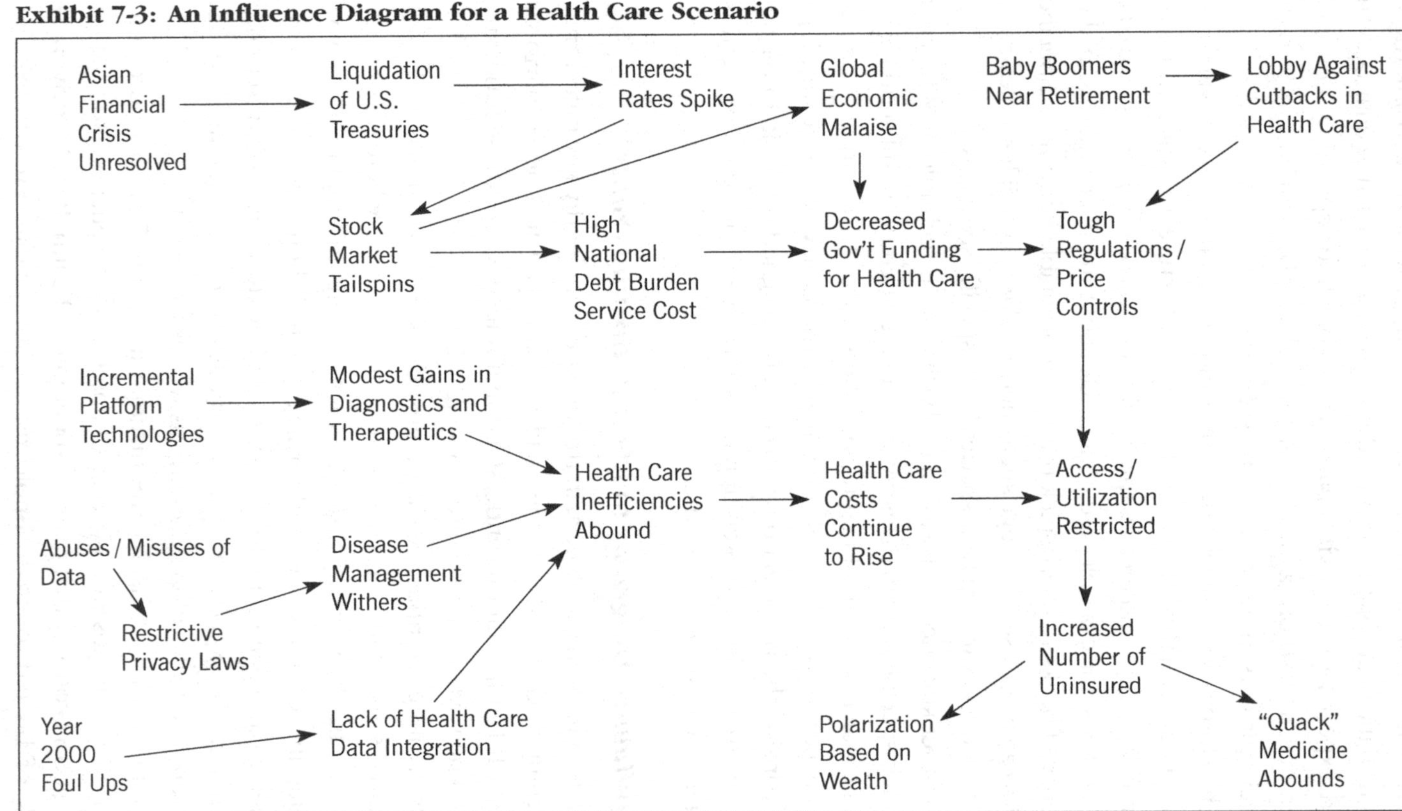

Source: *Decision Strategies International, Inc.*

changes in insurance reimbursement. These forces interact and build on one another to influence how this scenario unfolds. Drawing such a diagram can help you think through the causal relationships that drive the scenarios and can also help identify milestones that will signal whether the scenario is unfolding.

Make Your Assumptions Explicit

Many of the assumptions upon which we base our strategies are implicit or insufficiently examined. They can be assumptions about the scenarios (as discussed above) as well as assumptions underlying specific business strategies. What are you assuming to support your belief that a specific option will pay off for your company? The process of scenario planning (Chapter 3) offers a framework for making the assumptions underlying your plans more conscious. (You design strategies for specific futures, so you know that if these futures are not emerging, you probably need to change your plans.)

When the Walt Disney Company opened Euro Disney in 1992, it made an implicit assumption that visitors to the theme park would largely act the same way as visitors to its U.S. and Japanese parks. It assumed that it could charge a high entrance price, that visitors would stay an average of four days in hotels, that they would "graze" in restaurants all day, and that they would buy a similar mix of souvenirs. Instead, European visitors found the price high compared to much lower tickets for other theme park attractions in Europe. They stayed an average of two days in hotels, tended to all crowd into restaurants at noon instead of grazing, and they bought far fewer high-margin souvenirs than their peers at other Disney parks. By 1994 the company had lost more than $1 billion on the project.

Rita Gunther McGrath and Ian MacMillan, who analyzed the Euro Disney case, developed a systematic approach for identifying and monitoring underlying assumptions in business strategies.[9] In their discovery-driven planning process, managers identify and track key assumptions using an "assumptions checklist" and explicitly monitor these assumptions at specific milestones. In this way the assumptions are treated as hypotheses that are tested along the way, and the consequences of the tests are immediately translated into the bottom-line income statement. The main problem with Euro Disney was not just flawed assumptions going in, but slow detection and corrective action once new data became available.

Track Broader Measures

Once your organization has agreed upon good internal and external measures, you should assess the adequacy of the existing measures. Most companies carefully monitor their financial situation as well as their internal operations, from inbound logistics to inventory management to operational efficiency and quality metrics. The key challenge is to assess how well these traditional measures track the degree of progress of the particular vision and strategies you have crafted to profit from uncertainty. Does your organization have good measures to ascertain its agility in the face of change, its capacity to exercise options in a timely fashion, or its ability to improvise and adjust as circumstances warrant?

Many companies have embraced the Balanced Scorecard approach, which entails a healthy broadening of performance measures as well as a much tighter connection with the specific strategy involved.[10] In essence, this approach starts with the strategy and then decides what the organization should measure in four broad areas (covering internal, financial, customer, and renewal metrics) to track its progress. But the strategy or plan may not survive contact with reality, and so an additional challenge is to incorporate uncertainty. A good scorecard will quickly tell you when you are veering off the desired path, but it may not tell you whether a tactical adjustment is in order or whether a major strategic overhaul of the plan is called for. Similarly, the traditional budgeting process runs into trouble when significant uncertainty is present. What do you do when you are over or under budget due to allegedly unforeseen circumstances? If you continually adjust the budget depending on new contingencies, what's the purpose or value of budgetary discipline?

Ideally, the monitoring system should fully recognize that the world is quite uncertain and that this uncertainty is a source of opportunity rather than a failure to plan or execute. So a good dynamic monitoring system should quickly spot departures from expectations and gather sufficient information in real time to help managers decide whether embedded options should be exercised, tactical adjustment is called for, or a new (flexible) strategy should be devised for new external scenarios. This is a tall order and is best approached by examining the current monitoring system.

Focus on Leading Measures and the External Environment

Leading indicators are usually not tracked as carefully as present or lagging measures, which are needed for financial reporting. When I was at Shell in the early 1980s, I met with managers from the strategic planning department at IBM and asked them if they did scenario planning. They replied that they had such a good information system for their existing business that they didn't need it. They received sales information overnight from Stuttgart and other regional offices. They knew everything there was to know about their existing business. But a change in the part of the world that they were not in tune with sent the company into a tailspin in the 1990s. The personal computer shook up the computing world and undermined the validity of IBM's truckloads of positive data. As in the old joke about the man looking near the lantern for the coin he dropped down the street, we often look where the data are clearest rather than where we should really look—in shadows of our business and industry.

Detailed management information systems (MIS) may give a false sense of certainty by focusing on what the company knows, concentrating on the internal data of its existing business. This is the reason Russell Ackoff facetiously calls MIS "Mis-Information Systems." Comprehensive, up-to-date information may give managers an illusion of control, but these systems usually don't highlight the *unknown,* the hidden uncertainties that lurk around the edges of the existing business. And these uncertainties are often the most important source of potential challenges and new opportunities. Because many companies fail to see the changes or respond to them when they appear, they deal with them reactively, only after their symptoms show up in the corporate monitoring system.

As IBM found out in the 1980s, and as Cisco learned in 2001, it is not enough to be good at monitoring your business closely. Even the best early warning system will not let you know trouble is headed your way if you don't monitor the right things—and this often means looking at the bigger picture (the forest, not the trees). As discussed throughout the book, scenario planning allows managers to put the disparate pieces of information into a strategic context, to see how they add up to a coherent whole. This is especially important for organizations that become blinded by their success or their existing worldview. If IBM had monitored how all its customers were using computers, including educational users and not just current mainframe customers, would the company have been able to anticipate the PC revolution more clearly and move more quickly? Would a more detailed view of the compounding factors that sent the U.S. economy reeling have sobered Cisco's overconfident view of the future? If Cisco had developed, explored, and prepared for a true downturn scenario, would it have been quicker to recognize and respond to the early warning signals?

Why do companies spend most of their energies tracking trailing indicators? First, these measures are more reliable. The past is hard and fixed, while the future is fuzzy and uncertain. Second, these are the measures that accounting systems and regulators require. Third, the data for these measures are much more easily gathered.

At a deeper level, managers desire certainty and a sense of control. Having reliable and consistent data can satisfy this longing for predictability, and slowly the illusion creeps in that the numbers are the reality (rather than an imperfect reflection). The philosopher West Churchman studied the nature of inquiring systems and noted that most people prefer the certainty of universal truth and reality rather than philosophies that highlight contradictions and the limitations of human experience. Most companies want an information system that is consistent and free of contradiction. The numbers must add up, and estimates should be based on common and internally consistent assumptions. This was a philosophy favored by Leibniz, who invented calculus. Scenario planning, however, is much more sympathetic to the philosophical perspective of Hegel or Kant, creating a dialectical tension by courting mutually incompatible views of the future that need to be synthesized. Managers who seek precision about the world may have some philosophical and conceptual difficulty with the approach advanced in this book.

Dynamic monitoring calls for tracking the leading indicators that will affect future performance rather than analyzing the past or projecting the past forward linearly. How quickly can you see that a small dip in sales is the start of extended downturn in the industry? How quickly can you detect that a sudden interest in a particular product is the start of a huge surge in demand as the product takes off?

Information systems such as customer relationship management

(CRM) now create the possibility of channeling data from every conversation that a salesperson has with a prospective client into an overall projection of the future sales of the firm. When a prospect shrugs his shoulders, it should ripple through the entire system. Data mining can similarly detect weak signals before the trend is evident to all.

Companies devote many resources to measuring their internal performance but relatively few to tracking the external environment and even fewer to connecting the internal and external. Teams of accountants pore over their books, but few managers scan the horizon. Do you understand the trends that drive your business as well as you understand the internal data? How can you create systems to gather and track this external information with the same rigor that you gather and track internal numbers and progress? And how can you then draw the connections between external change and internal progress (or lack thereof)?

How to Monitor

How can your organization engage in dynamic monitoring of the future environment, to be aware of changes when they occur? Most corporate monitoring is centralized and event-driven and takes place in a fairly homogeneous culture. To monitor more effectively, you need to diffuse the process across the entire organization, design continuous planning processes, and create a nonconformist culture.

We are in the very early stages of developing systems for effective dynamic monitoring, but the emergence of systems for Enterprise Resource Planning (ERP), Customer Relationship Management (CRM), and Enterprise Risk Management (ERM) are all steps in the direction of building a "central nervous system" for the organization. This will allow it to be truly aware of its internal and external environment so it can react to and anticipate dynamic changes and develop forward-looking strategies. Advances in information processing power and communications speeds hold the promise to increase the reach and depth of these systems enormously, provided this power is harnessed strategically (see box).

Diffuse the Process across the Entire Organization

The more eyes you have looking for change, the more likely you will spot it. But to have the entire organization engaged in this process, people

The Future of Monitoring

When the CEO walks into the office five or ten years from now, the traditional polished mahogany desktop and blotter may be replaced by a flat-screen desktop providing multiple windows on the company, the world, and the future. In this vision of the CEO office of the future—described by entrepreneur, venture capitalist, and strategy consultant V. Michael Mavaddat—today's systems that are just beginning to monitor company performance will be made broader and deeper to pay attention to weaker signals, both inside and outside the firm.

Mavaddat highlights key characteristics of these systems that will utilize increasingly powerful computational engines, software tools, and networks for both storage and communications:

- **Bringing the outside in:** In contrast to today's internally focused systems, the future monitoring system will highlight key weak signals from the outside environment. For example, rather than reporting on the most frequent and prevalent customer complaints, CRM systems will be monitoring and highlighting the infrequent complaints of customers and raise red flags when the rate of increase of a certain complaint starts accelerating. In today's environment, the infrequent occurrences are dismissed as "outliers" or "anecdotes." However, there may be a great deal of strategic insight in these so-called outliers. They could very well be the weak signals that grow stronger over time. By the time the importance of these weak signals is recognized in the internally generated information (e.g., sales) it will be too late for the organization to be proactive. By bringing the outside information in, the organization can be better prepared to adapt itself. These weak signals can have any source: employees, suppliers, customers, and partners. The challenge is to build intelligent systems that are capable of relating and integrating these disparate sources of weak signals into a holistic and strategic view of the enterprise.
- **Tracking scenarios and dynamic metrics:** Most of the performance metrics used by managers today are static and backward-looking. Even the Balanced Scorecard, which looks beyond simple financial metrics, still defines a fixed set of dimensions to measure. The future monitoring system would allow for much more dynamic and forward-looking measures. It would track key assumptions and driving forces of the various scenarios, alerting the CEO when a particular scenario is starting to play out. The system, with built-in simulation capabilities, would allow the CEO to engage in "what if" analyses with the live data inside and outside the firm.

- **Taking the pulse of the organization:** Many important issues are raised in conversations throughout the organization, but this organizational discourse rarely makes it to the level of the CEO until there are serious problems. Systems would help monitor key dialogues across the organization and identify common threads of critical issues to highlight for the CEO. Sophisticated natural language software would continually analyze all kinds of communications and detect patterns, such as issues of increasing concern.
- **Aligning the decision processes of the organization:** Often in large organizations, different business areas act under very different assumptions. For example, Ford Motor Company took a $1 billion write-off because the purchasing department stockpiled precious metals such as palladium at the same time that the Ford research engineers were developing catalytic converters to use less of that expensive material. The monitoring system would make decisions across the organization more transparent and allow business leaders to compare decision processes side-by-side to make sure they are coherent.

This strategic monitoring system would not be limited to the chief executive, but similar systems would be available to managers throughout the organization. The difference would be that they would only see the parts of the company and the outside world that are most relevant to the issues they need to address. "Managers will be able to understand the discourse that is happening in and around [the] organization—who is talking about what," observes Mavaddat. "Where are the signals coming from, and how can they affect the future of the organization?" Technology will enable much deeper and wider monitoring of both internal and external events, and in addition will help create meaning from it all. This would all take place in real time and in a highly user-friendly manner.

need to know what they are looking for. The culture has to become one of sense and respond, which by definition includes a strong external orientation.[11]

The process of monitoring key trends can benefit from broad dissemination. Lucent Technologies created a quarterly publication called *Focus on the Future* in which it explored emerging technologies, management and workplace trends, and other future-oriented topics that could have an influence on its business. The stated goal of the publication was to "stimulate employees to think about the future and what it might be."

- *Communicate the scenarios broadly:* You should communicate the scenarios you have developed clearly and broadly throughout the organization. The more people who understand the scenarios, the more eyes you have looking for confirming or disconfirming evidence. When it developed its scenarios, *The Miami Herald* published summaries in the newspaper and invited employees and readers to comment on them. The developers of economic-political scenarios for South Africa in the early 1990s also created a fourteen-page insert in a major weekly newspaper. Then they went one step further by developing a thirty-minute video with cartoons illustrating the four scenarios. They also held sessions with approximately a hundred groups throughout the country, including political parties, companies, academics, trade unions, and civic organizations. This communication effort helped ensure that the scenarios were firmly embedded in the consciousness of the society and formed a common language for national discussion.[12] Some organizations have used artistic maps to broadly disseminate and focus attention on their scenarios (See Exhibit 9-7). These illustrations, which are often displayed prominently as mural-sized graphics, provide a creative way to keep the scenarios in front of employees and to help them to understand the key drivers and characteristics of each scenario.

- *Encourage the whole organization to assemble evidence:* If the scenarios are broadly disseminated, communication can then flow both ways. The organization can be actively gathering evidence that supports or opposes particular scenarios. At the simplest level, some companies use a bulletin board to monitor different scenarios. They divide the bulletin board into quarters and post the title and description of each scenario in one quarter of the bulletin board. Employees are asked to post news clippings or other information they find that supports each scenario. At the end of a few weeks, one or two scenarios often have many pieces of paper while others have few. One problem with this approach is that the mainstream media tend to be biased toward the sensational, so the clippings will reflect the evidence that is on the public radar screen. Depending on how broadly employees read and how deeply they dig into these issues, they may be able to counterbalance the sometimes-superficial perspectives of the media to offer a more even view. This approach provides a rather low-cost way to keep the organization focused on the scenarios and to continuously test whether they are coming to pass. In organizations that are dispersed more broadly, employees, customers, and other stakeholders could be encouraged to add data to a "virtual bulletin board" online.

- *Track trends across your industry:* Pooling resources across an industry can help to monitor key emerging trends. The Credit Union Executives Society (CUES) has developed industry-wide scenarios that have been periodically updated (as discussed later in this chapter). These broader scenarios are then used to shape the strategies of individual firms. The California Institute of Food and Agriculture at the University of California, Davis, and consulting firm Nuffer, Smith, Tucker, Inc. have created a trends intelligence system for the agri-food chain. This "Food Foresight" system assembles a blue-ribbon panel twice per year to identify the five to ten top trends in the industry. Partner firms then use this information to develop their own strategies. In monitoring the trends, associations can also help identify key warning signs that a certain scenario is unfolding.[13]

- *Use shadow teams:* Rather than inviting the whole organization to track all the scenarios, some companies assign shadow teams to track particular scenarios. These shadow teams gain depth in the issues related to the scenarios and provide periodic updates. This process is similar to the use of shadow cabinets in government, a form of devil's advocacy in the spirit of loyal opposition. The teams may usefully debate the meaning of key developments as seen through different scenario lenses. This is where the art of constructive dialogue is key, which in turn requires trust and mutual respect. Good dialogue goes beyond initial impressions and explores matters at a deeper level.[14]

- *Clipping services:* Various companies offer clipping services that can track specific topics across diverse media or identify provocative new trends that might affect the business. These services can help your organization monitor its environment, and they can challenge the thinking of managers by sending in a steady stream of reports on forces changing the environment.

- *Engage in periodic reassessments:* Your organization can also benefit from a periodic reassessment of the scenarios. By creating a regularly scheduled review process, your managers can be sure to continue to look for changes and keep the scenarios current. Depending upon the changes that have occurred since their development, this assessment could be a fairly minor update or a more substantial creation of new scenarios.

- *Look at the information through multiple lenses:* In addition to looking at how specific information either confirms or disconfirms a given scenario, you can also use each scenario as a lens for examining the implications of each piece of new information. For example, a newspaper company learned in 1999 that Xerox was planning to offer a new Pressline service to deliver newspapers electronically to hotels, offering customized onsite printing to give travelers their local newspapers or deliver national newspapers in different languages.[15] What does this information mean for the newspaper company? It depends on what scenario it expects to emerge in the future:
  - In a "business as usual" scenario in which the Internet makes limited progress, the new Pressline service will likely represent only a niche market (the traveler's market) and an alternative channel of newspaper distribution to physical delivery. Under this scenario, this service might offer an expansion opportunity for newspapers beyond their natural urban domain as well as a means of enhancing customer loyalty.
  - In a "cybermedia" scenario in which there is widespread proliferation of online media, Pressline could be the start of a customized home printing trend of newspapers. This development could undermine the very asset base upon which newspapers depend today (their printing presses and physical distribution network). Furthermore, as the market segments into finer clusters, the mass publication model of newspapers—imposed upon them by the constraints of printing presses—may give way to a new world of truly individualized newspapers in which the terms *reach* and *penetration* lose their traditional meaning. The implications of these changes for the way newspapers sell and price advertising, manage the newsroom, produce and package their product, and distribute it are indeed pro-

> found and uncertain. In this world, newspaper presses, delivery trucks, or broadband mass advertising messages are no longer needed nor valued.

As this example illustrates, the same piece of information can have very different meanings depending on the scenario considered. By examining significant new pieces of information through multiple lenses, managers can gain a deeper understanding of their implications for the scenarios and the organization.

If one piece of information is studied through different conceptual lenses, its meaning can shift; but if many pieces of information are thus examined, a totally new picture may emerge. For example, through careful analysis of the data, Dr. John Snow's celebrated analysis of a cholera epidemic in London in 1854 was able to pinpoint its probable source. While cholera deaths were typically reported chronologically, Snow instead plotted the deaths on a map, allowing him to determine that the source of the outbreak was the public water pump at Broad Street. Snow also conducted extensive interviews, particularly looking at outliers that did not fit his theory of the pump as the source of the outbreak. These interviews revealed that most of the more distant households with cholera outbreaks drew their water from the Broad Street pump because they preferred it to closer sources. Further, he found that a brewery near the pump, in which employees were spared from the outbreak, had its own well and offered its workers free liquor, so they did not have cause to drink water from the pump in the street. This more thorough analysis of disconfirming evidence ultimately strengthened his case for the removal of the handle from the Broad Street pump.[16]

Snow's creative mapping of information, his gathering of additional data, and his hypothesis that cholera was spread through water allowed him to see patterns that others had missed. If he had accepted a chronological report of deaths or failed to explore the disconfirming evidence in more detail, he would not have been able to reach the conclusion that the Broad Street pump was the source of the epidemic. By diffusing the monitoring process across the organization, you are more likely to gather the relevant information from diverse sources and come up with creative insights about what this information means.

Design Continuous Planning Processes

Traditional planning and budget cycles are annual events that can take three to seven months to complete in a large organization. In a rapidly changing environment, by the time the plan and budget are nailed down, they are often out of date. The weaknesses of episodic planning have long been recognized, and there were calls even in the 1950s if not before for a more incremental approach.[17] The idea is to proceed flexibly, experimentally, and in small steps, from broad objectives to specific commitments. This was easier said than done, however, particularly in large complex organizations, and it could easily devolve into chaos. Today better systems and tools allow continuous and ongoing planning while sustaining discipline and rigor. A variety of strategies can make planning more continuous, including:

- *Use active financial planning:* A new set of computer-based financial tools is emerging for "active financial planning," drawing together financial planning, competitive intelligence, and collaboration into an integrated system.[18] Your company's goals are set annually, but the software platform allows your managers to use a system of continuous rolling forecasts to assess past results and profitability drivers. Based on this assessment, the managers develop incentives, take actions, and measure results. The cycle operates continuously. The system helps your organization adapt its budgets and actions in real time, based on a continuous flow of new information. These systems build upon traditional enterprise resource planning (ERP), adding layers of financial consolidation, business analysis, business intelligence, and Web-based enterprise planning and decision support.

- *Use options valuation to put uncertainty on the balance sheet:* As discussed in Chapter 6, the valuation of real options can be a way to actively reflect uncertainty in the balance sheet. In this way, the potential for the future is given a real value, and that value is lost only if the options are destroyed or are not exercised. This means the budgeting process is much more directly linked to the future rather than remaining focused on the past. It also means that, in conjunction with a real-time monitoring of these options, the cost and value of uncertainty can be reflected directly in the balance sheet on an ongoing basis.

Create a Nonconformist Culture

The culture of an organization will affect its ability to identify outlying information and develop creative responses. A culture that is in lock-step agreement will be very efficient but will tend to be locked into a common mindset. The pharmaceutical company that tolerates a devotee of holistic medicine on its staff, or the oil company that invites a committed environmentalist into the organization, is far more likely to see changes outside the industry's normal field of vision. Becoming a learning culture is key to achieving excellence in strategic monitoring and real-time adjustment.[19]

A conformist culture can create deadly blindspots. "Rien"—*nothing*—was the final entry of King Louis XVI of France in his diary on July 14, 1789. This was the day the Bastille fell in a bloody uprising that launched the French Revolution and ultimately cost Louis his crown and his head. Shouldn't he have seen this coming? The signs of unrest were everywhere, but Louis was surrounded by aristocrats of the same mind, ensconced in his palace with sycophants while the nation was headed for revolution.

Uniform thinking poses tremendous danger to an organization. For example, in developing its global scenarios in the 1980s, Royal Dutch/Shell failed to see the fall of the Berlin Wall. Perhaps the team developing the scenarios was too rational or too heavily weighted with engineers or economists. A few historians or others who might have been able to draw upon the lessons of the French Revolution might have seen alternative outcomes and more chaotic possibilities. It can often be uncomfortable for organizations to invite revolutionaries into the palace. But it can be even more uncomfortable, and outright dangerous, for them to arrive uninvited.

One of the greatest perils of organizations is the tendency toward groupthink,[20] when "concurrence seeking" becomes so dominant in group dynamics that it overrides realistic appraisals of alternative courses of action. When groupthink develops, the overall organizational IQ is *less* than the sum of its parts because half-baked ideas are embraced prematurely. Your organization needs to consciously fight this tendency toward conformity by encouraging *disagreement,* so it can fully explore the information that falls outside the currently accepted view of the world. As General Motors CEO Alfred Sloan, Jr., once said, "Gentlemen, I take it we are all in complete agreement on the decision here. . . . Then I propose we postpone further discussion of this matter until our next meeting to give ourselves time to develop disagreement and perhaps gain some understanding of what the decision is all about."

Among the strategies for creating a collective open mind are:

- *Become a learning (as well as a performance) organization:* Most organizations are focused primarily on improving their performance and delivering bottom-line results. This is important but can lead to doing the wrong thing very efficiently. Today companies are increasingly recognizing that their future strength lies in how well they are able to learn. While building your performance organization, you also need to create a "learning culture." Two types of learning are important. The first, learning that reinforces the current paradigm and business, is something that most performance organizations are good at: How can you do what you currently do better, faster, or cheaper? But the learning organization is also concerned with a second type of learning, about how the organization needs to change to succeed in the future. The first type of learning is what a tennis player does on the court. The second is what a good coach does standing on the sidelines. Both types of learning are vital to organizational success, but most companies are far better at learning how to improve their existing game than they are at learning how to play a new game. Creating a learning mindset can help your organization balance its performance orientation with a focus on creatively learning from the environment.

- *Bring in outside perspectives:* Soliciting the insights of outside perspectives can help to ensure that a rich pool of information flows into your organization. These outside perspectives are critical to creating dynamic scenarios for the future, and they are also crucial to continuing to monitor the world. Managers need to consciously go outside their circles to monitor the periphery, where most of the dramatic changes in the industry will originate. For instance, Procter & Gamble used proactive monitoring to detect and respond swiftly to a swell of negative consumer reaction associated with its new spray deodorizer for clothing called Febreze. An unsubstantiated Internet rumor began circulating in December 1998 that the product was harmful to pets.

Some consumers claimed that their canaries had suddenly died and blamed it on spraying with Febreze. Others argued that Febreze was affecting their dogs or cats, but all without proof. By monitoring such complaints in public chat rooms (using filters to search for keywords such as the product and company name), the company became alerted to these concerns and got its message out quickly, gathering support from the American Society for Prevention of Cruelty to Animals and other respected authorities as it entered into a dialogue with consumers. By monitoring these small-scale early complaints carefully, the company was able to avert a large-scale negative consumer backlash, and the product was a success. Sometimes these "outside" perspectives are right inside the organization.

- *Celebrate deviance of thought:* To sense and adapt to the environment, you have to have requisite variety in your organization. This requires tolerating people who are quite different from you. One male engineer at Hewlett-Packard preferred to wear an airy sundress in the summer, because he found the lighter garment much more comfortable in humid, sticky weather than traditional male attire. Most organizations might have criticized or ridiculed this departure from the norm, but by embracing diversity, Hewlett-Packard promoted a culture that celebrates new perspectives and radical thinking. Diversity is vital to seeing and understanding new information that comes into your organization.

Revisiting Scenarios

The general approaches described above can help you create an organizational mindset and systems that permit your managers to see the implications of new information and incorporate these changes while executing their strategic plans. This process is crucial to dynamic monitoring. It is also important to continue to specifically monitor the unfolding of the specific scenarios for the future. How do you dynamically monitor these scenarios? Are they reinforced by new information from the environment or undermined by it?

Scenarios are by their nature built upon assumptions that key uncertainties will be resolved in one way or another. As time passes, these key uncertainties become less uncertain (and new ones may arise). Regulations that could shape the competitive environment are moving either toward passage or defeat. Technology that is crucial to the development of a particular scenario is on track either to being developed or to being delayed. Early market pilots may give an indication of whether customers or employees are going to adopt a particular technology as was assumed in a given scenario.

Scenarios take a lot of work and organizational attention to develop, so most organizations are reluctant to go through the process more than once every few years. Shell conducts yearly updates until a major change occurs. But in the meantime the world may change significantly. It is important to continue to monitor and adapt your scenarios and consider the ripple effects of these views of the external future on the strategic vision and options that your company is pursuing.

How do you know it is time to reinvent your scenarios? If the three or four scenarios you have developed still define a useful range of possible worlds, you are okay and your managers can continue to update and revise them. But anointing one of the scenarios the clear winner or eliminating another one is usually a sign that you need to create new visions for possible futures. Otherwise the organizations will once again become limited by the blinders of the new "official future."

An Ever-Changing Chameleon

Two years after developing a set of four scenarios for credit unions, members of the Credit Union Executives Society (CUES), which sponsored the project, updated one of its four scenarios. This scenario, called "Chameleon," was one of rapid regulatory and technological change. The simultaneous deregulation of the banking industry and rapid advance of online banking and other technologies meant that many new threats and opportunities were created. By its nature, the "Chameleon" scenario was one that would change very quickly. In surveys, CUES members also reported that it was the scenario that they considered most likely to happen—and the one for which they were least prepared.

Updating the scenario added detail and explored its implications for developing new business models. It also identified a variety of new developments. The most significant was that taxation of credit unions, which had played a central role in the original scenarios, was a nonstarter. At the time when the scenarios were first created, credit unions faced a serious legal challenge from the American Bankers Association that went all the way to the U.S. Supreme Court. The Supreme Court sided with the American Bankers Association on the definition of field membership, and it looked like credit unions might face taxation. But the impact of the case was muted by a grassroots campaign of industry organizations (the Credit Union National Association and National Association of Federal Credit Unions) that ended in Congress passing legislation (HR 1151) that protected the tax exemption of credit unions and accepted expansion. While it placed restrictions on the business growth opportunities of credit unions, its impact was not nearly as dramatic as what CUES had anticipated when it developed the original scenario.

In addition, other parts of the scenarios became clearer or shifted. The official repeal of the Glass-Steagall Act moved deregulation forward, accelerating consolidation and a move toward "open finance" (where best-of-breed financial products could be offered through any single provider). There also had been a shift in deposits, a rise in nontraditional competitors, and a boom in merger activity. The technology landscape likewise had shifted, with increased spending on technology, the emergence of the e-consumer, and the success of "clicks and mortar" strategies. Credit union data processing was consolidated through technology, and new Internet services were launched.

The monitoring and extensive updating of scenarios does not have to occur evenly across the board. Some scenarios may appear more likely at a certain point, become more complex, or just change much more rapidly than others. CUES did a thorough update of just one of the scenarios, but it continued to monitor all four of them. The "Chameleon" scenario could eventually splinter into several subscenarios, especially after the dot-com bubble burst. Such dynamic change is in the spirit of scenario planning.

Above all, it is important to continue to focus on all the scenarios, to avoid being locked into a single vision. This was made very clear after the release of the new report on credit union scenarios. The shake-out of the dot-coms, and the resulting slowing of the economy and the pace of technology development, seemed to make the status quo scenario more likely. Focusing on a range of scenarios can better prepare your organization for the many possibilities that lie in between.

Organizing for Uncertainty

The monitoring of specific metrics ultimately needs to be brought together into a coherent picture. It is not enough to just track a list of measures—you need to make sense of them. The power of Susquehanna International Group is that it can capitalize on the monitoring of its employees in diverse industries to create a coherent strategy for investing. The tragedy of September 11 highlights that early warning signals existed in disparate parts of the system, from enrollees in a flight training program who only wanted to learn how to fly a plane horizontally to a flurry of activity within the Osama Bin Laden network. But not enough pieces had been coded and recognized as relevant to complete the puzzle. These tragic events remind us that intelligence gathering and monitoring remain very human activities, fraught with biases, blind spots, and misinterpretations.

Measures must also assign people responsible for their development as well as those tasked with acting upon them. And both these groups must examine their measures in light of the flexible strategies developed and the external scenarios on which they were initially based. Good measures that are not acted upon are a wasted opportunity. In the movie *Tora! Tora! Tora!*, which depicts the Japanese attack on Pearl Harbor, a key telegram alerting senior officers about the impending onslaught of planes slowly winds its way through the bureaucracy and fails to reach the key decision makers in time. Implementation is crucial.

Even as your organization monitors its own progress and the changes in the environment, it needs in parallel to update the scenarios, fine-tune the strategic vision, and shape new options. Managers need to move forward in environments of high uncertainty, rather than get stuck or become paralyzed.[21] They also need to develop a capacity for continuously evolving new insights on how to profit from uncertainty. In other words, your organization needs to be designed to live with uncertainty, day after day, year after year. Chapter 8 explores strategies and stumbling blocks for the successful implementation of ongoing planning for uncertainty.

Stop Trying to Figure Out the Future: Do Something About It

Russell Ackoff, a distinguished management consultant and author of *Creating the Corporate Future: Plan or Be Planned For* (New York: John Wiley, 1981), has been an outspoken critic of forecasting and planning. While he acknowledges that preparing for a range of possible futures is better than preparing for just one, he contends that even scenario planning may fail to highlight the active role that companies play in shaping their own futures.

Since one of the goals of scenario planning is to draw in alternative views and examine the future from many different perspectives, I've invited a critic to the table. In his dialogue with me, Ackoff presents his thoughtful perspectives on the subject, emphasizing that understanding the future should not be a passive process.

Schoemaker: What do you see as the primary limitations of scenarios in corporate planning?

Ackoff: Scenarios are too passive. Scenario planning assumes that the environment is out of the control of the company. This sets planners off in the wrong direction—planning for a future they believe to be out of their control. In fact, much of the environment is in their control.

Schoemaker: But what about OPEC and its impact on world oil prices? Certainly, the decisions of oil ministers in the Middle East were not in the control of Shell.

Ackoff: Yes, you are right. But many other decisions made the company more or less vulnerable to OPEC's demands. Shell had control over the development of new oil fields, the creation of new processes for discovering and extracting oil, and a wide range of other actions that meant it was hardly a passive victim of edicts from OPEC. Emphasizing the search for external scenarios leads to a passivity about controlling the future.

Schoemaker: Admittedly, companies can control some of the future, but parts of it are still uncertain. How can a newspaper, for example, know how the Internet will develop or control whether it will be accepted? Even some of the leaders of e-commerce are very uncertain about how this will play out, and they appear to have more control over it than old-line newspapers.

Ackoff: Not all uncertainty about the future can be controlled, but significant parts of it can. There are a wide range of mechanisms for controlling the future. Consider just a few of them. Companies can reduce uncertainty or its negative effects. They can use vertical integration to absorb sources of uncertainty (from a supplier, for example). Or they can use horizontal integration to balance other sources of uncertainty. For example, a company that makes both nipples for baby bottles and condoms is much less sensitive to changes in the birth rate than a company that makes either one of them alone. Cooperation and conflict reduction can reduce uncertainty of customer demand or rival moves. These are just a few of the methods that can be used to actively influence and design the futures in which the company will operate.

Schoemaker: If you don't use scenarios, what methods would you use to get your hands around the future?

Ackoff: One very useful approach is the use of reference projections. Instead of creating scenarios, take current trends and project them out to their logical conclusions. For example, a projection prepared for one of the districts of the Federal Reserve Bank in 1973 looked at the increasing number of checks being processed. The study projected that if exponential growth continued, as it had since the end of World War II, the number of people needed to clear checks would exceed the U.S. population. This, of course, is impossible. But the bankers used this impossible forecast to begin examining ways to avert this impossibility. This led to the development of electronic funds transfers, which ultimately reduced the need for check processing. It was not a scenario but rather a projection. Scenarios would look at ways to cope with this future. But here, once the outrageous projection was made, the challenge then became to find ways to actively change that future to avert that outcome.

Schoemaker: Why do managers fail to see that they have control over the future?

Ackoff: They don't recognize that organizations are part of a system. The design of a system is a synthesizing process, putting things together to form wholes. You can't understand a system by analysis. Analysis of systems takes them apart, reveals how they work, and reveals structure and know-how. This knowledge will allow us to increase the efficiency of the system—to fine-tune it—but it will not allow us to increase its effectiveness. Increasing effectiveness requires understanding, an explanation of why the system was designed to work the way it does, and how it can be made to function better in the larger system of which it is a part. If you see the organization as part of a system, then you will recognize that it simultaneously influences and is influenced by its future through its impact on this system.

A last word: This discussion points out that managers need to be careful not to take a passive view of the future when creating scenarios. It is possible for scenario planners to see themselves as tourists taking snapshots of the future rather than active participants in shaping the future. Ackoff's strategy of focusing on creating the future helps to overcome this tendency toward passivity, and can be a great way to think more creatively about future opportunities. Ultimately, however, the future is neither completely determined by our actions nor completely out of our control. We need a judicious balancing of the unbounded opportunities that the future holds with the realization that we need to somehow get from the present to that future. This balance offers the best of both worlds.

Chapter 8

Implementation: Living with Uncertainty

"No plan survives contact with the enemy."
—Prussian field marshal Helmuth von Moltke

The fuel cell idea had come up at DuPont three times over a span of twenty years, but the company didn't turn it into a business until Terry Fadem was able to put a convincing story around it. He pointed out that fuel cells could be a billion-dollar business for the company in the next decade. "I don't know what technology exactly, nor which companies, but it will be big," he said. "Alternative power markets will grow, and fuel cells will take off. We studied the energy market and competing technologies and mapped out scenarios for alternative energy. There is a $1.5 trillion global power market." He also pointed out that DuPont, as a large consumer of energy, could benefit directly from fuel cells as well as building a business. He presented the idea only to managers who could make a financial commitment to it. DuPont launched a major fuel cell initiative in February 2001.

As director of new business development at DuPont, Fadem was a champion of lost causes and forgotten ideas. He kept things going when others had given up, and his story contains important lessons about how to implement strategies when faced with doubt and uncertainty. Fadem mastered a process he calls "sifting for gold," searching for the overlooked innovations in the company and recognizing their future value when circumstances have changed. He specialized in reassessing the kind of risky projects that many more conservative managers shy away from or completely overlook. This persistence is often the key to effective implementation, since many projects look like failures when you are in the midst of them, when harsh realities rear their ugly heads.

With four thousand scientists, each one of whom might have several major *ahas* a year that don't get acted upon, ideas are literally sitting on the lab benches of a large company like DuPont. The challenge is to initially see and keep seeing their potential value without being foolhardy. Fadem points out that most of the major innovations of the future are right under the noses of companies today, just like those of the past. When was the liquid crystal (used in liquid crystal displays) discovered? 1888. The fax machine? 1843. The fuel cell? 1839.[1] These innovations were right there, but they required 99 percent perspiration after that 1 percent inspiration had flagged their potential. The challenge was to see not just their possibility but to doggedly pursue them. The genius of Thomas Edison, the great inventor of the lightbulb, was not just his vision but his tenacity in trying no fewer than six thousand different filaments before finding one that could burn at the right temperature and for a long enough duration.[2] Effective implementation is the key.

Fadem fondly recalls the day he discovered a $10 million business sitting on the desk of a DuPont researcher: a new gel that had a potential application as a specialized lubricant. But the entire global market for the product category was just $100 million, and DuPont's hope to capture $10 million was hardly worth looking at in a company so large. So Fadem struck an alliance with another company and built a very profitable business that generated cash for shareholders. Again persistence, guided by a vision of what could be, paid off handsomely.

Whether a company pursues a niche idea or a big audacious goal, it must be willing to fail in order to succeed. More often than not "sifting for gold" results in a pan full of silt. Fadem pulls out of his briefcase a black object that looks like a large hockey puck and places it on the table. It is a "phase change material" that can generate heat without any external source of power. It seems like a perfect power source for the third of the world that is not connected to energy grids. But despite his best efforts, it has never taken off—at least not to date.

A Chart Room in an Uncharted World

The challenge facing champions of new and radical ideas in large organizations is that the existing business is based on facts while the new ideas are largely based on speculation. When Fadem started at DuPont, presentations for new businesses were made in the "chart room." This citadel of facts was the most feared room in the entire company: huge charts of economic information for every part of the world slid out vertically from every wall. Many a manager making a presentation had been interrupted as his listeners pulled out a chart to challenge his facts in midstream. But then the world began changing too quickly for the chart room to keep up. In the 1990s the room fell into disuse, and facts were no longer the sole guarantor of good strategies.

The irony is that some of the most significant business decisions were not built upon detailed analysis. "Most business decisions are based on belief, not on fact," Fadem says. "When DuPont built the nylon business in the 1920s, there was a belief that nylon would substitute for natural fibers. There were no facts for that. In reality, you often cannot know until someone does the hard work of delivering it. Nylon was a prime historical example of the value of futuristic thinking within DuPont itself."

Similarly, somewhere in the organization there is someone who recognizes the possibility of another future breakthrough scenario, but many organizations do not have a process for tapping into these insights. DuPont has had its share of surprises. Fadem points to speculation in the silver markets in the 1980s, when the Hunt brothers tried to corner the market. They drove prices from two dollars per ounce up to more than thirty, which seriously affected DuPont's business in silver halide film used in X-rays and photography. Like many companies, DuPont was also caught off guard by disruptions in the Asian currency markets in the 1990s.

It's not that these events were complete surprises, but the company had not seriously considered them in its strategy. "There are people who do see and warn about these things inside companies," Fadem says. "I don't think any business the size of DuPont is totally blind to these risks. But even though people talk about it, it doesn't get serious top-level attention. Management is considering today's business and putting out fires."

Fadem likens strategic planning to a practice session for a sports team. It is not the real thing but an opportunity to build the skills and reflexes needed to play. The problem, he says, is that many companies ignore practice because they are so busy playing. Or they mistake the practice for the game. "Sports teams have practices Monday through Friday," he said. "The only type of practice businesses can get is planning. And many businesses fail to recognize or use it fully."

The Challenge of Implementation

Organizations are, for the most part, not designed for uncertainty. More often than not, implementing a process of planning under uncertainty goes against the grain of an organization's culture and processes. As Fadem found, in a large organization raised on chart rooms, the compelling story about tomorrow is often crushed by the cold facts of today. Managers are so engrossed in running the business that they don't take the time to engage in practice.

In a finely tuned machine, predictability is what greases an organization's wheels, while uncertainty is the grit that gums up the works. The more certainty there is, the more easily managers can move forward with confidence. In most organizations, uncertainty leads to delays in making decisions so more study can take place. Consultants are brought in to increase the feeling (often an illusion) of certainty. Opportunities are missed in an effort to avoid mistakes. Traditional accounting doesn't measure opportunities missed (sins of omission); it focuses on mistakes made (sins of commission) and usually underestimates the value of options. On top of it all, people have incentives to hide uncertainty, to avoid surprises, and to filter bad news. All these factors tend to create a strong bias against acting under uncertainty in a timely manner, let alone anticipating it. Is it possible to create an organization that actively embraces uncertainty?

The organizational and psychological bias against uncertainty is one of the most significant obstacles to profiting from it (see Appendix A). People want to operate within their comfort zone, whereas the real opportunities lie outside of it.

Thus far we have explored the process of creating scenarios, determining Key Success Factors, identifying a robust strategic vision, and finding flexible options to get us there. Now let's turn to the messy problem of implementation in the face of uncertainty. What is required is not just a great plan on paper but rather a change in the thinking of the organization. We need to work at involving the organization in the process of creating the scenarios and strategic vision and, indeed, change how the entire organization relates to uncertainty. This often goes against the training of managers, against the experiences that led to their success in the organization and against the grain of the organizational culture.

Think of scenarios as creating surrogate crises. They plunge the organization into uncomfortable environments. The first response to a crisis is often denial or anger, until these emotions are turned, ideally, into bold action. Along the way, people have to be pushed past their comfort zones and challenged to think outside the "official future." Admittedly this is painful, but it is not as painful as dealing with a real crisis when jobs and profits are at risk.

The obstacles inherent in organizations and our own psychology make successful implementation of this planning process a real challenge. Many promising plans on paper never see the light of day because too little attention was given to implementation. On the other hand, what may be considered mediocre plans on paper have been phenomenally successful in implementation because managers invested the time and energy to do it carefully. In addition to the up-front planning process, deciding who will be involved in the implementation phase is key. As some like to say, "The plan is nothing; planning is everything." In this chapter, I'll examine how different organizations have created unique solutions to the challenge of implementation, highlight some common pitfalls, and offer guidance for designing your own implementation.

Different Strokes for Different Folks

Across hundreds of companies, I have found that even though managers apply a common set of frameworks, every planning process is unique. The approach you take depends upon the challenges of your industry and organization, as well as the resources you have to devote to it. For some organizations, the planning process is a deep, transformational initiative that is fully integrated into strategy and budgeting. Other organizations step back to look at scenarios and then move into their traditional budgeting and planning process. The following examples offer a few snapshots of the implementation challenges that different organizations faced and how they addressed them:

- *Small and agile:* A midsize street sweeper manufacturer in the Midwest faced serious challenges in the mid-1980s. Its labor costs were higher than those of its East Coast competitors, and it faced new competition from Asian manufacturers. The federal government was reducing its funding for state and municipal governments, the company's primary customers. Local governments had less money and so were decreasing their spending on new equipment. There was a clear trend toward leasing equipment with a maintenance contract rather than buying it outright. Also, new technologies were changing the design of the equipment, a further argument for leasing and upgrading later. The company, which was a typical operationally focused firm, clearly had to broaden its vision. In three or four meetings, the management team worked through the entire process just using flip charts. They created a new strategic vision, which included approaching the union about labor costs, developing a maintenance shop for clients, and recognizing that the firm might need to make changes in its management team. Because it was a small, agile company, implementation was fairly swift. Within a month it had acted on the strategy, which started with an ugly strike that ultimately brought labor costs down. Also, key members of the management team were replaced, to get a better alignment of visions.
- *In the barracks:* A division of a major agricultural equipment manufacturer needed to rethink its strategy. The company had made a major acquisition, and as it integrated the new business, the managers realized that they needed to address significant changes in the industry. The process of farming was changing fundamentally with new technology, genetic engineering, and changes in the global business environment (as discussed in Chapter 5). The managers leading the process, many of whom had military backgrounds, set up a special facility in a barrack far removed from headquarters. They holed up there for half a year. Because of time pressures, the company used parallel teams: one assessed the external environment, another worked on the industry, and a third studied the organization itself.

They examined the process of farming and changes in the industry in depth. They interviewed experts inside and outside the company. Once they identified the forces shaping the future, the team brought the project back to senior management to select the key uncertainties that were shaping future scenarios. From that planning meeting, they created smaller task forces to bullet out all the scenarios. The small teams regrouped to create a new strategy. They also codified their learning, which facilitated moving the process out to other parts of the company.

- *Top down and bottom up:* Driven by external forces, a division of a major government agency decided that it needed to make better decisions about its programs and reshape strategic thinking among its line managers. Key civilians started a division-level pilot project in scenario planning. The cross-functional task force involved staff and managers from the division and its districts in a series of strategy working sessions. Although the top division executives were not involved in the day-to-day activities of the process, they gave it their full commitment and resource support, allowing it to be successful. Congress had enacted legislation requiring the division to formulate an annual strategic performance plan. The program gained credibility with internal and external stakeholders. In addition, the agency decided to adopt and roll out scenario-based strategic planning as its overall strategic planning process. Today this agency has engaged its senior leadership by using planning as a tool to renew learning and improve performance. This new planning process is the start of reshaping the culture: a new challenge facing this large public agency that has diverse mission areas and multiple constituents with a wide variety of interests.
- *Perils of mergers:* A global pharmaceutical firm wrestled with the right time frame and industry definition for its planning. Should it be global or regional? Should it reflect the long time frames of R&D and regulatory dug approvals or the shorter time frames of the competitive environment? The managers chose an intermediate time frame of ten years, then established three regional teams (for Europe, the United States, and Asia), each of which developed its own set of scenarios. The teams were geographically dispersed but kept in touch by e-mail

and conference calls, and they also held occasional face-to-face meetings. The process was intellectually very successful, but as the organization entered a new megamerger and a new CEO took over, implementation and follow-up were put on hold until key managers knew what would happen to them in the short term.

Royal Dutch/Shell: A Fully Developed System

One of the most highly developed and tightly integrated scenario-planning processes was created at Royal Dutch/Shell. While Shell's process of *building* scenarios has been well documented—see the excellent discussion in Peter Schwartz's *The Art of the Long View*—it is less well known how the scenarios were actually integrated into the company's business planning and budgeting process. I worked with Shell on how to strengthen this connection in the early 1980s and published some of the key insights in an article with Shell colleague Kees van der Heijden.[3] While the process has continued to evolve at Shell and the details are rather intricate, the following overview offers a useful model for a fully developed scenario-planning process in a large complex organization, with multiple divisions, functions, and business units.

To understand the design of Shell's planning process, we must first appreciate some of the complexity of Shell's organizational structure. The company essentially consists of two holding companies (Royal Dutch and Shell Transport and Trading), under which reside nearly a hundred operating companies that largely function as independent businesses in their respective countries. To coordinate activities of the operating companies, Shell at that time used a matrix design. This matrix consisted of three types of support organizations, organized by (1) business sector (oil, natural gas, chemicals, coal, etc.), (2) region (Europe, Western Hemisphere, Middle East, etc.), and (3) function (finance, planning, legal, etc.). These three service organizations—which resided in Shell's two central offices in the Hague and London—interacted with the operating companies whenever necessary. Although the overall company is very decentralized, its planning process was driven from the central offices in London. In particular, Group Planning in London included experts on the business environment and strategic planning who helped to provide insights for the broader scenarios and to drive the planning process throughout the organization.

The first part of the planning cycle consisted of a *qualitative* process of exploring scenarios and understanding the potential strategies drawn from those scenarios, as shown in the top "strategic planning" half of Exhibit 8-1. This was then linked to a more *quantitative* budgeting process shown in the bottom "business planning" half of the figure. Typically, the entire cycle took about two years to complete.

The qualitative process usually began in July, when top leadership issued a broad policy statement to set the stage. Based on this statement and its own extensive research of major economies, energy demand, energy supply, and other factors, Group Planning would develop a set of initial reports on key issues and uncertainties, as well as help write Shell's global scenarios about the future. These scenarios were issued every two to three years and updated in between as needed. The scenarios would be elaborated and discussed by the countries, sectors, and regional groups, to explore the implications of different strategies across these scenarios. The local management teams would offer their own weighting of the different scenarios. This process, which entailed extensive dialogues among senior managers between October and April, would result in a document of sector-preferred strategies and country-preferred strategies. Finally, in July of the following year, a group strategy review would articulate a strategic vision for the company as a whole, which in turn would set the stage for the next policy statement about future direction.

As this qualitative process unfolded, it created a context for the quantitative budgeting cycle of the company. But here Shell decided to do something creative that reduced the complexity of the initial budgeting process. Once the overall strategy had been agreed to for each operating company, sector, and region, there was no need any more to look at the full range of potential scenarios. They had already been reflected in the strategies themselves, in terms of how much commitment and flexibility to build in. So the budgeting process would simply start with the midpoint of all the scenarios as translated into a set of business premises concerning oil prices, economic growth rates, currency levels, prevailing regulations, and so on. This would allow all Shell managers to work with a single set of numbers, which was simply viewed as a reference case for the future. Shell would then aggregate these budgets to quantify the overall "call on resources" (human and capital) that would be needed to execute the projected strategies over the next five or ten years.

Exhibit 8-1: Shell's Group-Wide Planning System

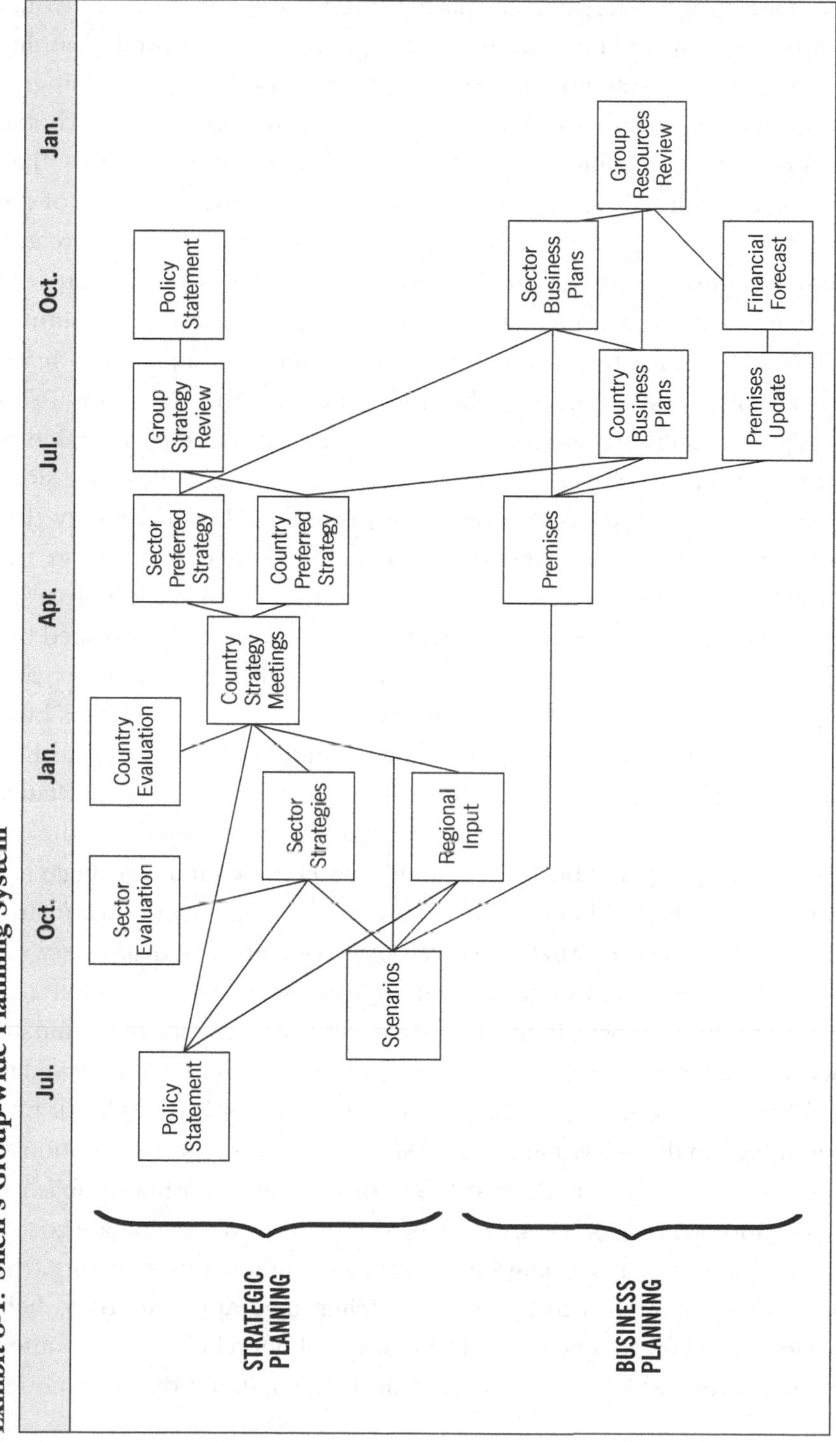

Once budgets were consolidated, Group Planning in London would reintroduce uncertainty back into the picture. This central planning function would carefully explore how the overall budget would change if a different set of premises had been adopted. But rather than trouble the operating companies with yet another budget cycle (one was challenging enough), Group Planning would trace out the full range of different assumptions implied by the scenarios. To do this, it created computer models that approximated the cash flows throughout the company under different premises and then used Monte Carlo simulation (see Appendix B) to trace out the implications of millions of different premise cases covering the full range of the scenarios. This simulation would provide a clear sense of the upside and downside of the proposed strategies and would further prompt valuable discussions about contingency plans and timely adjustment. The uncertainty that had temporarily been stripped out when turning the crank on the budget cycle would thus be reintroduced to round out the full picture.

The planning process at Royal Dutch/Shell is rather sophisticated but well-suited for a very complex organization. A smaller and simpler organization might be able to adopt a more streamlined approach. Also, a business without the long lead times of the oil industry might need to find ways to accelerate the cycle. But the basic approach of creating qualitative strategies that are scenario-based and then driving them down into the traditional budgeting and business planning process (assuming a single reference case)—with either qualitative contingency planning or quantitative computer simulation—can be followed by an organization of any size.

Shell's approach to strategic planning has evolved over many decades and continues to evolve. In the 1950s, like many of its peers, the company focused primarily on project and budget planning. In the 1960s it moved to sophisticated forecasting and optimization techniques (such as linear programming). In the 1970s it introduced scenarios, giving special attention to strategic issue analysis. In the late 1980s, once Shell had firmly established its scenario-planning process, the focus shifted toward the ultimate goal of faster organizational learning.[4] In order to instill a learning culture, the group experimented with dynamic modeling (see Appendix B) to help surface managers' mental maps. The real world often behaves in counterintuitive ways—which good scenarios capture. A system's dynamic modeling approach can help managers understand in greater detail how nonlinear feedback loops can create surprising outcomes.[5]

As managers throughout Shell have gained more experience with scenarios, the process has become increasingly decentralized. Shell has encouraged operating company planners to take more responsibility for the process themselves. This brings planning closer to the point of action and reduces the gap between planning and learning. It also gives the organization more agility, particularly with the rapid deregulation of the energy industry. The role of Group Planning in London is now much more that of catalyst for scenario planning rather than conductor of the process.

Tailoring the Process to Your Goals

There are no hard-and-fast rules for tailoring the scenario-planning process to your organization. It is highly flexible and scalable. It can be conducted quickly or slowly, with intense senior involvement or more passive support. It can be an all-out assault on uncertainty or a leisurely afternoon stroll at an off-site meeting. In designing the process for your organization, you need to consider a series of key decisions:

- *Full scale or pilot?* Since the process is very scalable, it can be several short work sessions for a core management team or a process stretching out over years and involving a broad cross-section of the organization. Companies can gain benefits from both approaches. In general, the benefits are proportional to the time and energy invested in the process. Early in the process, however, it is particularly important for managers to be able to start small, achieve some distinct victories, and then broaden the scope as the benefits become evident. It also helps the organization to move slowly into icy and turbulent waters so people can more gradually adjust to the discomfort of uncertainty. They can figuratively put their big toes in the water before diving in to seek the treasures in the sea of uncertainty.

- *Quick or slow?* In an ideal world, you would have enough time to fully absorb and reflect on learning from the process, but the cycle can also be compressed into a much shorter period of time. Fast processes can be facilitated by teams working simultaneously, and they can offer much more intense focus that may complete the process before a new CEO or other event derails it. On the other hand, a fast process does not allow for as much between-session time for reflection, further study, or absorbing the results into the fiber of the organization. Sometimes it is important to allow time for communication and involvement of a broader group of stakeholders to internalize or legitimate potential scenarios prior to exploring strategic actions. Long processes, however, run the risk of lingering or losing energy. They need sustained support because they require ongoing time and resources that might be pulled away if leaders lose patience or have a shift in strategic focus.

- *Top down or bottom up?* At some point, top managers need to get involved lest the process be killed off or its results ignored. But the initial process can be a bottom-up initiative in a specific part of the organization. This "skunkworks" approach can lead to creative thinking and ensures diverse perspectives. Either way, the challenge is to keep the initiative from being snuffed out by senior managers who may be threatened by it as well as to demonstrate its value to organizational leaders who need to become its champions. The top-down approach ensures that the project will have strong support and be integrated into the overall planning process of the organization. The danger, however, is that it may encounter resistance in becoming embedded into the culture of the organization. In this case, care must be taken in communication and engagement of the organization with the process. What also matters in balancing the top-down and bottom-up forces is the diversity of businesses and issues encountered.

- *Internal or external?* The process can be facilitated using external resources or be carried forward by internal managers. The advantage of using consultants and other outsiders is that they will push the organization to think more creatively, beyond its traditional culture and industry. They will come with systematic tools and processes that they have honed across a variety of organizations. The downside challenge, however, is that with outsiders leading the initiative, internal managers may not feel as much responsibility and engagement in the process and may fail to take ultimate ownership. On the other hand, a fully internal process may suffer from lack of expertise in the planning process and an inability to ask the challenging questions that are needed to develop creative scenarios and strategies. In the end, your organization needs to seek the right balance between internal and external players, with a goal of developing the capabilities within the organization to continue the process effectively in the future.

- *Integrated or separate?* Should the planning process be carried by a separate group within the organization, or should it be an integral part of the strategy process? This choice depends upon your organization's experience in scenario planning and managers' comfort level in taking a high-visibility organizational risk. Unless the organization has a very strong top commitment to the process, it often works better to start small with a single business unit or separate division, then slowly build on successes to integrate the process into the organization's mainstream, as illustrated by Royal Dutch/Shell's experience.

Pixie Dust: The Art and Magic of Successful Planning

While designing the implementation of a new planning process has a scientific component, remember that it has a strong art component as well. The best plans in the world still have to survive the crucible of transforming deeply rooted thinking patterns and encrusted organizational decision-making processes. The buy-in from senior managers, the board, and employees is crucial to success, but changing old thinking patterns is often harder than creating a great set of scenarios or plans. Success or failure often turns on the dynamics of a single meeting. A certain magic, chemistry, and mastery of change management is involved in this process, as the leaders of the Vista Federal Credit Union, serving 55,000 Disney employees with $220 million in assets, learned.

The Vista managers had developed a set of scenarios for the future and needed to take their new vision to the board at its annual three-day planning meeting in August 2000. It was clear this would be a planning session like none other. The planning retreat typically consisted of serving up a completed plan and bringing it in for the blessing of the board. Usually the real work was done by the end of the first day, with plenty of time left for golf. This time it was different as managers presented several provocative scenarios for the future. Would the board buy management's view of impending technological and regulatory change as depicted in two scenarios (labeled "Chameleon" and "Technocracy")? Or would they want to stick to the status quo reflected in the "Credit Union Power" scenario that had implicitly guided much of their thinking in the past? This was the moment of truth.

Jeff York, vice president of marketing at Vista, had carefully prepared the senior managers and the nine-member board. They had now met for three days in a conference room at a Santa Barbara hotel. On the first day they considered changes in the external environment. On the second day they described how the four scenarios had been developed. Senior managers believed that the radical views of "Technocracy" and "Chameleon" were the ones the company should prepare for. In fact, they believed this so strongly that they hadn't really developed a presentation for the status quo scenario of "Credit Union Power." But would the board agree?

Near the end of the third day, after reviewing the scenarios, the facilitator asked the board members: "Where do you think we are going to fall in this set of scenarios?" The managers exchanged nervous glances. If the board chose the status quo, the meeting would be over, and it would be back to business as usual—there wouldn't be much more to say.

The facilitator polled the board around the conference table. About half the board members chose the "Technocracy" scenario as most likely, and all of them cited the rapidly changing "Chameleon" environment as a scenario they needed to prepare for. This time, the managers exchanged happy glances. "All six of us let out a sigh of relief," York told me. "Things were *not* going to stay the same. We knew right then that we were on the right track."

Then something unusual happened. The board began discussing uncertainties in its business environment that it had never discussed before. What if something happened to Disney CEO Michael Eisner? Without a clear succession plan, it could be a tremendous blow to the company and also to Vista, whose fortunes rise and fall with Disney's. What if another company bought Disney? "We had never had these kinds of discussions before," York explained. It was a deep and meaningful discussion of key strategic issues for the organization. "We were actually engaged in collective strategic thinking." The vice-chairman of the board commented afterward that it was the best planning session they had ever had.

"It was a departure from our old way of doing business," York recalled.

"We realized that we didn't need some of our old goals anymore, because they didn't fit into the 'Technocracy' or 'Chameleon' environment. The landscape was going to change more quickly."

Strategic planning is an art. Like jazz or modern dance, it works within a broad and systematic framework but cannot be unduly mechanistic; it should be inductive and holistic. The goal is not to produce a deterministic vision of the future but to engage in deep and meaningful discussions that address the real issues. If the initial scaffolding becomes an obstacle to that process, it can be modified or set aside. Analysis gives managers a feeling of control, and they are understandably reluctant to give up this crutch. But in an environment of rapid change, this feeling of control is an illusion. What is needed most is not control but deeper understanding. The process used by Jeff York at Vista and by hundreds of other companies augments linear analysis with systems thinking and disciplined imagination.

Jazz groups actually practice as much and sometimes more than classical orchestras, to gain the flexibility and understanding needed for spontaneous interactions during performances. The planning process described in this book can be viewed as a systematic way of improvising—the true source of its magic.

Ten Common Pitfalls

The change process involved in addressing uncertainty, like any organizational change, requires courage and perseverance. As Rosabeth Moss Kanter and colleagues wrote after studying organizational change processes, "Everything looks like a failure in the middle. In nearly every change project, doubt is cast on the original vision because problems are mounting and the end is nowhere in sight."[6] The scenarios you develop will be dismissed by naysayers. The process can be derailed or slowed by internal politics, particularly by managers who might see their own domain changing as a result of these scenarios.

Shell created its first set of global energy scenarios in 1969, and one of them brilliantly anticipated the rise of OPEC. But these great scenarios had no impact because the process had not engaged the top leadership. The scenarios had been developed by staff planners, and even though they accurately anticipated the 1973 OPEC oil embargo, the line managers did not take the warning seriously. Only after Shell's leaders became champions of the process was scenario thinking deeply infused throughout the organization.

In addition to senior support, you need expansive thinking, as opposed to tunnel vision. An oil services company that developed drilling forecasts based on internal experts, came up with a range of estimates (lines I to III in Exhibit 8-2). The company planned for this rather narrow range after having experienced a sharp drilling increase in 1979. They simply extrapolated the recent past and then engaged in some sensitivity analysis. They failed to recognize the temporary nature of this sudden spike by ignoring the deeper forces at work and adopting a longer historical perspective. As the graph shows, reality was far removed from their projections. Might a more diverse group of forecasters, engaging in deeper dialogue, have given a more accurate perspective on the true uncertainties?

In 1991 and 1992, when South African leaders met in Mont Fleur to create political scenarios, they drew together a highly diverse group that included twenty-two prominent leaders from across the political spectrum—politicians on all sides of the issue, activists, academics, and executives. This broad representation ensured that diverse stories of the future would be considered. These diverse thinkers found a common language in four scenarios for South Africa's future. Even more important, however, their diversity ensured that many constituencies within South Africa would take the results of this process seriously and would use them as a basis for creating a common future. The resulting scenarios would not have been as deep, nor their impact as broad, if they had been created independently by the African National Congress, by the National Party government, or by say the Anglo-American Corporation alone. As a result, the Mont Fleur scenarios played a powerful role in shaping a peaceful transition to all-race elections in April 1994.

It is important at the beginning to identify the specific obstacles that might derail the process in your organization. If you do, these obstacles will not be a surprise when they arrive, and you will have prepared strategies for overcoming them when they surface. What are the obstacles that can undermine planning for uncertainty? How can you overcome them? Here are ten common pitfalls to watch out for:[7]

Exhibit 8-2: How Not to Do It

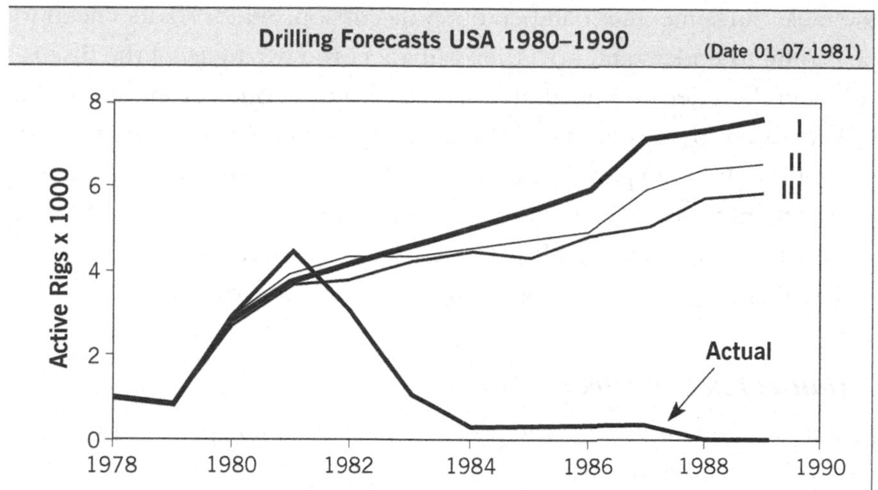

Pitfall 1: Failure to Gain Top Management Support Early On

Because planning for uncertainty is often so challenging to the core values and special interests of an organization, it needs, at a minimum, top management's blessing to succeed. Otherwise the antibodies in the organization will seek out and kill this foreign activity quickly. The process of planning for uncertainty can also be time consuming, and the results are, needless to say, *uncertain.* The process is fraught with failure by its nature and might require short-term investments for uncertain long-term payoffs. For all of these reasons, the senior leaders of your organization must be 100 percent behind the process for it to succeed.

Ideally top leaders should do more than passively bless the process. The more actively senior management is involved in the process, the more their decisions and overall strategies will be permeated with perspectives on how the company can profit from uncertainty.

Antidote: If the process is not initiated by leaders in your company, try to engage them early on and keep them engaged. Draw them in at critical points to help define scenarios and strategic vision. Also work to integrate insights from the process into the larger strategic planning of the organization by building bridges to existing processes. At the same time, top leaders need to be careful about the role they play. Because they are reluctant to look foolish or to challenge the CEO, the very presence of the CEO at the table can sometimes dampen open discussion. Senior leaders need to be careful to understand how they will affect the dynamics of the discussion and then decide how they will participate. In one organization, the CEO decided to stay out of early brainstorming completely. In another organization, the CEO participated but explicitly told managers that he expected them to share their true opinions freely and not be inhibited by his presence. He also deliberately played a more passive role in the session to ensure that the voices of the other managers were heard.

Pitfall 2: Lack of Diverse Inputs

Managers often undermine the power of their planning process by failing to seek diverse inputs. The process should be challenging and uncomfortable, but most managers feel more at ease gathering with the same set of familiar people to think about the future. In this case, the resulting perspectives are likely to be too timid and predictable. Everyone has been singing from the same hymnbook for so long that you are unlikely to hear any new tunes.

The process of creating insights into future uncertainties will be quite different if it includes younger members of the company, environmental protesters, customers, regulators, analysts, and proponents of radically new technologies or different views of the future. The goals should be both to shake things up and to gain the widest possible view of the future. And, as in the case of the Mont Fleur scenarios in South Africa, diverse participation up front leads to stronger buy-in during implementation.

Antidote: Draw together the broadest possible group of people in developing your scenarios and strategic vision. If you can't bring them into the room physically, then engage them through the Internet, internal publications, or other channels. One newspaper company went out and talked with journalism students about their views of the future. Or you can use surveys to collect systematic feedback to set the stage for the planning process. Look for ways to create dialogues with your enemies, whether they are regulators, consumer activists, Wall Street analysts, originators of disruptive technology, or industry doomsayers. Invite the radical fringe inside, and listen seriously to what they have to say.

Pitfall 3: Unrealistic Goals and Expectations

While many organizations reap immediate benefits and insights from this process, focusing on the future by its nature takes time. If managers are looking for a quick return on their investment within two weeks, they may be disappointed. Many organizations begin the process enthusiastically but then do not have the patience to stay the course.

Antidote: It is important to make a strong commitment to the process at the outset. It is also important to manage expectations about the process so that the participants don't see it as a quick fix or a one-shot initiative, before the organization moves on to the next fad of the month. Try to point to past planning sessions that yielded fruit, and remind people of the time lags between ideation, choice, implementation, and results.

Pitfall 4: Failure to Develop a Clear Road Map

If the roles of participants are not clearly established at the outset, the process will drift. It will be put on the back burner as the present certainties take precedence over future uncertainties. To keep everyone focused, you need a clear road map.

Antidote: Clearly establish roles and the steps in the process. It is generally a good idea to create a core group responsible for carrying the process through. Other participants can then be assigned roles for specific parts, and senior leaders can be brought in at key points. Establish clear time frames, milestones, and deliverables as well as review points. Although you start with a clear road map, the core group has to be flexible enough to change this map when necessary, especially when confronting organizational resistance.

Pitfall 5: Lack of Strategic Focus

The process of examining future uncertainties is inherently expansive, and many organizations become swamped by its complexity. Instead of focusing on a few meaningful scenarios, they look at dozens of scenarios in extensive detail. Or they get sidetracked and fail to appreciate the truly strategic issues. Many companies accumulate truckloads of data and never are able to see the forest for the trees. They are data rich and synthesis poor.

Antidote: The key is to acknowledge and embrace the full complexity, then to distill it into a simple set of three to five scenarios. The team might identify dozens of scenarios in the initial brainstorming, but it needs to agree on a limited set of scenarios that bounds the full complexity of the situation. The key is not to cover everything there is to know about the future but to know enough to create credible and useful scenarios for what lies ahead. Again, it is about seeing the forest, not all the trees.

Pitfall 6: Insufficient Time for Reflection and Learning

Most companies have a strong action bias, so they are uncomfortable with the slow, simmering process necessary to wrestle with future uncertainty. They want to race out after developing scenarios or a strategic vision and immediately put these ideas into action. They are focused more on performance than on learning.

Self-renewal requires a careful balance between the harvesting mode of the performance organization and the quest for experimentation of the learning organization. Recall how the publisher of *The Miami Herald* characterized the process in Chapter 1: he viewed it as a "liberal arts education," not a crash course. Each company has to strike its own balance, depending on the competitive circumstances it faces, the stage of its industry's evolution, and its appetite for learning.

Antidote: Allow time for people in the organization to absorb the scenarios and strategic vision and to learn from the process. Organize small, informal lunch sessions where people can absorb and debate the issues. Focus attention on learning rather than on the specific actions or visions that are the outcomes of the process. At the end of every session, ask how the learning can be deepened. Set up different teams to take up individual scenarios, and compete in making plausible cases for them. This interaction and competition can lead to fresh insights and can push the learning deeper into the organization.

Pitfall 7: Failure to Link into the Planning Process

In some organizations, the process of planning for the future is divorced from overall strategic planning. This ensures that future planning will be a peripheral activity and will have little impact on the direction of the organization. The overall process outlined in this book is designed to make scenario planning central to the overall strategic planning effort. The process at Royal Dutch/Shell, as described earlier in this chapter, is deeply integrated into its overall business planning and budgeting. If planning is conducted in a small part of the organization or as a stand-alone activity, it will still have little traction in the organization. This may be a good (low-risk) way to get started, however, and to try it on for size.

Antidote: Eventually the process of scenario planning and creating a strategic vision should be directly tied to the existing planning and budgeting process. Even if it starts off as a separate project, managers should actively work to build bridges to strategy making in the organization. Techniques such as risk assessment, simulation, and real-options analysis offer ways to apply the insights from scenario planning directly in corporate or business unit strategy. Staff managers can play the role of internal consultants, helping business unit managers to sharpen their strategies, tactics, competencies, and strategic options.

Pitfall 8: Failure to Dynamically Monitor through Signposts

The scenarios you create today may be obsolete tomorrow. New information is coming in, and new technologies are being developed. For many organizations, however, the stories created by the scenarios become the new conventional wisdom. At this point, rigor mortis sets in. Scenarios and the strategic vision need to be kept alive by constantly assessing and updating them.

Antidote: As discussed in Chapter 7, you need to identify clear signposts that confirm or deny the progress toward a given scenario. Also, actively monitor the outside environment to look for new information that does not fit easily into any of the current views of the future. What are the new uncertainties? How are the existing uncertainties becoming more certain?

Pitfall 9: Failure to Change the Paradigm

Some organizations expend extensive time and energy in creating new scenarios and strategic vision but still fail to reach "escape velocity" from their existing worldview. They end up with views of the future that confirm their conventional wisdom. There are no surprises, and so there is little original thinking.

Antidote: Start the process expecting to be surprised and even terrified by what you find. Be sure to cast the net widely, and ask yourself and others at key points whether the results are truly shocking or challenging. You'll know you are breaking out of the old view by watching people's reactions. If they don't exhibit denial, confusion, discomfort, and outright anger, your views of the future are too predictable and too cold. You need to turn up the heat until it is at least mildly uncomfortable. At the same time, one of the key balances of the process is that you can't push too far beyond the understanding of the audience. The story can't be so "off the wall" that it will be immediately dismissed. The more radical the view, the more evidence is needed to make the case for it.

Pitfall 10: Failure to Stimulate New Strategic Options

The proof of the process is in the harvest. If the result is to go back to the same old strategies, it has probably not reached its full potential. Some organizations may have already developed such broad and flexible strategic options that scenario planning doesn't add much to them, but the lack of fresh, new options is usually a sign that the planning process is weak.

Antidote: As I've noted, you have to be careful not to expect too much too soon. Still, the process should ultimately result in some original strategies that have not been previously identified. Try to list, at the end, how many new ideas can be credited to the new process. The list should have many items, including some genuine breakthrough ideas.

Implementing a Strategy

To keep the process moving forward, you need a clear overview of where you are headed. There are several practical steps for implementing specific strategic options, including:

- *Identify key tasks:* It is important to develop a clear plan based on the strategic vision and the options created. The plan should be tailored to the goals and the strategic environment in which it will be implemented. Develop a detailed action plan with time lines for each strategic option, clarifying the purpose of the project, identifying major tasks to be completed, and agreeing on resources (time, money, information, equipment, skills, and the like). Finally, you need to set up milestones and review points, as well as early warning signals when the project is off track. As discussed in Chapter 7, you should monitor both for the implementation of options and for the unfolding of the scenarios.

- *Assign responsibility:* Identify who has ownership of the specific strategic options and dynamic monitoring. The first step is to identify the critical stakeholders who should be involved in the process, both inside and outside the organization. Then you need to determine the task leaders and discuss how the teams will function. Who has the knowledge, experience, and skills essential for success? Who controls the personnel and resources essential to this task? How much decision-making authority will the team, project leader, and project members have? Finally you need to clarify the roles of outsiders such as consultants, customers, partners, vendors, and regulators. Who needs to be involved in the process, and what roles should they play?
- *Align performance review and rewards:* How do you know if you are succeeding and if the managers are individually benefiting? Strategies that are aligned with incentives and rewards will be much more likely to be completed. A plan that does not have strong incentives is unlikely to be achieved, particularly if doing so creates greater risks for compensation under the current package. You need to clearly indicate the deliverables for each option and carefully assess the competency, team function, and dedication of key project personnel. Then you need to ensure that they are rewarded for achieving project goals. How do you know you are making progress toward fulfilling your vision? How can you reward this progress? You might create a Balanced Scorecard, designed to measure and manage achievement of the vision.[8]

Developing a Strategic Capacity

Planning is not a one-shot process. It needs to be ongoing. The ability to plan today and rethink your strategy tomorrow depends upon developing capabilities that will facilitate carrying out the vision today and the dynamic capacity for change to meet the challenges of the future. The steps for developing this strategic capacity are:

- *Reshape the corporate culture to support the new vision:* Corporate culture is the collective pattern of behaviors, values, and unwritten rules developed by an organization over time. If the culture is rigid and discourages experimentation and creative thinking, it will be difficult to think expansively about the future. If the culture focuses on and rewards certainty, it will be difficult to ask employees to focus on the possibilities created by uncertainty. Determine your current culture and what elements need to change to support your new strategic vision. In particular, corporate leadership is critical to shaping the culture and developing a mindset that is open to exploring the opportunities in diverse views of the future. The goal is to create a learning organization in addition to a performance organization.

- *Strategically develop systems and processes to support the vision:* The systems and processes of the organization can either reinforce or inhibit the creation and implementation of a dynamic vision for the future. These processes include reward and incentive systems, information systems, personnel development and promotion, strategic planning, organizational structure, communication pattern and methods, and financial and accounting systems. Managers should consciously undertake the process of redesigning the systems and processes so they are aligned with the vision—and are flexible enough to adapt to the next vision. One way to do this is to create a task force to develop and implement the changes needed to complement the new vision.

- *Develop the knowledge and skills necessary for strategic insight and competitive success:* We have already examined the competencies that will be needed for success under different scenarios. If the company does not currently have the competencies that are critical to the strategic vision, you need to develop them. You can establish development plans to identify and eliminate gaps in your current competencies to build the organizational competencies you will need for the future. At the same time, you need to create the metacompetencies needed to carry forward the dynamic process of profiting from uncertainty. These include the capacity for scenario planning, expertise in the development and evaluation of options, and capabilities for strategic monitoring.

The goal of all this work is to create an ongoing strategic dialogue about the future and the organization's role in it. The environment is constantly changing, so this is not a process with a clear beginning or end. It is an organic process involving art and science. It is a continuous process that should engage the best thoughts and creative insights of the organization. Ideally, it will encourage managers and all stakeholders to focus more energy on examining the potential dangers and possibilities of the uncertain future while they manage the certainty of the present. It is in future uncertainty that the greatest threats and opportunities lie.

Chapter 9

Case Study: Flying through Turbulence

"There is beauty in space, and it is orderly. There is no weather, and there is regularity. It is predictable . . . Everything in space obeys the laws of physics. If you know these laws and obey them, space will treat you kindly."

—WERNHER VON BRAUN[1]

The Hughes Aircraft Employees Federal Credit Union began its life in October 1940 in a secure and protected environment. With branches in Hughes Aircraft buildings, the credit union had access to a captive market of Hughes employees. As the defense industry continued to expand in the cold war era, these employees swelled to 93,000, and the Credit Union rode this wave to become one of the largest credit unions in the United States. Hughes was one of the largest employers in California. Like von Braun's view of space, it was regular and predictable.

Then the dark clouds began gathering. The cold war ended, and the Berlin Wall fell along with the Soviet Union. The defense industry consolidated, and the number of Hughes employees was reduced accordingly. The Credit Union, which had so long tied its fortunes to Hughes Aircraft, was now concerned about its future growth opportunities.

At the same time, in the late 1990s, technology was transforming financial services. In 1999 WingspanBank.com had burst onto the scene with an aggressive national advertising campaign as the most visible of an advancing host of online banking initiatives. Managers of the Hughes Aircraft Employees Federal Credit Union discussed whether they needed to create their own "greenfield" project similar to Wingspan. While this electronic market was initially relatively small, it posed a disproportionate threat. The Credit Unions' most profitable borrowers are most likely to be targeted by these services. But how much of the market would migrate from the teller's window to the computer window? How fast would the changes occur?

Regulatory and competitive changes were also reshaping the industry. There were proposals to remove the tax-exempt status of credit unions, a change that would place significant new pressures on margins and could change the dynamics of the industry. In 1998 commercial banks made a failed attempt to revoke the tax exemption of the credit unions, and they could go on the offensive again as credit unions continued to expand their fields of membership aggressively. The industry structure in financial services was being deeply transformed, with barriers falling between long-term bond markets, money markets, and stock markets. Megamergers and acquisitions were reorganizing the competitive landscape. The direction and pace of these changes were as uncertain as the shifts in technology. Which changes would occur? Which competitors would join forces, and what kind of new entrants might appear?

The customer base, the regulatory environment, and the technological context of the credit union business were all changing at once. The Hughes Aircraft Employees Federal Credit Union, which had long been one of the largest and highest-flying credit unions in the United States, was flying into turbulent weather.

At the annual employee meeting in October 1999, President and Chief Executive Officer Thomas R. Graham sadly announced to employees that the Credit Union had slipped out of the ranks of the top ten credit unions in the United States, down from sixth place in 1990 to eleventh place. One weekend at home, Graham (who is trained as a CPA) sat down and started cranking through the numbers. By Monday morning, he told his senior staff that if the organization kept on its current course, it would be in nineteenth place within five years. Could it pull out of this seemingly inevitable dive?

Teaching an Old Dog New Tricks

The organization was not designed for this environment. Credit union CIO Rudy Pereira, a member of the strategy team, notes that surveys of members found that they viewed the credit union as "a golden retriever: lovable and loyal, but a bit slow." The organization was a product of its comfortable environment. "You didn't have to be the quickest or best because you were convenient," Pereira says. "Now we have to be as swift, intelligent, quick and nimble as any financial organization we are competing against. We needed to become more like a greyhound."

And the Credit Union has. Over lunch Graham pulls out his handheld Palm VII and calls up the screen that gives him wireless access to his credit union accounts. The organization was one of the first credit unions, or any financial institution for that matter, to offer wireless access. So far, only about three or four hundred of the credit union's members have taken advantage of this service. But the publicity alone has been worth the small investment, and Graham notes that with teenagers leading the use of cell phones around the world, this technology will help secure the future of the business. It also sends a clear message, in Graham's words, that this credit union is "not your father's Oldsmobile."

Wireless access is the least visible of the changes, which become clear just by walking into the five-story credit union headquarters on Rosecrans Avenue in Manhattan Beach, California. Outside the building is the image of the past, the silhouette of a face and hat of a Western "paymaster" and the name "Hughes Aircraft Employees Federal Credit Union." Inside is the announcement of the company's new name and logo, rolled out just days before in July 2001. The new name, "Kinecta Federal Credit Union," is represented by a new colorful and dynamic logo (as shown in Exhibit 9-1). The company changed its name to reflect the declining role of Hughes as a sponsor (the Credit Union now serves employees from a wide range of sponsors), its new sense of energy and direction, and its stronger member focus.

Even the design of the lobby of the flagship branch speaks volumes about the changes. When Graham joined the company as senior vice president in 1990, the lobby was dimly lit (a product of the Carter administration energy crisis), furnished with 1970s-era brown carpets and orange chairs. It was organized around the company's needs, not the

Exhibit 9-1: Old and New Logos: Leaving Behind the Paymaster

The new logo at the bottom right is clearly more dynamic and is not tied to a single corporate sponsor.

members'. To get a credit card, members needed to go to the fourth floor; for a loan, the third floor. "You needed to leave a trail of bread crumbs," Graham says.

Today the branch is organized as a "member mall," with bright blue signage designating areas for "member services," "mortgages," and "auto loans." Two greeters welcome visitors at a counter at the entrance. At the side of the room are computer terminals that link users to an online loan application form, and a telephone that connects directly to the telephone banking system. One of the teller windows is used by members of other credit unions, who can use the branch and ATMs as part of an alliance strategy. This opens up many more channels for Graham's organization, which in turn has opened branches in Albertsons supermarkets.

While many of the new initiatives are investments for the long term, the short-term impact of this new momentum is already apparent a year or two into their implementation. The Credit Union has pulled out of its dive, and all its key indicators are on the rise (see Exhibit 9-2). In one year, it went from being one of the slowest-growing credit unions in the nation to one of the fastest. Most notably membership growth, which had been nearly flat and even negative for the past five years, rocketed above 16 percent in 2000 (see Exhibit 9-3).

Exhibit 9-2: From Bottom to Top Ranking among Top 100 Credit Unions

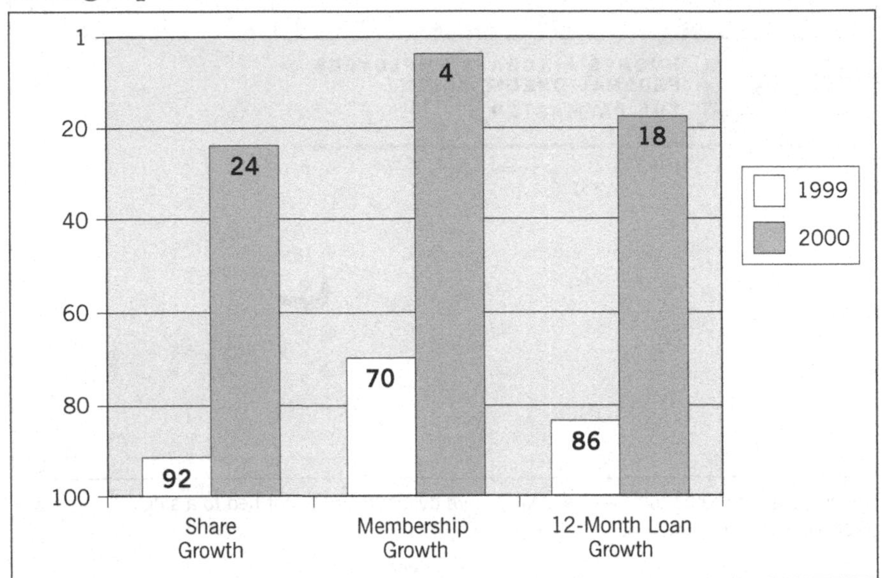

Note: Ranking is shown from best (=1) to worst (=100) in this list of 100 largest credit unions (in assets).

"There have been a lot of changes," says Graham, the son of an Ohio minister with a knack for midwestern directness. "Some people would say we've been nuts, and I would have to say: I guess you are right. Real change happens when you have a sense of urgency. But you have to recognize the crisis, you can't make it up. I realized that maybe we could find the crisis if we could see things differently."

A New Approach to Planning: Seeing Things Differently

The organization has a new name, a new vision, and a variety of bold new initiatives. How did they get to this point? How did the leaders of the credit union, like Louis Arnitz in Chapter 1, manage "to see things differently"?

In addition to thoughtful and bold leadership, the Credit Union employed the scenario-based approach to strategic planning. Over the years, the Credit Union's Leadership Team (comprised of executive management and Board of Directors) had moved from a traditional budget planning process, focused primarily on next year's budgets, to a more strategic orientation that it called FAST (Fundamentals, Assumptions, Strategy, and Tactics). As it looked at fundamentals and assumptions, the

Exhibit 9-3: Membership Growth Rate

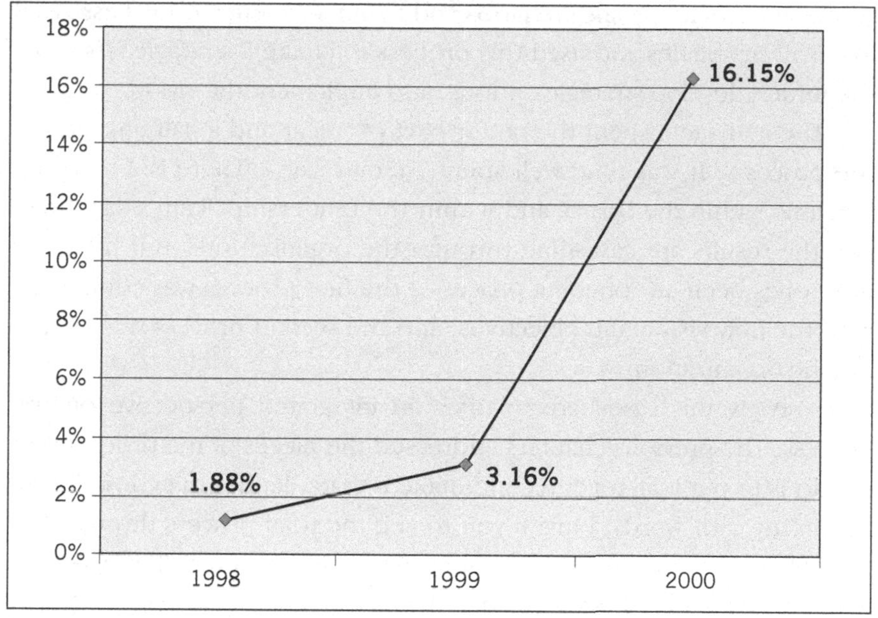

Source: *Kinecta Federal Credit Union*

Leadership Team scanned the environment and drew in speakers who offered novel perspectives on the industry. In the context of these insights, including an examination of its mission and vision, the Leadership Team then moved to developing strategy and tactics. This exploration of the future was largely intuitive and was not yet systematically linked to the planning process.

In 1998 the organization began to implement a deeper approach to examining its fundamentals and assumptions based on the scenario-planning approach. "This was the next level," says Paul A. James, chair of the board. "Scenario planning helped evaluate assumptions and look at priorities, since it asks you to think about the possibilities within those assumptions. This ensures you have sound strategic thinking about what needs to be done. The value of that is that you have a clearer understanding of what the future could look like under various scenarios, and what you need to do to be successful within them. The process also allows the Leadership Team to get much closer to a shared sense of reality."

The process the Credit Union used (described in the previous chapters of this book) was to identify the main scenarios for the future, define its strategic segments, and then identify the Key Success Factors needed to win across the specific scenarios and target segments. Also, it assessed internal capabilities and used this process to create a strategic vision for the future, develop strategic options, and implement the vision.[2]

The managers spent the better part of a year and a half engaged in the process. "It was time well spent," James says. "There is a changed dynamic within the Board, and within the Leadership Team as a whole, and the results are cascading through the organization." But he notes that it has been an "ongoing process": the first process was coming up with the new vision and objectives, and the second process was changing the organization.

I review this case here to offer an integrated perspective on the process. The previous chapters addressed the pieces of the process, but the art is to put it all together and make it work. Rather than describe all this in my own words, I invite you to see the total process through the eyes of senior managers who have implemented it. After all, it was they who brought about the remarkable turnaround charted above.

Getting Off the Runway

Graham compares the initiating process to taking off in an airplane. "My analogy is that you are sitting in a small Piper Cub airplane at the end of a small runway," he says. "What do you see? I can see to the end of the runway. What do you see beyond that? All I see is trees. Okay, let's take off. You get fifty feet off the ground, and all of a sudden you can see the highway beyond the trees. Let's keep going. Pretty soon you can see the farm beyond the highway. Let's keep going. Now you can see multiple farms. The better your vision gets, the more you can really see and the more things fall into place. We've actually gotten a much clearer vision of what we want to do and how we want to do it.

"Once you get there, now all of a sudden you realize what you might have missed before," he continues. "We were in that phase of budget planning, not strategic planning. We were worried about whether we could guess what might happen next year. We had to get to this level of strategic planning to say: What are some of the options for the future? What are the things that hold true for all those potential futures so that no matter which one occurs, we have the opportunity to be successful? Like most everybody else, we were stuck in an old model."

Four Scenarios for the Future of Credit Unions

The first step in challenging this old model was to take a long hard look at the competitive environment and examine how it might change in the future. The Hughes Aircraft Employees Federal Credit Union explored several potential scenarios for the future, building on a set of industry scenarios that we had developed for the Credit Union Executives Society (CUES) using the process discussed in Chapter 3.[3]

Credit unions were born of necessity in 19th-century Europe, which was then reeling from a global economic crisis. As agricultural imports from the Americas flooded European markets, prices fell. Farmers in Germany and elsewhere faced bankruptcy, and banks would not lend them what they needed. In response, a grassroots movement for credit unions formed as an innovative way to address their financial crisis. Neighbors joined forces to pool their resources and support one another financially, as they had always done physically in building barns and fences in their communities. Credit unions offered small, short-term consumer loans that would never have been considered by large financial institutions.

In the United States credit unions found relative peace and security under the regulatory umbrella of the federal government. They took off following the Great Depression, when the government offered the protection of the Credit Union Act in 1934. Thereafter corporate sponsors began offering credit union membership as a convenient benefit to their workers. Credit unions continued to expand, and by the end of the twentieth century there were 77 million credit union members in the United States, served by more than 11,000 credit unions.

But offering security to credit unions also allowed them to become complacent. "Until several years ago, the industry overall was characterized by insularity, risk aversion, and conservatism," says Franck Schuurmans, vice president of professional development at CUES, whose Ph.D. in history favors taking the broad view. "This was true of the traditional retail banking environment in general, but even more so for credit unions, protected by tax exemption and a captive customer base. Now there is a sense of competition. People are waking up. There are still too many credit union managers who think they can thrive just making car loans, but there is an emerging interest in new approaches and in challenging long-held ideas."

Which of the forces shaping the environment could have the greatest impact on the future of the credit union business? we asked. In creating the initial industry scenarios, we identified two primary drivers—shifting technology and a changing competitive playing field—as the major forces of change for credit unions overall. While the change in sponsorship was one of the most significant factors shaping the future of the Hughes Aircraft Employees Federal Credit Union, it was not really an uncertainty but a trend, and thus it was woven into the stories of all four scenarios.

The two key uncertainties—when bracketed in terms of their outcome range—define a set of four very different futures for credit unions, as summarized in Exhibit 9-4. The outcome range was set wide enough to properly bound the possibilities of each dimension within the time frame considered. These four future scenarios were:

- *Scenario A: Credit Union Power:* This is the most stable scenario, resting on assumptions of only moderate change in both technology and the playing field. The credit unions' current capabilities remain strong, and they can continue to succeed with a status quo strategy. Yet, changes in the basis of competition, new business models, human resource challenges, and industry dynamics occur as they are the baseline trends for all scenarios.

Exhibit 9-4: Credit Union Scenario Matrix

		CHANGES IN PLAYING FIELD?	
		Minor	**Radical**
CHANGES IN TECHNOLOGY?	**Minor**	Credit Union Power	Wallet Wars
	Radical	Technocracy	Chameleon

Source: *Credit Union Executives Society and Decision Strategies International, Inc.*

- *Scenario B: Wallet Wars:* While the technology is still advancing slowly, deregulation and free-market economics have led to an intense battle for customer wallets. Credit unions, banks, brokerage houses, mutual fund companies, and insurance companies are increasingly encroaching on one another's turf. Credit unions lose their tax exemption and hence their related price advantage.
- *Scenario C: Technocracy:* The wide-scale adoption of the Internet by U.S. consumers has led to massive technological innovation for financial service companies, increasing the range of distribution channels and the products, services, and geographic scope of financial services organizations. Deregulation and other changes in the playing field, however, have been slow to follow.
- *Scenario D: Chameleon:* Radical changes occurring both in the playing field and in the technology make this scenario tumultuous for all credit unions. The nature of competition has changed such that banks and credit unions compete directly, under the same rules of the game. This has caused a wide-scale convergence of cultures among the various financial services providers, testing the boundaries of the long-standing credit union philosophy of cooperation and member service.

The purpose of developing these four diverse scenarios was not to select one in order to predict the future but rather to provide a broad range of outcomes to help prepare for success across multiple possible futures. Rather than placing a big bet on a Wingspan-like initiative, premised on the view that the "Technocracy" or "Chameleon" future was going to emerge rapidly, the Hughes Aircraft Employees Federal Credit Union took a more balanced approach. This allowed it to better maintain an even keel across the hype of the dot-com run-up and collapse. The Credit Union could identify and build the capabilities it would need across diverse futures.

"Even though 'Chameleon' looked like it would be important for the future at the time, the key was to find ways to be successful no matter what scenario came to pass," Pereira recalls. "I'm a strong believer that twenty years from now, we won't have as many bricks and mortar. The millennium generation won't want to step into a physical branch. But when we developed the scenarios, we realized that the scenarios did not depict any future that would actually occur. Not one of the scenarios would play out exactly as stated. Pinpointing the future wasn't nearly as important as creating some diverse scenarios to understand future Key Success Factors."

Strategic Segmentation

Once scenarios for the future were created, the next challenge was to identify key strategic segments and Key Success Factors needed to win in these segments across multiple futures (see Chapter 4). Examining these distinct segments (as opposed to whole industries) was indeed important, because the KSFs differed considerably by segments as well as scenario.

The Hughes Aircraft Employees Federal Credit Union looked not only at age demographics (the traditional dimensions for credit unions) but also at the different needs of member groups, as shown in Exhibit 9-5. Upon considering various segmentation schemes, it settled on the following strategic segments:

- *Teach me:* The younger generation (eighteen years and younger) want to be taught about all aspects of finances and financial management, from transactions to wealth accumulation. In identifying this segment, the Credit Union Leadership Team realized that it had virtually ignored these children of members, even though they represent the future. The Credit Union created a new youth strategy to draw them in.

- *Show me:* This segment of nineteen-to-twenty-five-year-olds wants information about wealth accumulation, protection, financing, and other financial advice.

- *Max me:* This segment of members, age twenty-six to over sixty-five, is focused on wealth accumulation and wants advice in preparation for retirement. They are particularly interested in mutual funds and retirement vehicles.

- *Protect me:* Another group, in the same age group as the "Max me" members, is interested less in wealth accumulation than in preservation. This group is interested in insurance and other protection vehicles that the Credit Union offers through a separate organization that is not tax exempt. In identifying this group, the Credit Union realized it needed to find ways to more closely integrate marketing of these services into credit union channels.

- *Finance me:* This group, in the prime home-buying years of twenty-six to sixty-five, is primarily interested in financing homes, cars, and other consumer purchases.
- *Serve me:* Finally, there is a broad segment (nineteen to over sixty-five) that is interested primarily in completing transactions with the Credit Union. There is an opportunity to move these members to other services.

These strategic segments were created by crossing two key dimensions—age versus needs satisfied. Rather than consider every cell of this matrix (in Exhibit 9-5) to be a separate segment, the company combined certain cells (letters A, B, C, and D) to arrive at segments that truly differ strategically. Within each segment, members were quite homogeneous in terms of needs, preferences, and profiles.

Exhibit 9-5: Strategic Segmentation Map

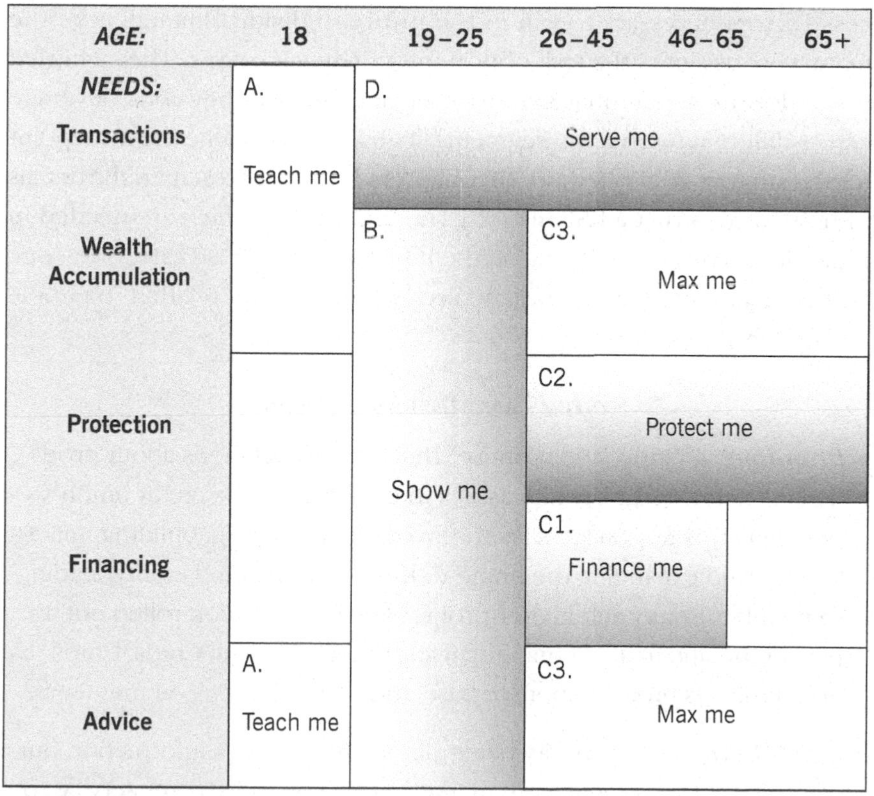

<table>
<tr><th>AGE:</th><th>18</th><th>19–25</th><th>26–45</th><th>46–65</th><th>65+</th></tr>
<tr><td>NEEDS:
Transactions</td><td rowspan="2">A.
Teach me</td><td colspan="4">D.
Serve me</td></tr>
<tr><td>Wealth Accumulation</td><td rowspan="4">B.
Show me</td><td colspan="3">C3.
Max me</td></tr>
<tr><td>Protection</td><td rowspan="2"></td><td colspan="3">C2.
Protect me</td></tr>
<tr><td>Financing</td><td colspan="2">C1.
Finance me</td><td></td></tr>
<tr><td>Advice</td><td>A.
Teach me</td><td colspan="3">C3.
Max me</td></tr>
</table>

Source: *Kinecta Federal Credit Union*

While this process helped identify neglected segments and offered insights on new strategies for reaching particular segments, it also was the most uncomfortable part of the process for the Credit Union's management. They realized they had limited information about some of these customer segments. The segments were based 60 percent on hard information and 40 percent on gut. Management tried to gather more information about the new segments, but they still had to become comfortable moving ahead with their best guess rather than precise information. This is the nature of segmentation. And the more creative or unusual your segments are, the fewer hard data you may have to go on. But often it pays to think differently.

Key Success Factors

The next question in the process was: Given this set of scenarios and strategic segments, what will it take to win in the future? The Leadership Team now began to wrestle with the challenge of identifying the Key Success Factors necessary to win in the future. Individual members of the team were assigned the task of fleshing out specific KSFs. They whittled down dozens of potential KSFs to a set of eight that they could leverage across different futures and segments. These KSFs became the focal point for the strategy going forward. (In Chapters 5 and 6, I presented the details of how to construct a KSF matrix.) The eight KSFs, which are needed in multiple scenarios and several segments, fit into two broad categories, one addressing systems and infrastructure and the second relating to people and culture.

Systems and Infrastructure

- *Branding:* A brand is a "promise" that sets expectations about product and service delivery and assists in establishing the credit union's position. This Key Success Factor involves developing, building, maintaining, and expanding the brand to build strong brand equity, leading to member loyalty and higher profits. The Credit Union rolled out a new brand and image, renaming itself Kinecta Federal Credit Union, to emphasize its broader sponsor base and dynamic focus on members.
- *Data Mining:* The capacity to extract useful business information out of large databases can inform marketing and provide better service to

members. To develop this capability, the Credit Union launched a major data-mining initiative, investing in building a new data warehouse that is normalized across the company. Also, it created data-mining tools to access this wealth of information.

- *New Delivery Channels:* Enhancing the existing channel mix and developing new channels for connecting members to the Credit Union helps them interact in any way they choose. There is now a seamless interaction across different channels. In addition to its branches, ATMs, and telephone banking systems, the Credit Union opened or enhanced its channels for wireless access, grocery store branches, and computer-accessed "home branching."

- *Targeted Product Development:* Products and services can be customized to meet individual member preferences and needs. For example, products can be developed for specific employee groups, using mass customization. This capability combines with data mining and new delivery channels to offer tailored solutions to specific members or groups of members.

A host of cultural imperatives were identified as well to help move the organization in the right direction quickly. Here is a sampling of the associated organizational KSFs.

People and Culture

- *Quick Action:* With rapid changes in the financial services industry, the organization needed the capacity to react quickly. The Credit Union worked on developing the capacity to be a flat, fast, and flexible organization (not a golden retriever but a greyhound!).

- *Strategic Alliances:* Leveraging relationships with other credit unions and key partners can enhance the growth and service of the credit union. The Credit Union joined with other credit unions to offer broader access to branches and ATMs.

- *Aggressive Marketing:* For an organization that had traditionally done little marketing, this credit union focused on providing timely and appropriate offers to members with innovative flair. Its rollout of its new brand and new channels was part of this aggressive marketing strategy.

- *Learning Organization:* The Credit Union sought to build an organization in which people continually expanded their capacity to create results they truly desire, where new and expansive patterns of thinking were nurtured, where collective aspiration was set free, where people were continually striving to learn together. By building and nurturing a learning culture, employees across the organization could become adept at reading the market and mobilizing a rapid response. As part of this initiative, the Credit Union involved all its employees in understanding and implementing the new strategy and vision (as discussed later in this chapter).

Refocusing the Strategic Vision

The segments and KSFs offered a road map for developing the capabilities that the credit union would need to succeed across a wide range of futures. This map would guide any future investments and initiatives in the coming year and, most likely, many years to come.

But there was a problem: the set of KSFs, and the discussion that led up to them, were out of sync with the Credit Union's current vision. That vision—to be "a global, multisponsor credit union"—had been approved only eighteen months earlier. It reflected the need to move away from its traditional association with the Hughes Aircraft company, but it now felt far too inwardly focused. The Credit Union needed to use its insights into scenarios, segments, and KSFs to refocus its strategic vision (as discussed in Chapter 5).

"We were making our presentations on the KSFs to our management staff, and we kept saying there is something wrong here," Graham recalls. He points out that it was like designing a car where one person goes out and designs an excellent fender, another the engine, and another the best suspension system. Then you go off and put the car together. "No one had stood back and said, this will be a Formula II racing car," Graham says.

They took the issue to the board. It was a difficult thing to consider changing a vision that had been developed such a short time earlier. Many Board members and executives had a personal investment in the current vision. To handle this sensitive issue, three teams developed separate presentations in support of the current vision, a neutral vision, and a new externally focused vision that seemed more closely aligned with the Key Success Factors.

"By the time we reached the last group, you could tell there was a shift in the room that we needed to change our focus," Graham says. The new vision, which is now framed on walls throughout the organization, was focused on credit union members: "We will provide an exceptional member experience by delivering unequaled value in meeting our members' needs. As a result, our members will make us their first choice for financial services."

The vision helped to crystallize the work that had gone into identifying the Key Success Factors and organizing them into a coherent statement of the Credit Union's larger goal. "By coming back and reexamining the vision, we found something that made sense and pulled together all the work we had done," Graham says.

Implementation: Bringing the Vision Down to Earth

At the entrance to the Credit Union's flagship Manhattan Beach branch, Graham stoops to pick up a piece of paper from the ground. He is meticulous about these details, realizing the battle for retaining members is won or lost not on a strong strategic vision alone but on details such as smiles, personal service, and cleanliness.

The success of the planning process ultimately depended upon bringing the Piper Cub back down out of the clouds, landing it at the airport, and driving the new perspectives deep into the heart of the organization. Once the KSFs and vision were created, the Leadership Team developed a systematic plan to put it into practice and carry it out across its five hundred employees. The goal was "to get all the hands on all the oars stroking in the right direction at the right cadence," Graham says. "If we could do this, no one would be able to catch us."

The challenge was to continue dynamic monitoring and adjustment and to systematically implement the vision (as discussed in Chapters 7 and 8). The organization posted descriptions of the KSFs on the company Intranet, using the image of a sailboat that contained the vision, the KSFs, and the fundamentals (see Exhibit 9-6). Employees could click on the names of any of the KSFs on the sailboat to find a description of it.

Exhibit 9-6: Kinecta Sets Sail with New Key Success Factors

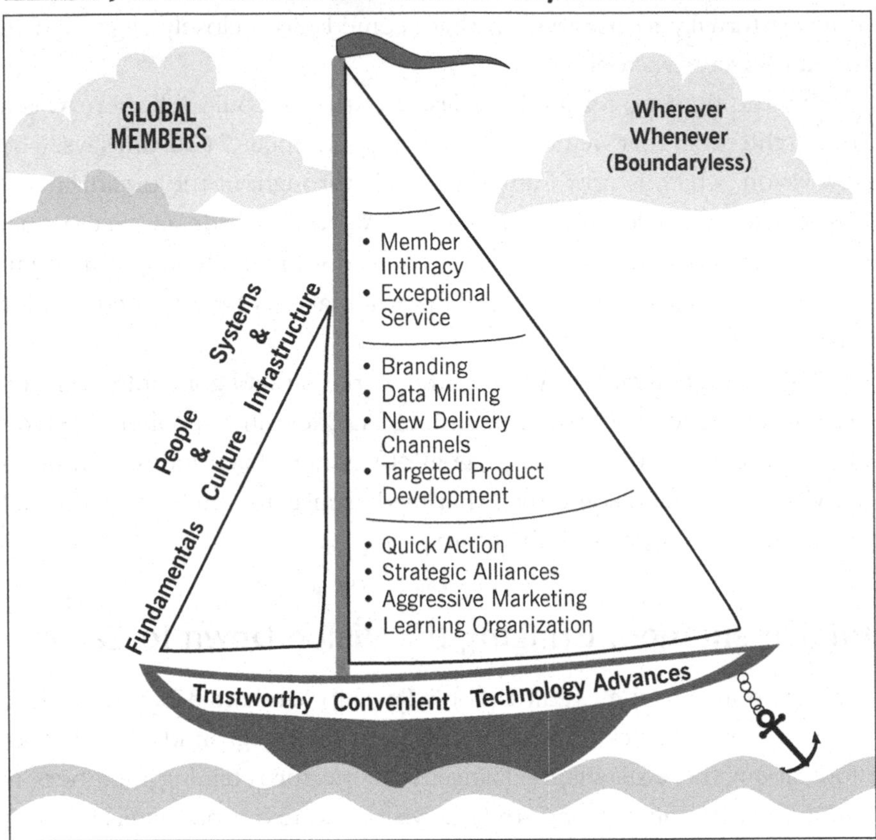

Source: *Kinecta Federal Credit Union*

The Credit Union also worked with an outside agency to develop a set of illustrations of its industry context, member relationships, strategy, and business model, using them in sessions with all its employees (see Exhibit 9-7). This ensured that nearly every employee had a deeper understanding of the business and current strategy.

After one of these sessions, the credit union's manager of records said that the map allowed him to put everything into place for the first time ever. He now felt he understood what the organization did and why. Why was that important? "When the records guy gets it, what is going to happen in the record center?" asks Graham. By the end of August 2001, the records center had created a system to allow tellers to access members' canceled checks online. "That is driven from the records center,

Exhibit 9-7: Visualizing the Strategy

©2002 **Root** *Learning® Inc.*, Maumee, Ohio

where they are now thinking creatively about how to improve member service. This is all part of the vision."

Looking Forward

What advice would the Credit Union give to others who contemplate undertaking this process? I asked Paul James, chairman of the board, who offers the following advice for senior managers:

- *Make a strong commitment:* "Be realistic about the level of engagement it will require," he advises. "We spent a considerable number of months and got a thorough, thoughtful result. You need to be committed to it."
- *Keep an open mind:* James also emphasizes that executives and volunteers must keep an open mind. The value of some parts of the process may not be immediately apparent, but they ultimately fit together into a coherent strategy for the future. "You have to be willing to test your assumptions," he says. "You have to be open minded."

Tom Graham, the president, adds the following recommendations:

- *Include everybody possible:* "Include your leadership team and your employees. The more you include people in this development, the more lieutenants are going to help you with implementation."
- *Take time to do it right:* "Don't do step B because it is now time for step B. Keep it flexible. If you want to do a day-long planning event, this isn't for you. We challenged people to help define what's possible in our future, and that took time."
- *Move with imperfect information:* "A lot of times during this process, we didn't have enough information. In segmentation, we just didn't have the information we needed. That was scary. We had to make stuff up and use our best judgments. That was one of the hardest things for managers used to working with precise data."
- *Use good facilitators:* "You need someone who understands not only the process but also the human relations. You're going to pull a lot of skeletons out of the closet in this process. You need someone who can pull these out and see that they are not so bad or deal with them."

The challenge for the Credit Union going forward is to balance implementation while continuing to monitor the environment and adjust the strategy. In July 2001 the Leadership Team prepared its agenda for its annual strategic business planning retreat. The focus of the retreat was on implementation of the vision and KSFs it had created the year before. In the future, however, the Leadership Team plans to update the scenarios and ensure that their KSFs and strategic vision are still on track.

"The challenge is to watch for early warning signals that would indicate which of the scenarios are likely to come true. The vision and strategy would then be adjusted accordingly," James says. "We have to continue to properly water and fertilize our growing organization so it continues to meet our members' needs."

The Kinecta case provides a good real-life illustration of the art and science that this process entails. What looks simple on paper is often very challenging in the real world of organizations. Issues of personality, culture, and politics invariably arise. For the process to flourish, you need a healthy organization, as the less fortunate case in the box below illustrates.

Without Top Support, You Could End up Banished to Micronesia

High-level support is vital to success. The absence of this support can be fatal, as I found out in the scenario-planning process we conducted with a financial services organization in the Far East. The top managers showed up for the cocktail parties but not the planning exercises. This was the first sign of impending trouble. The second was that in the course of the planning discussions, when managers were asked to come up with metaphors for their organization, the images they created were Roman galleys, three-ring circuses, and ocean liners with engines powering off in different directions. It was not a good sign.

Despite this lack of high-level support, the planning process was a great success intellectually, resulting in far-sighted scenarios. At a time of tremendous economic success in the Pacific Rim (circa 1993), no one else anticipated a prolonged economic downturn, but it was right there in the scenarios developed for the bank to see. The only problem was, these scenarios were never used because they lacked top leadership support. The scenarios were brilliant but irrelevant.

"People who went through the program were very stimulated and excited and in some cases shocked by what came out," recalls Michael Hostetler, director of executive education at Cornell University and one of the organizers of this program. "It was a new way of thinking. They were enthusiastic. It was such an eye-opening experience for them. They would have liked to have had the people higher up in the organization have the same experience."

But the organization had a culture that was averse to grassroots movements. It was rigidly hierarchical. Some processes required eleven signatures. To send a routine fax, a manager needed a signature from a supervisor. One manager who made the mistake of talking to the president on the elevator was called aside and told that "If the president wishes to speak to you, he will tell you."

The organization had "a highly politicized power structure," with complex interactions among different levels. Saving face was very important in this Asian culture, and the scenario-planning process was implicitly or explicitly viewed as inviting criticism. If learning from mistakes is uncomfortable in some organizations, it is unconscionable in an organization such as this one.

One of the champions of our process, who had been the director of strategy for the organization, was thanked politely for his brave scenario report and then exiled to a post in Micronesia. The division he headed up was eliminated and folded into the personnel office. All traces of the scenario-planning process were erased.

The absence of top management support, particularly in an organization of very rigid hierarchy, was the kiss of death. Even though top management allowed the activity to go on as part of an executive education initiative organized by Cornell, they did not allow it to penetrate the thinking of the organization because some of the scenarios raised doubts about the wisdom of senior management's current course of action.

The bottom-line insight from the experience is that no matter how thorough and insightful the scenario-planning process is, it will be pointless if it is not supported at the highest levels of the organization. Some less hierarchical organizations allow for grassroots scenario planning that eventually percolates up to the senior management and boardroom. But even here it is risky unless the top leadership can be brought on board.

"If you are really trying to give people tools that imply change, you can't be starting at the middle of the organization," Hostetler says. "You first have to convince people higher in the organization so it can cascade down. In trying to do that, you may find out that the top of the house is not willing to support the initiative. Then you have a judgment call to pull out or try to make the case."

Even a good planning process can work only with a healthy organization, since it requires trust across all levels to truthfully look at the future and change the organization to respond to it. It will not work well, nor will any other process, in a sick or cynical organization.

While frustrating, the Far Eastern experience offered a lot of learning—both to Hostetler and to ourselves. "It was a fascinating piece of work," he says. "Individually, we made great impact on some people. But for organizational impacts, I'm not sure we can point to them."

Conclusion
Navigating the Future

"Those who look only to the past or present are certain to miss the future."
—JOHN F. KENNEDY

For early mariners and the cities or principalities that supported them, the compass alone was not a sustainable source of competitive advantage in maritime trade. Only those that developed related capabilities in such key areas as shipbuilding, seamanship, and trading were truly able to take advantage of the new tools for navigation. For example, it was not just the compass and other navigation tools that made Venice a major global shipping center. Venice especially advanced as a result of breakthroughs in shipbuilding. It moved from building lagoon vessels and small ships of less-than-100-ton displacement to 200-ton ships and finally to a crowning achievement of 500 tons, the *Roccaforte,* in 1260. (This was roughly five times the size of Christopher Columbus's ship *Santa Maria,* which sailed across the Atlantic more than two centuries later.) At the same time, trading became increasingly sophisticated, with an expanded array of products. The Venetians also controlled islands along key trade routes, ensuring they would stay open and protecting their valuable cargo from pirates.[1]

Similarly, the frameworks and tools for navigating uncertainty discussed in this book do not confer advantage in a vacuum. They need to be combined and embedded in related organizational capabilities. All of them must be brought together into a coherent system and integrated into the planning and budgeting process of the organization, as seen in the experience of Hughes Aircraft Employees Federal Credit Union discussed in Chapter 9. I think of this framework as a strategic compass (as illustrated in Exhibit C-1) that provides direction through three key processes:

1. Developing multiple future scenarios that fully embrace the external uncertainty.
2. Creating a strategic vision and associated real options to properly balance commitment and flexibility.
3. Closely monitoring the external and internal environment to make real-time adjustments when needed.

These three processes in turn are deeply interrelated and reinforce each other when properly executed. The scenarios allow managers to test which strategies require flexibility, and the ensuing strategic options can be properly valued only in light of the full uncertainty range implied by

Exhibit C-1

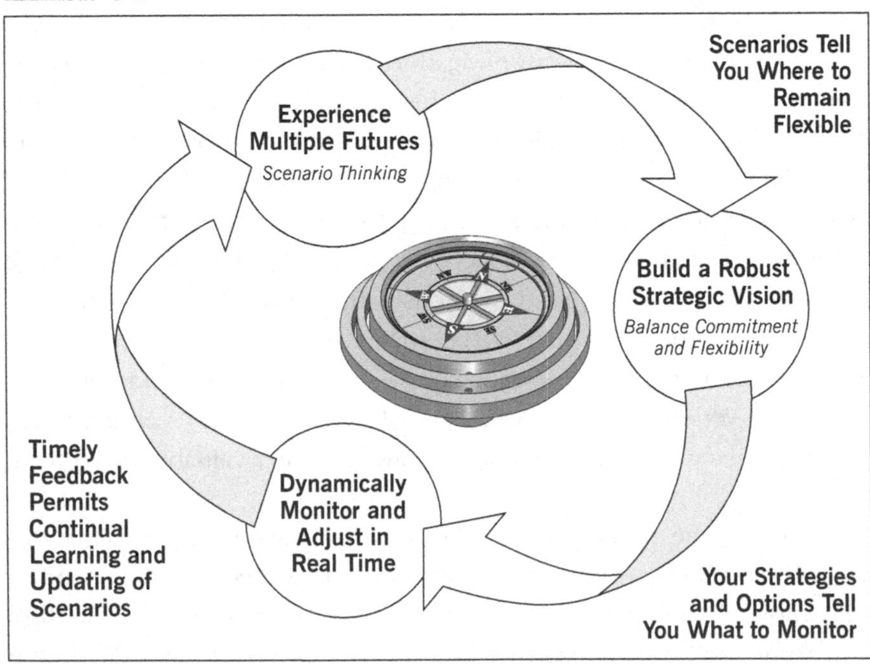

the scenarios. The flexible strategies and embedded options, in turn, emphasize which aspects of the external environment need close monitoring in real time. And the options themselves serve as a springboard for timely action since their value can be realized only if they are triggered at the appropriate moment. Furthermore, the broader scenarios will suggest an array of signposts and markers that will aid managers in scanning and canvassing the future as it unfolds. Thus, a self-reinforcing learning cycle is set in motion in which the total system is only as strong as its weakest link. For this reason, organizations must learn to master all three processes at comparable levels of proficiency lest they run on just one or two engines rather than firing all three.

Part of the reason that managers underutilize scenario planning, options thinking, and other frameworks and tools is that they view them as peripheral to running the business. Scenarios may seem an interesting diversion—a trip into a fascinating but useless fiction—because the insights that they generate are not directly linked to planning and budgeting. A more comprehensive and coherent approach to planning under uncertainty allows us to imbue our strategies and actions in the present with a broad and dynamically changing awareness of the future.

The highly scaleable process outlined here must be tailored to the strengths and constraints of your organization and industry. Various examples have illustrated how specific companies have benefited from different aspects of these approaches. This tailoring is by its very nature individual, idiosyncratic, and constantly evolving. The notion of continuous change is uncomfortable for many managers, but for success in an uncertain environment, is absolutely necessary. Companies need to continue to learn and refine their management processes based on current experience and their understanding of the shifting context of business.

The challenge in the long run is that the capabilities you develop for profiting from uncertainty today may become encrusted so that it is harder to adapt to changing circumstances. Venetian naval superiority sustained the city as a powerhouse for centuries, but it was completely unprepared for a land invasion by Napoleon in 1797. Venice surrendered without firing a shot. Any organization—no matter how successful—must keep looking ahead and periodically reconfigure the tools it uses to address uncertainty to meet emerging challenges. Success requires developing strengths and capabilities that are well adapted to the current environment while also nurturing the metacapability of dynamically changing the *process itself* to meet the new challenges that the future will surely bring.

Appendix A
The Psychology of Uncertainty

"You are—face it—a bunch of emotions,
prejudices, and twitches . . ."
—ADAM SMITH, *THE MONEY GAME*[1]

Most of us want certainty. That is why we find Nostradamus so attractive and our daily newspapers publish astrological columns. We want someone who will be able to tell us when to act and what will happen next. The truth is, however, that the future is unknowable and uncertain. Our desire for the certainty of Nostradamus may reveal more about ourselves than about the future.

Even the rational managers who would scorn the idea of visiting a fortune-teller or peering into a crystal ball still turn to sources to make the world more certain. They call in consultants and listen to analysts and other experts. Some of this information gathering and analysis is appropriate and actually helps to reduce uncertainty. But other activities are an attempt to wrap convincing data around vaporous enigma. (We have only to look at the rapid fall from grace of Internet analysts with the collapse of the dot-com bubble or the boom-and-bust cycles of innovations such as business process reengineering to see how quickly solid recommendations and strong convictions can be undermined.) Still, we seek certainty in an uncertain world.

Why we desire certainty, at least most of the time, is a complex question involving emotional and cognitive factors, as well as economic and cultural ones. As children, we needed structure and boundaries to develop. Those who lacked those boundaries may end up confused or scared. A sense of control is crucial to our feeling of well-being and particular kinds of uncertainty may disturb that sense. Also, we exhibit greater sensitivity to losses than gains and, so in general, would not welcome additional risk. From an economic perspective, we are taught that risk is negative and that we should consider buying insurance to get rid of it. In finance, we speak of the tradeoff between risk and return, highlighting that only a fool would welcome more risk without being compensated in return. Most of us prefer a fixed-rate mortgage over a variable one precisely because the former entails more predictable payments, even though it is more expensive. And culturally, we are taught to act responsibly and prudently in the face of risks to ourselves and especially those to others.

Society has ordained certain forms of risk-taking to be acceptable, however, such as betting on horses, football games, or the stock market—but all within reason. Even the government has gotten in on the act, through state lotteries, while still focusing on prudent risk management in more serious areas such as social security, federally insured banking deposits, and disaster relief.

I don't think we really know yet what makes us dislike uncertainty most of the time, whereas at other times we seek it out in the form of new experiences, adventures, or the casino. But it is clear, from numerous research studies, that humans have a hard time dealing with uncertainty.[2] In this Appendix, I examine some of the factors that make uncertainty so challenging. These human difficulties in handling uncertainty are important to understand, because they are the reason we often cannot rely upon instinct or tradition in uncertain times. These basic human limitations make tools and frameworks all the more important in overcoming the obstacles posed by uncertainty. We can improve our responses to uncertainty only if we better understand the fundamental human challenges it poses.

The research literature related to how people deal with uncertainty includes hundreds of academic papers that I cannot possibly review here. By necessity the following summary is incomplete and rather idiosyncratic in its selection of topics, but I think it suggests the extent of the challenges we face in making decisions under uncertainty. I refer to my academic writings on this subject for a more complete view[3] as well as the numerous other sources cited from the growing body of research in this area.

Myopic Eyes and Timid Souls

Our heads are not wired for uncertainty. Years of behavioral research on judgment and decision making have unearthed a variety of cognitive limitations in dealing with uncertainty.[4] I group them here into two broad categories: those concerning the *perception* of risk and those addressing how we *choose* when facing uncertainty. In general, we tend to have *myopic eyes* when assessing risks and rather *timid souls* when choosing among uncertain options. In what follows, I briefly review some of the biases in each of these categories.

Myopic Eyes

Our myopic eyes tend to narrow our range of view, and so we fail to appreciate the full scale of uncertainty. There are several reasons for this phenomenon. One of the central reasons is *overconfidence*. We are too sure of our single view about the future, and we fail to consider alternative views sufficiently. Overconfidence led Thomas Edison to dismiss his phonograph as "not of any commercial value." It seduced Digital Equipment Corporation president Ken Olson—one of the most technologically astute men of his time—to proclaim in 1977: "There is no reason for any individual to have a computer in their home." Few leaders have been as fatally wrong about their forecast as Civil War general John B. Sedgwick. He well understood the latest military technology, but his last words at the Battle of Spotsylvania were: "They couldn't hit an elephant at this dist—"[5] While most business leaders do not have to pay such a stiff or immediate price for their overconfidence, it nonetheless exacts a high toll on organizations and careers. Even experts tend to be overconfident in their predictions.[6] (To test your own overconfidence, try the questions in the box.)

We are overconfident, in part, because of our inability to envision all possible pathways into the future—a failure of imagination. Another reason we are often overconfident is that we have a deep-seated emotional need to feel in charge. Studies by Ellen Langer at Harvard University show that people harbor an insidious illusion of control that gets stronger the more effort they exert in predicting the future.[7] For example, lottery sales in Massachusetts increased markedly once people were allowed to pick their own lucky number (instead of being assigned a number at random). This need for an illusion of control is why gamblers blow on their dice or study the streaks in roulette.

Managers have a psychological need not only to feel in control but also to project the image that they have control to those they wish to influence. Investors, the media, and society at large tend to reward those who exude confidence, making it perilous for managers to admit what they don't know.

How Confident Are You?

A simple way to test whether you are overconfident is to put a range around any numerical estimate you make. For example, I'll ask you a question: how many private golf courses do you think there were in the United States at the end of 2000? Stop and write down your guess before proceeding further. In addition to providing your best guess, try to write down a very low guess as well as a very high guess so that you are 90 percent sure the true answer will fall in between. Typically, people make their ranges much too narrow and miss such questions about 70 percent of the time (when they should miss only 10 percent given their level of confidence).

There were 6,374 golf courses in the United States in 2000. If that number lies outside your 90 percent confidence range, don't feel too bad. You belong to that vast majority of people who don't know what they don't know.

For a more sobering lesson in overconfidence, try the quiz below, which I often use in executive education programs. Note that what counts in this quiz is not your ability to know the precise answers to these trivia questions, but rather your ability to gauge how accurate your estimates are. Unless you are an exception, this quiz will demonstrate what a hard time we have in assessing a confidence interval for our estimates.

For each of the following questions, provide a low and high guess such that you are 90 percent sure the correct answer falls between the two. Your challenge is to select a range that is neither too narrow (overconfident) nor too wide (underconfident). If you succeed, you should have nine hits and only one miss, that is, your answers should be correct 90 percent of the time.

	Low	**High**
1. Martin Luther King's age at death	____	____
2. Length of the Nile River (in miles)	____	____
3. Number of countries that are members of OPEC	____	____
4. Number of books in the Old Testament	____	____
5. Diameter of the moon in miles	____	____
6. Weight of an empty Boeing 747 in tons	____	____
7. Year in which Wolfgang Amadeus Mozart was born	____	____
8. Gestation period of an Asian elephant (in days)	____	____
9. Air distance from London to Tokyo	____	____
10. Deepest known point in the oceans (in feet)	____	____

(See answers in endnotes)[8]

As discussed in Chapter 1, part of the reason we are overconfident is that we suffer from *frame blindness.* Frames persist because they serve a very useful purpose, especially in a world of overwhelming complexity. Frames (like the closely related concepts of paradigms and mental models[9]) provide simplification, which is essential in making sense of the complex patterns presented by the world. Amid an avalanche of information, they help us filter out some things and focus on others. Instead of seeing a stream of disconnected pixels on our computer or television screens, we are able to see images and words. We use a process of "pattern matching" to connect the new stimulus to the models in our heads.

The problem is that we tend to become trapped by these frames. We see patterns that are not really there, or we fail to see when the environment is changing. When new information comes in, we try to jam it into the existing frame rather than shifting our frames. As Albert Einstein noted, "We should make things as simple as possible, but not simpler."

We further distort our perceptions of risk and uncertainty because of *skewed attention.* We are overly focused on the areas of the world that produce the most noise or are most readily in our line of sight. For example, when researchers asked subjects whether they thought lung cancer or automotive accidents caused the most deaths annually in the United States, the majority guessed auto accidents. In fact, at the time of the study, there were about 140,000 deaths per year from lung cancer compared to 40,000 from auto accidents. But people learn about auto accidents from the media every day, so their perception of risk was biased accordingly.[10]

Similarly, we overreact to shark attacks in the ocean or terrorist attacks in the sky and fail to put these risks in their proper statistical perspective. We dread most those risks we understand poorly (like radon gas in our basement) and those over which we have no control (such as flying versus driving). Risks that occur in clusters, such as an airplane crash in which all people are killed, instill far greater fear than risks that hit isolated individuals at random such as electrocution or falling from a ladder. Similarly, we react more strongly to uncertainties that are vividly portrayed or experienced, such as physical assault or a highly traumatic childbirth, than to less vivid statistical risks such as various kinds of cancer. Managers may favor kidnapping insurance over, say, additional car insurance when both are equally attractively priced from an actuarial perspective, just because reports of kidnappings are more vivid and memorable.

In general, people are not very good at assessing or weighing probabilities. And often they don't even look at information about them. Several studies asked people to choose among uncertain alternatives, and when given the opportunity to get additional information, few inquired about data on probabilities.[11] This problem is especially acute when dealing with very low probabilities, such as the chance of accidents or natural disasters, where people cannot really distinguish between a 0.001 risk vs. a 0.0001 risk, even though the latter is ten times less likely.[12]

Even when people actually do look at the probability dimension, they may greatly *distort the risk.* The meaning of a "small chance" of something happening will differ across individuals and across questions. For example, a person might view a 5 percent risk as a "small chance" of contracting a disease, while a "small chance" of rain might be a 15 percent probability. The same person might give very different assessments of the same risk on different occasions or when the risk is framed over different time periods. Breast cancer may be viewed as less likely than being in a car accident when evaluated on a yearly basis but deemed more probable across an entire lifespan.

Correlations among risk likewise suffer from notable distortions. Human beings underestimate correlations among risks when their perceptions are purely based on past data—say the correlation between being in a car accident and theft at home. We don't infer weak correlations well from the data, but we tend to overestimate correlations when they are primarily based on a causal theory.[13] If we can easily envision a causal pathway that makes one risk dependent on another—such as experiencing a car accident and breaking your leg in a given year—we estimate the correlation to be stronger than the data warrant.

Timid Souls

In addition to myopic and distorted perceptions about risk, humans also tend to have rather timid souls when acting upon risk (however they perceive it).[14] Part of the reason for this caution is our *strong aversion to losses.* From our infancy, we hate to lose things, and this persists into adult decisions. We register losses much more vividly than gains. Few people would flip a fair coin for, say, $1,000 because they consider a loss of $1,000 to be much more painful in absolute magnitude than the pleasure of a gain of $1,000. Most people will flip the coin only if the chance of winning is at least two in three (and the chance of loss one in three). Similarly, experiments show that people will ask for more to give up something (such as a mug) than they would be willing to pay for the exact same item.

This loss aversion contributes to people's general *risk aversion.* We value the "bird in the hand" much more than the "two in the bush." Even in a gamble that entails no loss, such as a coin flip that pays $0 with tails and $2,000 with heads, people would rather take $1,000 for sure.

Most people also *dislike ambiguity,* which is different from risk aversion. Ambiguity is technically defined as not knowing for sure what the probabilities are. In a standard gamble, such as playing roulette in a casino or a game of cards, there is general agreement on the odds of receiving a particular outcome. In the real world, however, most situations entail uncertainty about the probabilities attached to various outcomes. Such second-order uncertainty (assigning probabilities to different probability levels) should theoretically be reduced to simple probabilities by calculating an expected probability. But most human beings don't look at it this way.[15] To illustrate, read the jar problem in the box. Do you prefer the jar with the known or the unknown probability? Why?

Several studies show that people's degree of risk aversion bears little correlation to their degree of ambiguity aversion, suggesting that they are distinct concepts in practice as well as in theory.[16] Also, people's degree of ambiguity aversion (which can be measured by asking how much more they prefer jar A) may be different on the gain than on the loss side. Suppose the jars in the box now entailed losing (rather than winning) $100—which would you prefer?

Another reason for timid souls is that we also suffer from an *isolation bias.* People usually act on a particular risk in isolation from other risks that they may face at the same time. When you buy disability insurance, do you also think about other risks that influence your financial well-being? For example, if your spouse works, the impact of disability on your household income would be less, and you might need lower insurance, or perhaps your investments will do very well or poorly. Financial portfolio theory teaches that the risk of any single stock depends on how it correlates with the rest of the portfolio and that significant diversification of risk can be achieved by investing small amounts in many stocks rather than one big sum in a favorite stock. Likewise, people may fail to appreci-

How Well Do You Deal with Ambiguity?

You are faced with two jars, both of which contain a mix of red and white balls, as illustrated in Exhibit A-1. Jar A contains exactly fifty red balls and fifty white balls. You can draw one ball without looking. If it is white, you receive nothing, but if it is red, you receive a payoff of $100. In this case, you know you have exactly a fifty-fifty probability of drawing the desired color. Jar B also contains a hundred red and white balls, but in unknown proportion. Again, if you draw a white ball you receive nothing, but if you draw a red ball, you receive a certain payoff of $100.

You have an opportunity to draw a ball from either jar A or jar B. Which one would you choose? Most people favor jar A, where they know the probability precisely. Of course, jar B is, rationally speaking, the same. In the absence of further information, you cannot really assume that there are more red than white balls in jar B (or vice versa), so your chances are fifty-fifty for drawing red. But people don't average out the ambiguity in jar B and intuitively dislike its greater uncertainty. This, in turn, creates opportunity for those who recognize that the two jars are equally attractive in a statistical and economic sense.

Exhibit A-1: Which Mix Do You Prefer?

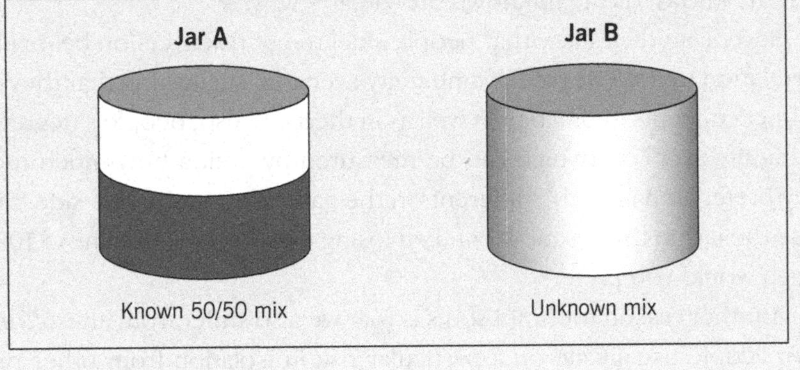

ate the effect of risk diversification over time. Being in the stock market may seem risky in any one year, but over the long run the yearly fluctuations cancel out, so investing in equities will seem safer. It is easier, however, to deal with risks one at a time even though that heightens the danger. Portfolio thinking elevates the level of analysis to a larger pool of risks and as such may reduce the anxiety associated with any single investment or project. The law of averages is usually on your side.

Finally, we suffer greatly from *context effects* when choosing among risky options. How a question is asked often determines the answer. When Internet visitors are asked to opt *in* to an online mailing list, far fewer say yes than if they are asked to opt *out.* If insurance buyers are asked if they want to give up tort protection, they are far less likely to do so than if they are asked if they want to add it on. Researchers also found strong context effects based on what other options are presented[17] and get different answers depending on whether the trade-offs among alternatives are expressed concretely in, say, dollars versus probabilities.[18]

Why We Need Help

Given the limitations of our perception and action in the face of uncertainty, we cannot rely upon intuition alone in uncertain environments. Pilots can fly airplanes on visual as long as the weather is clear, but when the fog and storm clouds roll in, they turn to instrumentation such as radar. We can't trust our intuition or perception in an uncertain environment. We need new tools and frameworks to address these challenges. While few pilots would ignore the instruments available to fly through foul weather, many managers—due to overconfidence and the lack of a Federal Aviation Administration for corporate navigation—trust their gut rather than applying the tools and frameworks that are available for making their way through turbulence.

The frameworks and approaches discussed in the book, as well as the specific tools outlined in Appendix B, are designed to address these limitations. They can help overcome the challenges of our myopic eyes and timid souls to see more effectively and act more intelligently in an uncertain future.

Appendix B
Uncertainty Tool Kit

"We should all be concerned about the future because we have to spend the rest of our lives there."
—C. F. KETTERING

While I have focused on an overall process for planning under uncertainty, a wide range of specific tools and methods can be brought to bear on this challenge. We use many of these approaches when implementing our framework, to deepen, quantify, and clarify issues in the process. This appendix offers a very quick summary of some of the tools that managers need in their arsenal. This list is by no means exhaustive; nor are the descriptions thorough, but they should point the reader in the direction of other useful resources.[1]

The list that follows ranges from highly quantitative tools to softer organizational approaches. First, I provide a brief description of each approach and in the second paragraph comment on its potential value in managing or coping with uncertainty. I assume that the reader is familiar with MBA terminology (which has been italicized).

The tools below are organized according to the "strategic compass" framework presented in Chapter 1 (see Exhibit 1-4), focusing on three primary processes:

- developing multiple views of the future to embrace uncertainty
- creating a strategic vision that balances commitment and flexibility
- monitoring in real time to adjust dynamically, when needed

Some of the tools are applicable in more than one area or across the entire process. They appear here in the section where they typically add the most value to the process.

The wide selection of tools, along with the dynamic nature of strategic planning, makes their implementation a complex challange, which probably explains why not many companies use them all and so few use them well. Tools such as NPV analysis are much more widely used than scenario planning in large part because they are fairly straightforward in concept and application. But as managers face increasingly sophisticated business environments, they need to be aware of more sophisticated tools as well. In many cases, these tools already exist in their organizations but are not widely used.

Ultimately, technology may offer a way to create a more user-friendly interface. This could give managers access to a broad array of tools and approaches in a highly user-friendly manner. These systems could also facilitate ongoing dynamic monitoring. That way managers can have access to sophisticated planning support without the trade-offs of overwhelming complexity and high cost in time and other resources. This is the largely unrealized promise of decision support systems, and a critical task for researchers and executives. Until then, managers have to pick and choose judiciously from these approaches to use tools that make the most sense given the nature of the problem, the skills in the organization, and available resources.

Experience Multiple Futures

The core tool we recommend in developing multiple views of the future is scenario planning, but there are many other tools and approaches that can generate fresh ideas, deepen insights or offer more rigorous analysis of the external environment.

Scenario Planning

Scenario planning explores the interaction of external conditions that may create vastly different futures (see Chapter 3). It is used to encourage creative thinking, to make informed decisions, and to develop creative strategies. This method separates predictable trends from unknowable uncertainties, and then plays out their possible interactions using a limited number of scenarios.

Scenario planning directly embraces uncertainty by identifying those unknowns that matter most in shaping the future. Rather than considering all variables and outcomes, it focuses on the most fundamental ones, then describes in some detail what range of futures lies ahead. The method can be used intuitively as well as quantitatively.

Analogies, History, and Reference Cases

This approach studies past experiences, similar industries, and analogous situations to derive learning and anticipate potential outcomes. The essence of this technique is pattern matching and case-based reasoning. It can either be used to develop automated responses as practiced in medicine, pilot training, and emergency work or as object lessons to develop new insights. The celebrated Harvard case method falls in this second category.

It may be especially useful in highly uncertain and novel environments to draw parallels, note similarities, surface insights, identify trends, and generate creative thinking. An example would be to compare the boom and bust of the dot-coms with early periods in history, or to compare and contrast the emerging field of genomics and proteomics with that of a more mature technology such as monoclonal antibodies.

Contingency Planning

A type of planning that seeks to identify key areas of uncertainty in strategies and projects to be ready with a plan B in case the future turns out differently than expected. The operative motto is that no plan survives contact with reality and that every plan is a basis for change. Apart from intellectual preparedness, contingency planning also requires organizational preparedness, in monitoring external change as well as having managers in place who can pull the trigger on plan B when needed.

As the title implies, this approach directly focuses on possible deviations from the plan by anticipating possible contingencies (i.e., uncertainties) that may arise. Of course, the most difficult part of this analysis lies in anticipating the unexpected—which by definition is hard. However, great value can be garnered by simply preparing plans for those uncertainties that everybody acknowledges and by building in some rapid response capability to deal with those things that were not on anybody's radar screen.

Extrapolative Forecasting

This approach predicts the future by identifying past trends. Predictions are sometimes based on sophisticated statistical analysis such as *regressions, econometric models,* or *neural nets* and other times more on visual interpretations. It is used most effectively when the future is reasonably predictable and can be bounded statistically.

The key premise of forecasting is that the future is not entirely random and that patterns can be inferred from past data once we remove layers of random noise that mask the underlying trends. The various tools available help manage uncertainty by distinguishing noise from signal or by detecting relationships not apparent to the eye.

Sensitivity Analysis

Any formal analysis is based on a set of assumptions and the optimal course of action may be more or less dependent on the accuracy of these underlying premises. By changing the nature of an assumption, or by varying numerical estimates across a wide range, insights can be obtained about which premises and parameters the final solution is most sensitive to. Once this is known, these critical estimates or parameters can then be approximated with greater precision. The easiest form of sensitivity analysis is to observe the effect of just one small change, while keeping all else constant. Larger changes may require corresponding changes in other parameters which often greatly complicate the analysis.

Whenever uncertainty is quantitatively modeled, it usually entails estimates of the mean and variance of various probability distributions, and perhaps of other distribution parameters as well. In project planning, for example, estimates may be made about the completion times and costs of all key tasks needed to finish the project. Since some tasks may become bottlenecks in the overall project, sensitivity analysis can be used to assess how much delay or cost overrun such critical component tasks may cause. Approaches such as *PERT* (Program Evaluation and Review Technique) combine *critical path analysis, simulation* and *sensitivity analysis* to better manage the inherent uncertainty of large-scale projects.

Management Flight Simulators

This approach uses computer-based simulation games to approximate business conditions and test key decisions dynamically. Sometimes they are used to play strategists against each other, and at other times strategists play against an assumed competitor. External shocks, or unknown relationships between, say, price and demand, are what makes such games challenging.

Although the complexity of a computer simulation can be purely deterministic in origin, the decision maker nonetheless faces multiple unknowns about the nature of the marketplace as well as the downstream consequences of actions taken. The creation of such uncertainty in a simulation game can help better understand the external environment.

Monte Carlo Simulation

Monte Carlo simulation is a quantitative tool to help evaluate the consequences of complex strategic initiatives by acknowledging the uncertainty associated with forecasts. Akin to spinning the ball millions of times in roulette to estimate the chance of getting a particular outcome, it combines computer models and *random number generators* to examine interactions among random variables that defy closed form analysis.

This tool can help manage uncertainty by estimating the probability distributions associated with variables of interest, such as the unknown completion time of a project, waiting time in a queue, or the rate of return on an uncertain investment project. In addition to bounding the uncertainty range on single variables, it can help estimate correlations among variables as well.

Develop a Robust Strategic Vision

The strategic vision is shaped by the Key Success Factors needed for the future and the capabilities the organization already possesses. In addition to developing rich scenarios, as discussed above, this process requires an understanding of internal core competencies and market needs. This vision is then used to analyze specific decisions and generate strategic options, which can be analyzed both through NPV and options frameworks.

Core Competency Analysis

This tool identifies an organization's capabilities (skills and resources) that underlie its current product, marketing, or technology strengths. It focuses on a limited number of capabilities that set firms apart from each other. These capabilities are often described in terms of the activities, skills and resources needed to deploy them. Core competency analysis can help firms decide which organizational activities should be outsourced and which to invest in further.

The link to uncertainty is two-fold. First, emphasizing core competencies instills a focus on flexibility, since organizational capabilities can usually be leveraged or reconfigured in new ways if circumstances change. As such, it enhances the organization's ability to deal with unexpected change. Second, the management of uncertainty could be studied as a core competence in its own right, whether as part of risk management, organizational agility or crisis management. In such industries as insurance and trading, risk management would naturally be considered a core competence.

Corporate Venturing Units

Corporate venturing is the creation of an internal investment group that funds new technologies and businesses (either fully or in partnership with other organizations) both inside and outside the company. The basic strategy here is one of organizational separation in order to better deal with high levels of uncertainty. The new unit may apply different investment criteria and failure tolerances. It may also engage in sophisticated hedging and risk-management techniques.

This organizational separation approach to managing uncertainty fosters learning and will likely create new strategies and options that would not survive in the old structure. It allows companies to place small bets in specific areas to hedge, experiment in new areas, and learn about non-core businesses that may grow in the future. Importantly, it may permit the organization to attract talent and skill sets that otherwise would not develop.

Decision Analysis

Decision analysis is a set of rigorous analytic methodologies that help decision makers clearly identify alternatives and assess potential outcomes plus their probabilities, as well as any relevant downstream choices. In addition, the decision makers are asked to become very explicit about their trade-offs among competing objectives, including attitude toward risk, such that the decision can be made in a rational deductive manner. Specific tools here include *decision trees, probability theory, expected utility analysis,* and *simulation.*

Decision analysis follows a divide-and-conquer strategy in tackling uncertainty. It seeks to isolate the residual uncertainty in the problem (that is, that part of the uncertainty that truly cannot be controlled) and then uses computational methods to choose the alternative that maximizes the decision maker's subjective expected payoff (called *utility*).

Insurance and Risk Management

Traditionally companies made isolated decisions about which exposures to insure and which not. Increasingly, the focus is now on total risk management, reflecting the myriad of risk-management solutions available in the market place. Complex hedging strategies, involving exotic derivatives, are commonly used by firms to manage their earnings and protect their assets.

To fully utilize these technologies, companies must adopt a total risk perspective in which both the gain and loss side are carefully assessed. In addition, a portfolio view must be adopted to reflect that the various risk exposures are not statistically independent. Decisions about insurance, hedging, self-protection, etc., should be made comprehensively rather than piecemeal. ERM (enterprise risk management) is an emerging organizational function focused on these issues.

Net Present Value (NPV)

This method values strategic projects by considering the present value of future cash flows by adjusting them for both time and risk. The time factor is dealt with by using appropriate interest rates for the time frame considered and recognizing the compound nature of interest. The risk adjustment requires estimates of both *expected values* of the cash flows and their correlations with the overall market portfolio.

Specifically, the treatment of risk in NPV consists of two main components. First, the uncertainty surrounding cash flow estimates in any one period is averaged out by computing an expected value in the numerator of the NPV formula. Second, a risk premium is added in the denominator (on top of the *risk-free rate*) that concerns only the *systematic risk* in a project. This market-based discount rate (called *beta*) ignores any risk that can be diversified away by investors in their portfolios.

Portfolio Analysis

Portfolio analysis explores the combined effects of having multiple eggs in one basket. The tool can be used quantitatively (as in financial portfolio analysis) or qualitatively to portray an array of options (as in the famous Boston Consulting Group matrices plotting business units in terms of growth vs. market share). The key notion is to identify a relevant set of investments and plot them with respects to some key attributes such as return and risk, and then study the behavior of the aggregate. Issues of diversification and balance, based on relationships that exist among the options within the portfolio, are central to this tool.

In financial portfolio theory, the overall risk of all investments combined is computed based on the mean and variance of each individual security as well as the *covariance matrix* across all securities. This permits an optimal portfolio weighing. Portfolio analysis is also central to *total risk management,* in which a firm's insurance policies, self-insurance, and risky investments are all considered simultaneously and in the aggregate. In strategic settings, portfolio analysis may address risk issues of cash flow balancing, strategic positioning, or the spacing of opportunities over time (such as the product pipeline of a pharmaceutical firm).

Real-Options Analysis

Real-options analysis values strategic initiatives by recognizing all the downstream choices that may be encountered over a project's life (see Chapter 6). Once it has identified them, it then tries to value the benefit of any such flexibility. This method recognizes that a project's value may change over time due to the introduction of new information plus the ability to act on that information.

Real-options analysis is especially suitable for staged investment decisions in highly uncertain environments, when clear milestone events or future decision-making points can be identified. The technique basically relies on *decision tree analysis* and computing the *value of information.*

Dynamically Monitor and Adjust

To monitor effectively, organizations need to create systems for tracking key changes internally and externally. Organizational nervous systems can be strengthened through knowledge management systems. Key assumptions and early warning signs can be identified through market research. Systems dynamic monitoring and war games can provide frameworks for continuing to explore changes in the competitive environment that will shape the company's future.

Knowledge Management

This approach refers to systems and processes that collect and codify an organization's information and other knowledge assets, about both the internal and the external environment. The aim is to provide broad, timely, and user-friendly access to information that is accurate, up to date, and within ready reach of those who need it.

Superior information, when obtained in a timely fashion, can help assess external uncertainties, from trends in sales data to patent filings or competitive actions. Since uncertainty ultimately stems from limited knowledge, managing and improving information can be directly relevant to assessing and coping with uncertainty.

Consumer and Market Research

Consumer and market research determine market needs through surveys, *conjoint analysis,* focus groups, lead user research and other means. These methods are used to unveil or better estimate consumer preferences for new products or markets, often using a combination of quantitative and qualitative information. They can also be used to track and monitor changes in the competitive and market landscape.

Market research tools can help estimate uncertain demand for a new product or service by generating new data to test key assumptions. Also, they can help implement and adjust strategies as markets change. When faced with high uncertainty—in cases of new product launch or an extension into new markets—using a combination of methods is often recommended (referred to as *triangulation*).

Organizational Benchmarking

Organizational benchmarking compares an organization's processes and performance with those of other organizations, either in the same industry or "best in breed." It is used to identify best practices, transfer learning and to set targets and goals. Benchmarking will encourage organizations to adopt a more holistic view about how they manage uncertainty, by conceptualizing it as a process that can be improved and monitored over time.

Benchmarking can be used to reduce competitive uncertainty by better understanding how rivals operate, or it could be focused on studying how the best firms manage uncertainty. Uncertainty can be studied at multiple levels here, from individual attitudes and skill to project-level techniques, as well as in terms of strategic and organizational orientation toward uncertainty, including leadership style, controls, and incentives.

System Dynamics Modeling

In order to explore relationships between cause and effect in complex business environments, this diagnostic tool requires substantial analysis and dissection of organizational processes. This method especially focuses on the role of feedback loops and the often-counterintuitive results they produce. *Influence diagrams* are usually the first step, followed by algebraic representations of the relationships in the form of a computer model.

Although the system dynamics model need not have uncertainty in it per se, the complex interactions it entails will often appear to the user as being uncertain. In addition, uncertainty can be explicitly introduced either as an input to the model (in the spirit of *Monte Carlo simulation*) or inside as a random coefficient denoting uncertain demand, interest rates, technological breakthroughs, or competitive reactions.

Game Theory

Game theory studies how strategic decisions will be affected by the actions of presumably rational opponents. The core notion is to anticipate the actions of parties whose interests and influences run counter to those of the decision maker. Game theory models can become quite complex analytically and may not always yield clear predictions.

The focus here is squarely on better understanding the uncertainties caused by the willful actions of others, in the hope of better responding to their moves. It can reduce uncertainty by showing that certain competitive interactions are unlikely or irrational, or highlight the inherent unpredictability of the situation being faced. It can also help prepare for real-time adjustments in the heat of battle.

Fuzzy Logic / Artificial Intelligence

Increasingly researchers are creating intelligent systems that can deal with real-world challenges. Whereas the initial focus was on handling complexity (for example, in chess or medical diagnosis), more recent methods are tackling uncertainty as well. I classify under this large rubric expert systems, neural nets, genetic algorithms, and fuzzy logic, as well as related tools or methods.

Neural nets have been used, for example, to reprice complex securitized mortgage portfolios as interest rates change. Genetic algorithms introduce random elements in dynamic Darwinian simulations to see which variations will survive. And fuzzy logic tries to mimic the human capacity to deal with ill-defined constructs and uncertain boundaries. It is used, for instance, to operate elevators and in auto-focus cameras.

War Rooms / Opportunity Centers

This approach uses the visual display (either online or offline) of opportunities, threats, and issues that an organization is monitoring. The emphasis here is on visually organizing a large amount of complex information and making it accessible in a user-friendly form to groups who periodically discuss the meaning and implications of the ever-changing picture.

It is used to encourage learning and information sharing in highly uncertain or complex environments. The focus is on creating a context and place where uncertainty can be better tracked, assessed, and managed, with perhaps a central command center to allow for fast decision making. The military metaphor of a war room captures well the spirit of dynamic monitoring.

Notes

Preface: Tumultuous Times

1. Calmetta Coleman, "Buffett Says Insurers Made Mistake on Terror as Berkshire Posts Loss," *Wall Street Journal,* November 12, 2001, B-3.

Chapter 1: Embracing Uncertainty

1. Frank H. Knight, *Risk, Uncertainty and Profits* (1921; Chicago: University of Chicago Press, 1972), 310–11.
2. Almar Latour, "A Blaze in Albuquerque Sets Off Major Crisis for Cell-Phone Giants," *Wall Street Journal,* January 29, 2001, A-1.
3. George Anders, "John Chambers After the Deluge," *Fast Company,* July 2001, p. 102; Stephanie N. Mehta, "Cisco Fractures Its Own Fairy Tale," *Fortune,* May 14, 2001.
4. "Nokia Succumbs," *Economist,* June 16, 2001, 65.
5. Roger Lowenstein, *When Genius Failed: The Rise and Fall of Long-Term Capital Management* (New York: Random House, 2000).
6. As the book *When Genius Failed* chronicles in vivid detail, former Salomon Brothers bond traders and leading academics teamed up in LTCM to apply the most sophisticated arbitrage models to the worlds of fixed-income bonds and related indexes. Their so-called hedge fund, however, was more like a highly leveraged gamble that eliminated (via the hedge) many common risk factors in order to invest all capital in a highly focused bet on a particular spread in interest rates getting smaller. These convergence predictions were based on historical patterns and required enough staying power to see markets return to relative equilibrium. At times LTCM was leveraged more than a hundred times. Its capital base of $3 to $5 billion provided the foundation for a highly complex portfolio of exotic trading positions (calls, paths, straddles, and the like) numbering well over a hundred at any time and representing over $100 billion in balance sheet assets (and liabilities). The LTCM team viewed itself as the ultimate master of uncertainty, using complex quantitative models and Nobel-laureate brain power. But the team was courting disaster, and in the fall of 1997 it all collapsed. One of the head traders (Larry Hildebrandt) saw his net worth go from well over $700 million in May to negative in October. He filed for bankruptcy.
7. Research in the field of strategy has examined the relative importance of various sources of profitability following Richard Rumelt's finding that returns on assets vary far more within industries than across industries. The data shown in the table are from Jaime A. Roquebert, Robert L. Phillips

and Peter A. Westfall, "Markets vs. Management: What 'Drives' Profitability?" *Strategic Management Journal,* 17, 8 (October 1996), 653–664. For a summary of eleven different empirical studies on this complex question see Edward H. Bowman and Constance E. Helfat, "Does Corporate Strategy Matter?" *Strategic Management Journal,* 22, 1, Jan. 2001, 1–23. For some earlier data of return generating models, plus more accessible explanations of how they are constructed, see George Foster, *Financial Statement Analysis,* Prentice Hall, 1978, Chapter 5.

8. The self-serving rationalizations in CEOs' letters to shareholders can be found in Gerald Salancik and James Meindl, "Corporate Attributions as Strategic Illusions of Management Control," *Administrative Science Quarterly* 29 (1984): 238–54.
9. Gary Hamel and C. K. Prahalad, *Competing for the Future* (Boston: Harvard Business School Press, 1994), 4.
10. For behavioral research on the hindsight bias, see Baruch Fischhoff and Ruth Beyth, "'I Knew It Would Happen'—Remembered Probabilities of Once-Future Things," *Organizational Behavior and Human Performance* 13 (1975): 1–16. For causes of hindsight bias, see Terry Connolly and Edward W. Bukszar, "Hindsight Bias: Self-Flattery or Cognitive Error?" *Journal of Behavioral Decision Making* 3 (1990): 205–11.
11. The idea of prospective hindsight is discussed and documented in Deborah J. Mitchell, J. Edward Russo, and Nancy Pennington, "Back to the Future: Temporal Perspective in the Explanation of Events," *Journal of Behavioral Decision Making* 2 (1989): 25–39. Prospective hindsight works to increase the number and specificity of the reasons generated by increasing the certainty of the event. What matters most is not the time perspective, looking back versus looking forward, but the implied certainty of the event. People work more effectively to generate reasons for an event when it is certain than when it is still uncertain. This is true even if the event is in the past but the person generating reasons for it is not certain which way it turned out. In the real world, the temporal setting correlates highly with people's perceived degree of certainty about what happened or may happen.
12. See Joseph L. Bower and Clayton M. Christensen, "Disruptive Technologies: Catching the Wave," *Harvard Business Review* (January–February 1995): 43–53; Clayton M. Christensen, *The Innovator's Dilemma* (Boston: Harvard Business School Press, 1997); and Richard Foster and Sarah Kaplan, *Creative Destruction* (New York: Currency Doubleday, 2001).
13. I use the term *volatility* here in the colloquial sense. In finance and economics, volatility is usually measured as variance or standard deviation. A similar picture would emerge if using those metrics. I use the range measure here for ease of explanation as well as to accentuate the full extent of variability observed in the Nasdaq index from year to year.
14. Susquehanna compares a stock's current price level with its thirty- or sixty-day call option price, and then uses the Black-Scholes option pricing formula to impute an implied variance for that stock. This variance measures

the uncertainty the market is assuming for the stock over the time period of the option. These implied volatility measures have greatly increased over the past few years according to Susquehanna's Brian Kanaga.

15. C. West Churchman, *The Design of Inquiring Systems* (New York: Basic Books, 1971).
16. For a more detailed discussion of epistemic risk see Yakov Ben-Haim, *Information Gap Decision Theory: Decisions under Severe Uncertainty* (New York: Academic Press, 2001). The term epistemic risk has been used in seismic risk assessment to distinguish risks that arise from of our lack of knowledge about the applicable family of probability distributions (e.g., to characterize the recurrence of earthquakes in given fault fields) from so-called aleatory risk that arises from a *known* stochastic process (like gases in a confined space following Boyle's Law). The distinction is essentially one between unspecifiable uncertainty and quantifiable risk.
17. For a more detailed discussion, see Paul J. H. Schoemaker, "Strategy, Complexity, and Economic Rent," *Management Science* 36 (October 1990): 1178–92.
18. See Michael E. Porter, *Competitive Strategy* (New York: Free Press, 1980) as well as his *Competitive Advantage* (New York: Free Press, 1985).
19. Richard D'Aveni, *Hypercompetition* (New York: Free Press, 1994).
20. Gary Hamel and C. K. Prahalad, *Competing for the Future* (Boston: Harvard Business School Press, 1994).
21. Although not all scholars agree on how to distinguish risk, uncertainty, and ambiguity, and some even question whether these distinctions are useful, I favor the following definitions. In the case of risk, there is agreement on the probabilities of various outcomes occurring, such as when flipping a coin. In the case of uncertainty, there is no agreement about these probabilities—as when flipping a thumbtack—but there is agreement on the potential outcomes. In the case of ambiguity, there is agreement neither on the outcome space nor on the probabilities for those outcomes acknowledged. In the case of ignorance, we lack any confidence or agreement in even defining the problem. For behavioral research on risk versus ambiguity, see Hillel J. Einhorn and Robin M. Hogarth, "Ambiguity and Uncertainty in Probabilistic Inference," *Psychological Review* 92 (1985): 433–61; Hillel J. Einhorn and Robin M. Hogarth, "Decision-Making under Ambiguity," *Journal of Business* 59 (1986): 225–50; C. Fox and Amos Tversky, "Ambiguity Aversion and Comparative Ignorance," *Quarterly Journal of Economics* 110 (1995): 585–603. The issue of ignorance is addressed in Robin Hogarth and Howard Kunreuther, "Decision Making Under Ignorance: Arguing with Yourself," *Journal of Risk and Uncertainty* 10 (1995): 15–36. For a deeper discussion about the various meanings of probability—and the difficulty people have deciding under risk—see Paul J. H. Schoemaker, "The Expected Utility Model: Its Variants, Purposes, Evidence and Limitations," *Journal of Economic Literature* 20 (June 1982): 529–63.
22. J. Edward Russo and Paul J. H. Schoemaker, "Managing Overconfidence," *Sloan Management Review* 33, 2 (Winter 1992): 7–18.

23. Paul Slovic, Baruch Fischhoff, and Sarah Lichtenstein, "Accident Probabilities and Seat Belt Usage: A Psychological Perspective," *Accident Analysis and Prevention* 10 (1978): 281–85.
24. In actuality, people's risk preferences are much more complicated than my cursory discussion allows. When faced with pure losses, people are often risk seeking. Further complicating the picture is people's overweighting of low probabilities and underweighting of high ones. A parsimonious account of these tendencies is offered in D. Kahneman and A. Tversky, "Prospect Theory: An Analysis of Decision under Risk," *Econometrica* 47 (1979): 263–92. For a less technical discussion see D. Kahneman and A. Tversky, "Choices, Values and Frames," *American Psychologist* 39 (1984): 341–50.
25. See M. Cohen, J. Jaffray, and T. Said, "Individual Behavior under Risk and under Uncertainty: An Experimental Study," *Theory and Decisions* 18 (1985): 203–28; P. J. H. Schoemaker, "Choices Involving Uncertain Probabilities: Tests of Generalized Utility Models," *Journal of Economic and Organizational Behavior* 16 (1991): 295–317.
26. P. J. H. Schoemaker, "Multiple Scenario Development: Its Conceptual and Behavioral Foundation," *Strategic Management Journal* 14 (1993): 193–213.
27. Hugh Courtney, *20/20 Foresight* (Boston: Harvard Business School Press, 2001).
28. For a comprehensive review of the literature on intuition see Robin Hogarth, *Educating Intuition,* 2001, University of Chicago Press, and an article in the *Harvard Business Review* by Alden M. Hayashi, "When to Trust Your Gut," February 2001; Vol. 79, pg. 59. The view of intuition as tacit knowledge is well stated by Herbert A. Simon and Michael J. Prietula, "The Experts in Your Midst," *Harvard Business Review,* 1989, Jan.–Feb., 120–124. For a wide range of managerial views on intuition, see Weston H. Agor (ed.), *Intuition in Organizations* (New York: Sage Publications, 1989).
29. Arie de Geus, "Planning as Learning," *Harvard Business Review,* March–April 1988, pp. 70–74.
30. W. R. Ashby, *Introduction to Cybernetics* (New York: Basic Books, 1956).
31. F. Scott Fitzgerald, *The Crack Up* (New York: New Directions, 1945).
32. Amir D. Aczel, *The Riddle of the Compass* (New York: Harcourt, 2001), xi–xii, 103–104.
33. P. J. H. Schoemaker and C. A. J. M. van der Heijden, "Integrating Scenarios into Strategic Planning at Royal Dutch/Shell," *Planning Review* 20 (1992): 41–46.
34. For some well-known sources on scenario planning, see Pierre Wack, "Scenarios: Uncharted Waters Ahead," *Harvard Business Review* (September–October 1985); Peter Schwartz, *The Art of the Long View* (New York: Doubleday, 1991); Paul J. H. Schoemaker, "Scenario Planning: A Tool for Strategic Thinking," *Sloan Management Review* 36 (Winter 1995): 25–40; Cornelius van der Heijden, *The Art of Strategic Conversation* (New York: John Wiley, 1998); Gil Ringland, *Scenario Planning* (New York: John Wiley,

1998); L. Fahey and R. Randall, eds., *Learning from the Future* (New York: John Wiley, 1998); and Michel Godet, *Creating Futures: Scenario Planning as a Strategic Management Tool* (London: Economica, 2001).

Chapter 2: Preparing the Mind

1. Mary Gentile, Jeffery F. Rayport, and Sara B. Gant, *Miami Herald Publishing Co.,* Harvard Business School case no. 9-395-022 (Boston: Harvard Business School Press, 1995), 35–36.
2. David Lawrence, "A Once Optimistic Soul Is Discouraged," *Editor and Publisher,* January 20, 1996, 48.
3. Michael Mavaddat and I conducted most of the strategy sessions with *The Miami Herald,* with David Landsberg serving as the client's project leader. I thank both for their substantial contributions to this case.
4. J. Gilovich, "Seeing the Past in the Present: The Effect of Associations to Familiar Events on Judgments and Decisions," *Journal of Personality and Social Psychology* 40 (1981): 797–808.
5. Paul J. Schoemaker and J. Edward Russo, "Managing Frames to Make Better Decisions," in S. Hoch and H. Kunreuther, eds., *Wharton on Making Decisions* (New York: John Wiley, 2001), 131–55. The classic references to mental models and their cognitive functions are: Dedre Gentner and Albert L. Stevens, eds., *Mental Models* (Mahway, NJ: Lawrence Erlbaum Associates, 1983), and Philip N. Johnson-Laird, ed., *Mental Models,* 2nd ed. (Cambridge, MA: Harvard University Press, 1983).
6. The assumptions about how General Motors looked at its world in the late 1960s are from Peter Senge, *The Fifth Discipline* (New York: Currency Doubleday, 1990).
7. The concept of *thinking frame* as used here is much closer to the original notion of *frame* as it appeared in the field of artificial intelligence (AI) in the mid-1970s than to the *decision frame* concept currently popular in behavioral decision research. *Frame* was originally defined in AI as a method of organizing our knowledge about a concept to help focus attention and facilitate recall and inference. See Marvin L. Minsky, "A Framework for Presenting Knowledge," in P. Winston, ed., *The Psychology of Computer Vision* (New York: McGraw-Hill, 1975). In this view, frames are the mental structures and frameworks within which new information is interpreted through concepts acquired via previous experience. This notion of *thinking frames* is also closely related to what are called *schema* and *scripts* in cognitive psychology. Like frames in AI, schemas organize into a coherent whole a multitude of different component concepts and events. In the field of decision making, Amos Tversky and Daniel Kahneman brought the decision frame concept to great prominence by demonstrating that changes in the surface features of a decision frame can alter choices. Their specific definition is: "We use the term 'decision frame' to refer to the decision-

maker's conceptions of the acts, outcomes, and contingencies associated with a particular choice. The frame that a decision-maker adopts is controlled partly by the formulation of the problem and partly by the norms, habits, and personal characteristics of the decision-maker" (Amos Tversky and Daniel Kahneman, "The Framing of Decisions and the Psychology of Choice," *Science* 211 (1981): 453–58).

Chapter 3: Experiencing Multiple Futures

1. R. Thaler, "Toward a Positive Theory of Consumer Choice," *Journal of Economic Behavior and Organization* 1 (1980): 39–60.
2. I thank Michael Mavaddat for his contributions to the health care scenarios presented here, which constitute a synthesis of various DSI client projects we have worked on over the years.
3. P. J. H. Schoemaker, "When and How to Use Scenario Planning: A Heuristic Approach with Illustration," *Journal of Forecasting* 10 (1991): 549–64.
4. Howard Perlmutter, "On Deep Dialog," working paper for the Emerging Global Civilization Project, Wharton School, University of Pennsylvania, 1999.
5. Kees van der Heijden, *The Art of Strategic Conversation* (New York: John Wiley, 1998).
6. P. Ghemawat, *Commitment: The Dynamic of Strategy* (New York: Free Press, 1991).
7. J. Morecroft and J. Sterman, *Modeling for Learning Organizations* (Portland, OR: Productivity Press, 1994).
8. G. Shaw, R. Brown, and P. Bromiley, "Strategic Stories: How 3M is Rewriting Business Planning," *Harvard Business Review* (May–June 1998).

Chapter 4: Preparing for the Unknown

1. Roald Amundsen, *My Life as an Explorer* (New York: Doubleday, 1927), 236–37.
2. Roland Huntford, *The Last Place on Earth: Scott and Amundsen's Race to the South Pole* (New York: Modern Library, 1999). Huntford's criticisms of Scott's expedition have been controversial from the start. More recently, meteorologist Susan Solomon has proposed that the March winter Scott faced was much harsher than average (*The Coldest March,* New Haven: Yale University Press, 2001). I do not intend to enter into the running historical debate about Scott's and Amundsen's relative leadership skills; however one assesses their strengths in planning and leadership in retrospect, the fact remains that they made very different choices in resources and capabilities, which had a significant impact on their outcomes. Exploring these choices offers important lessons for business leaders.
3. The resource-based view of the firm was first formalized by B. Wernerfelt, "A Resource-Based View of the Firm," *Strategic Management Journal* 5 (1984): 171–80. Other key articles are: D. J. Teece, "Toward an Economic

Theory of the Multiproduct Firm," *Journal of Economic Behavior and Organization* 3 (1981): 39–63; J. Barney, "Firm Resources and Sustained Competitive Advantage," *Journal of Management* 17 (1991): 99–120; R. Amit and P. J. H. Schoemaker, "Strategic Assets and Organizational Rent," *Strategic Management Journal* 14 (1993): 33–46; D. J. Teece, G. Pisano, and A. Shuen, "Dynamic Capabilities and Strategic Management," *Strategic Management Journal* 18 (1997): 509–33.

4. C. K. Prahalad and G. Hamel, "The Core Competence of the Corporation," *Harvard Business Review* (May–June 1990): 79–91.
5. J. A. deVasconcellos and D. C. Hambrick, "Key Success Factors: Test of a General Theory in the Mature Industrial-Product Sector," *Strategic Management Journal* 10 (1989): 367–82.
6. R. Rumelt, "How Much Does Industry Matter?" *Strategic Management Journal* 12 (1991): 167–85.
7. J. S. Bain, *Industrial Organization,* 2d ed. (New York: John Wiley, 1968); R. A. Garda, "A Strategic Approach to Market Segmentation," *McKinsey Quarterly* (Autumn 1981): 16–29.
8. Paul E. Green and Abba M. Krieger, "Using Conjoint Analysis to View Competitive Interaction through the Customer's Eyes," in George S. Day and David J. Reibstein, eds., *Wharton on Dynamic Competitive Strategy* (New York: John Wiley, 1997), 343–67.
9. The chart showing the changing segment boundaries in the computing industry was taken from David B. Yoffe, *Apple Computer—1992,* Harvard Business School case no. 792-081 (Boston: Harvard Business School Press, 1993), based on a presentation by John Sculley, then the CEO of Apple.
10. Thomas B. Rosenstiel, "Old Demons at Bay—U.S. Newspapers Face Future with New Confidence," *Los Angeles Times,* April 30, 1986.
11. George S. Day, "Assessing Future Markets for New Technologies," in George S. Day and Paul J. H. Schoemaker, eds., *Wharton on Managing Emerging Technologies* (New York: John Wiley, 2000), 127–49.
12. This example is adapted from Vincent Barabba, *Meeting of the Minds: Creating the Market-Based Enterprise* (Boston: Harvard Business School Press, 1995).

Chapter 5: Building a Robust Strategic Vision

1. Richard Melcher and Amy Barrett, "Fields of Genes," *Business Week,* April 12, 1999.
2. Joan Magretta, "Growth through Global Sustainability: An Interview with Monsanto's CEO, Robert Shapiro," *Harvard Business Review* (January–February 1997): 81.
3. Sam Jaffe, "Why Monsanto and American Home Are Pooling Their Genes," *BusinessWeek,* June 2, 1989.
4. Heesun Wee, "The Missing Synergy That's Killing Life Sciences," *BusinessWeek Online,* January 2, 2001.

5. David P. Baron, "Integrated Strategy: Market and Nonmarket Components," *California Management Review* 37 (Winter 1995): 5.
6. Karl Weick, *Sensemaking in Organizations* (New York: Sage Publications, 1995), 54–56.
7. Gerard H. Langeler, "The Vision Trap," *Harvard Business Review* (March–April 1992): 46–55. See also Michael E. Raynor, "That Vision Thing: Do We Need It?" *Long Range Planning* 31 (1998): 368–76. The power of a sound strategic vision is amply documented in James C. Collins, *Built to Last: Successful Habits of Visionary Companies* (New York: HarperBusiness, 1997).
8. Ray A. Goldberg and Thomas N. Urban, *Monsanto Co.: The Coming of Age of Biotechnology,* Harvard Business School case no. 9-596-034 (Boston: Harvard Business School Press, 1996), 14.
9. Alfred D. Chandler, *Strategy and Structure: Chapters in the History of the American Industrial Enterprise* (Cambridge, MA: MIT Press, 1962).
10. George Stalk, "Time—The Next Source of Competitive Advantage," *Harvard Business Review* (July–August 1988): 41–51.
11. See Corporate Leadership Council *Vision of the Future* (Washington, DC: Advisory Board Co., 1995), 31, as well as C. K. Prahalad and Gary Hamel, "The Core Competence of the Corporation," *Harvard Business Review* (May–June 1990): 79–91.
12. C.K. Prahalad and Gary Hamel, "The Core Competence of the Corporation," see note 11.
13. H. Itami, *Mobilizing Invisible Assets* (Cambridge, MA: Harvard University Press, 1987).
14. I thank Michael Mavaddat and Doug Randall for their great help with this client project.
15. Ilya Prigogene and Isabelle Stengers, *Order Out of Chaos: Man's New Dialogue with Nature* (New York: Bantam Doubleday Dell, 1989).

Chapter 6: Creating Flexible Options

1. Pankaj Ghemawat and Patricio del Sol, "Commitment versus Flexibility?" *California Management Review* 40 (Summer 1998): 26–42.
2. "Telecoms Debt: Unburdening," *Economist,* May 12, 2001, 71.
3. For more specific techniques, numerous excellent books on creativity can be consulted. See in particular Paul Watzlawick, John H. Weakland, and Richard Fisch, *Change: Principles of Problem Formulation and Problem Resolution* (New York: W.W. Norton, 1974); James L. Adams, *Conceptual Blockbusting* (Reading, MA: Addison Wesley Longman, 1986); Edward de Bono, *Lateral Thinking: Creativity Step by Step* (New York: Harper & Row, 1973); and Roger van Oech, *A Whack on the Side of the Head: How You Can Be More Creative,* rev. ed. (New York: Warner Books, 1998), which even comes with a Wack Pack of cards. For creativity in an organizational context, see Robert Lawrence Kuhn, ed., *Handbook for Creative and Innovative Managers* (New York: McGraw-Hill, 1987); Jane Henry, ed., *Creative Management* (Thousand Oaks, CA: Sage Publications, 1991); and Alan G.

Robinson and Sam Stern, *Corporate Creativity* (San Francisco: Berrett-Koehler, 1998), 9–11. For a comparison of techniques, see Kenneth R. MacCrimmon and Christian Wagner, "Stimulating Ideas Through Creativity Software," *Management Science* 40 (November 1994): 1514–32.

4. Michael Gazzaniga, *The Mind's Past* (Berkeley and Los Angeles: University of California Press, 1998).
5. Xerox's PARC "Workscapes of the Future" project was described in Elizabeth Weil, "Brainstorming the Future," *Fast Company* 8 (April 1997): 100. The BrainStore's BrainNet is described in Anna Muoio, "Great Ideas in Aisle 9," *Fast Company* 33 (April 2000): 46.
6. See Vincent Barabba, *Meeting of the Minds: Creating the Market-Based Enterprise* (Boston: Harvard Business School Press, 1995). The study of the potential for copiers also overlooked the huge demand for the copying of copies, beyond simply copying originals.
7. "Exploiting Uncertainty," *BusinessWeek,* June 7, 1999, 118–24.
8. See Paul E. Green and Abba M. Krieger, "Using Conjoint Analysis to View Competitive Interaction through the Customer's Eyes," in George S. Day and David Reibstein, eds., *Wharton on Dynamic Competitive Strategy* (New York: John Wiley, 1997), 343–67.
9. See Glen L. Urban, Bruce D. Weinberg, and John R. Hauser, "Premarket Forecasting of Really-New Products," *Journal of Marketing* 60 (January 1996): 47–60, for a description of the method, and Eric Almquist and Gordon Wyner, "Identifying the Opportunities of the Future," *Mercer Management Journal* 10 (1998): 31–40 for its application to the broadband market.
10. Avinash K. Dixit and Barry J. Nalebuff, *Thinking Strategically* (New York: W.W. Norton, 1991), provides a nontechnical overview of game theory. See also Adam M. Brandenburger and Barry J. Nalebuff, *Coopetition* (New York: Doubleday, 1997).
11. David J. Reibstein and Mark J. Chussil, "Putting the Lesson Before the Test: Using Simulation to Analyze and Develop Competitive Strategies," in George S. Day and David Reibstein, eds., *Wharton on Dynamic Competitive Strategy,* (New York, John Wiley, 1997).
12. Paul R. Kleindorfer, Howard C. Kunreuther, and Paul J. H. Schoemaker, *Decision Sciences: An Integrative Perspective* (New York: Cambridge University Press, 1993), 233–36.
13. Kathleen M. Eisenhardt and Donald N. Sull, "Strategy as Simple Rules," *Harvard Business Review* (January 2001): 10.
14. William F. Hamilton and Graham R. Mitchell, "Managing R&D as a Strategic Option," *Research Technology Management* 31 (May–June 1988): 15–22; Edward H. Bowman and Dileep Hurry, "Strategy Through the Options Lens: An Integrated View of Resource Investments and the Incremental-Choice Process," *Academy of Management Review* 18 (1993): 760–82; Rita G. McGrath, "A Real Options Logic for Initiation Technology Positioning Investments," *Academy of Management Review* 22 (1997): 974–96.
15. For further detail on how to manage project-level uncertainty, see Arnoud

De Meyer et al. "Managing Project Uncertainty," *Sloan Management Review* 43, 2, (Winter 2002), 60–68.

16. Various studies show that people may reject gambles in isolation that they would gladly accept in combination (or vice versa). Consider this simple example: Option A involves a fifty-fifty chance of gaining $100 or losing $100. Option B offers a one-in-three chance at gaining $200 and a two-in-three chance of losing $100. When examined in isolation, neither of these two options may be attractive. However, when combined into option C, the new gamble entails four possible payoffs, namely getting $300, $100, or $0 or losing $200, with probabilities of one in six, one in six, two in six, and two in six respectively. The combined option is clearly different from either of its components, offering just a one-in-three chance of loss compared to one-in-two for A and two-in-three for B. The combined gamble may be attractive to people, whereas its components may not.
17. Eric D. Beinhocker, "Robust Adaptive Strategies," *Sloan Management Review* 40 (Spring 1999): 95–106.

Chapter 7: Dynamic Monitoring and Adjustment

1. Gambling Forum Archive, General Poker Theory. http://www.twoplustwo.com/digests/genpokarch_may00_msg.html.
2. Example provided by Sidney Winter, adapted from Roberta Wohlstetter, *Pearl Harbor: Warning and Decision* (Stanford, CA: Stanford University Press, 1963), and Gordon Prange, *At Dawn We Slept* (New York: McGraw-Hill, 1981).
3. Clayton M. Christensen, *The Innovator's Dilemma* (New York: HarperBusiness, 1997).
4. *Forbes,* September 15, 1967.
5. J. Edward Russo and Paul J. H. Schoemaker, *Decision Traps* (New York: Fireside, 1989), 197–98.
6. A penetrating analysis of the bias toward confirming evidence has been presented by Joshua Klayman and Young-Won Ha, "Confirmation, Disconfirmation and Information in Hypothesis Testing," *Psychological Review* 94 (1987): 211–28. Klayman and Ha argue that whether disconfirmation or confirmation is most suitable depends in complex ways on the kind of task one faces. See also Joshua Klayman, "Varieties of Confirmation Bias" in Jerome Busemeyer, Reid Hastie, and Douglas L. Medin, eds., *Decision Making from a Cognitive Perspective* (New York: Academic Press, 1995), 365–418.
7. The article describing the moon rock study can be found in Ian I. Mitroff and Richard O. Mason, "On Evaluating the Scientific Contribution of the Apollo Moon Missions via Information Theory," *Management Science* 20 (August 1974): 1501–13. A total of ten hypotheses were examined relating to the origin of the moon, its temperature history, and so on. The authors found that more well-known scientists were less open-minded about new evidence, and that the data overall belie the myth of the objective, rational scientist.

They argue that the lunar science community, like all scientific communities, is "best described as a hierarchy rather than as a democracy" (1511).

8. Malcolm Gladwell, *The Tipping Point: How Little Things Can Make a Big Difference* (New York: Little, Brown, 2000).
9. Rita Gunther McGrath and Ian MacMillan, "Discovery-Driven Planning," *Harvard Business Review* (July–August 1995): 4–12.
10. Robert S. Kaplan and David P. Norton, "Using the Balanced Scorecard as a Strategic Management System," *Harvard Business Review* (January–February 1996): 75–87, or Robert S. Kaplan and David P. Norton, *Balanced Scorecard: Translating Strategy into Action* (Boston: Harvard Business School Press, 1996).
11. Two important recent books explore the organizational aspects of developing such an external orientation: George S. Day, *The Market-Driven Organization: Understanding, Attracting and Keeping Valuable Customers* (New York: Free Press, 1999), and Stephan Haeckel and Adrian J. Slywotzky, *Adaptive Enterprise: Creating and Leading Sense-and-Respond Organizations* (Boston: Harvard Business School Press, 1999).
12. Adam Kahane, "Imagining South Africa's Future: How Scenarios Helped Discover Common Ground," *Learning from the Future* (New York: John Wiley, 1998).
13. Tucker, Kerry, "Scenario Planning: Visualizing a Broader World of Possibilities Can Help Associations Anticipate and Prepare for Change," *Association Management*, April 1999, 71–75, 126.
14. Good references on dialogue are David Bohm, *On Dialogue* (London and New York: Routledge, 1996); Daniel Yankelovich, *The Magic of Dialogue: Transforming Conflict into Cooperation* (New York: Simon & Schuster, 1999); and William Isaacs, *Dialogue and the Art of Thinking Together* (New York: Currency, 1999).
15. Paul J. H. Schoemaker and V. Michael Mavaddat, "Scenario Planning for Disruptive Technologies," in George S. Day and Paul J. H. Schoemaker, eds., *Wharton on Managing Emerging Technologies* (New York: John Wiley, 2000), 239–40.
16. Edward R. Tufte, *Visual and Statistical Thinking: Displays of Evidence for Making Decisions* (Cheshire, CT: Graphics Press, 1997).
17. Brian J. Loasby, "Long-Range Formal Planning in Perspective," *Journal of Management Studies* (October 1967), reprinted in James Brian Quinn, Henry Mintzberg, and Robert M. James, eds., *The Strategy Process* (Englewood Cliffs, NJ: Prentice Hall, 1988), 89–104.
18. Betinna Zwerdling, "The ABCs of Active Enterprise Financial Planning," AMR Research Report on Enterprise Management Strategies, February 2001.
19. The emphasis on creating learning cultures was pioneered by Peter Senge in his well-known book, *The Fifth Discipline* (New York: Currency/Doubleday, 1990). For a shorter version, see Peter Senge, "The Leader's New Work: Building Learning Organization," *Sloan Management Review* (Fall 1990), 7–23, and for elaborated essays, see Sarita Chawla and John Renesch, *Learning*

Organizations: Developing Cultures for Tomorrow's Workplace (Portland, OR: Productivity Press, 1995). The strategic significance of learning—especially about the future—was well underscored in Gary Hamel and C. K. Prahalad, *Competing for the Future* (Boston: Harvard Business School Press, 1994). Organizational obstacles to learning and change—especially concerning new technologies—are thoroughly addressed in Clayton Christensen, *The Innovator's Dilemma* (Boston: Harvard Business School Press, 1997).

20. For a short introduction to groupthink, see Irving Janis, "Groupthink," *Psychology Today,* November 1971, 84–90. Further analysis is provided in Irving Janis, *Groupthink: Psychological Studies of Policy Decisions and Fiascos,* 2d ed. (Boston: Houghton Mifflin, 1982). For a critical review of groupthink as a behavioral decision making model, see Won-Woo Park, "A Review of Research on Groupthink," *Journal of Behavioral Decision Making* 3 (October–December 1990): 229–46.
21. For insights about how Silicon Valley companies succeed in fast-changing environments, see Homa Bahrami, "The Emerging Flexible Organization: Perspectives from Silicon Valley," *California Management Review* 34 (Summer 1992): 33–52, or Kathleen Eisenhardt and Shona Brown, *Competing on the Edge: Strategy as Structured Chaos* (Boston: Harvard Business School Press, 1998). For further insight into the design of organizations that exchange information well, see Andrew Campbell and Michael Goold, *The Collaborative Enterprise: Why Links Across the Corporation Often Fail and How to Make Them Work* (Cambridge, MA: Perseus Press, 2000).

Chapter 8: Implementation: Living with Uncertainty

1. The first liquid crystals were discovered in 1888 by Austrian Friedrich Reinitzer (see http://moebius.physik.tu-berlin.de/lc/lcs.html and www.howstuffworks.com). It was not until 1968 that researcher James Fergason patented the first workable liquid crystal display (see http://web.mit.edu/invent/www/investorsA-H/fergason.html). Scottish inventor Alexander Bain patented the original concept for the fax machine in 1843, using a telegraph wire to transmit signals from a two-dimensional surface (metal type) and a clock mechanism to transfer an image from one electrically conductive paper to another. In the early 1920s, AT&T developed telephone facsimile technology (www.worldfax.com). Fuel cells were first conceived and invented in 1839 by William Grove, a British inventor.
2. http:/www.ideafinder.com/history/inventions/story074.htm.
3. P. J. H. Schoemaker and C. A. J. M. van der Heijden, "Strategic Planning at Royal Dutch/Shell," *Journal of Strategic Change* 2 (1993): 157–71.
4. Arie de Geus, "Planning as Learning," *Harvard Business Review* (March–April 1988): 70–74.
5. For a detailed study of how poorly humans understand a dynamic feedback environment, see John D. Sterman, "Modeling Managerial Behavior: Misperceptions of Feedback in a Dynamic Decision Making Environment,"

Management Science 35 (1989): 321–39 as well as John D. Sterman, "Boom, Bust, and Failures to Learn in Experimental Markets," *Management Science* 39 (1999): 1439–58.

6. Rosabeth Moss Kanter, Barry A. Stein, and Todd D. Jick, *The Challenge of Organizational Change: How Companies Experience It and Leaders Guide It* (New York: Free Press, 1992).
7. This section is adapted from Paul J. H. Schoemaker, "Twenty Common Pitfalls in Scenario Planning," in Liam Fahey and Robert M. Randall, eds., *Learning from the Future* (New York: John Wiley, 1998), 422–31.
8. Robert S. Kaplan and David P. Norton, "Using the Balanced Scorecard as a Strategic Management System," *Harvard Business Review* (January–February 1996): 75–87; and Robert S. Kaplan and David P. Norton, *Balanced Scorecard: Translating Strategy into Action* (Boston: Harvard Business School Press, 1996).

Chapter 9: Case Study: Flying through Turbulence

1. *Instant Quotation Dictionary,* Varner Bolander, et. al. New York: Dell, 1990, 278.
2. Michael Mavaddat, Roch Parayre, and Doug Randall were the primary DSI consultants conducting this engagement, following a kickoff section led by Paul Schoemaker and Tom Tucker (the Credit Union's former chairman).
3. Decision Strategies International and Credit Union Executives Society, *2005: Scenarios for Credit Unions—An Executive Report* (1999).

Conclusion: Navigating the Future

1. Amir D. Aczel, *The Riddle of the Compass* (New York: Harcourt, 2000), 105–107.

Appendix A: The Psychology of Uncertainty

1. New York: Random House, 1968.
2. It remains an open question to what extent our overall dislike of uncertainty is a consequence of, versus a cause of, our limited ability to cope with uncertainty. Things that are hard to cope with may generally not be liked by people, and conversely, things we don't especially like are not ones we usually get very good at. Whichever way the causality runs, it is clear that we need help in coming to terms with uncertainty.
3. P. J. H. Schoemaker, "The Expected Utility Model: Its Variants, Purposes, Evidence and Limitations," *Journal of Economic Literature* 20 (June 1982): 529–63; J. C. Hershey, H. C. Kunreuther, and P. J. H. Schoemaker, "Sources of Bias in Assessment Procedures for Utility Functions," *Management Science* 28 (August 1982): 936–54; P. J. H. Schoemaker, "Preferences for Information on Probabilities versus Prizes: The Role of Risk-Taking Attitudes,"

Journal of Risk and Uncertainty 2 (1989): 37–60; and P. J. H. Schoemaker, "Determinants of Risk-Taking: Behavioral and Economic Views," *Journal of Risk and Uncertainty* 6, (1993): 49–73. See also Paul Kleindorfer, Howard Kunreuther, and Paul J. H. Schoemaker, *Decision Sciences: An Integrative Perspective,* (New York: Cambridge University Press, 1993) 470.

4. For those who want a managerial review of behavioral decision research, I recommend Max H. Bazerman, *Judgment in Managerial Decision Making,* 7th ed. (New York: John Wiley, 1998); Reid Hastie and Robyn M. Dawes, *Rational Choice in an Uncertain World: The Psychology of Judgment and Decision Making* (Thousand Oaks, CA: Sage Publications, 2001); John S. Hammond, Ralph L. Keeney, and Howard Raiffa, *Smart Choices* (Cambridge, MA: Harvard Business School Press, 1998) and *Winning Decisions* by Edward Russo and Paul J. H. Schoemaker (New York: Doubleday, 2001). The most influential articles of the scholarly literature have been reprinted in various anthologies: Daniel Kahneman, Paul Slovic, and Amos Tversky, eds., *Judgment Under Uncertainty: Heuristics and Biases* (New York: Cambridge University Press, 1982); Terry Connolly, Hal R. Arkes, and Kenneth R. Hammond, eds., *Judgment and Decision Making: An Interdisciplinary Reader* (New York: Cambridge University Press, 2000); and William M. Goldstein and Robin M. Hogarth, eds., *Research on Judgment and Decision Making: Currents, Connections, and Controversies* (New York: Cambridge University Press, 1997). A broader, integrative perspective is offered in David Bell, Howard Raiffa, and Amos Tversky, eds., *Decision Making: Descriptive, Normative and Prescriptive Interactions* (New York: Cambridge University Press, 1988). For a broad graduate-level text, see Paul Kleindorfer, Howard Kunreuther, and Paul J. H. Schoemaker, *Decision Sciences: An Integrative Perspective,* (New York: Cambridge University Press, 1993). I also highly recommend the seminal writings of James G. March as collected in *Decisions and Organizations* (London: Basil Blackwell, 1998). For more wide-ranging views, see Stephen J. Hoch and Howard C. Kunreuther, eds., *Wharton on Making Decisions* (New York: John Wiley, 2001).
5. C. Cerf and N. Navasky, *The Experts Speak* (New York: Pantheon Books, 1984).
6. The literature on overconfidence is extensive. A recent authoritative discussion can be found in Joshua Klayman, Jack-B Soll, Claudia Gonzalez-Vallejo, and Sema Barlas, "Overconfidence: It Depends on How, What, and Whom You Ask," *Organizational Behavior and Human Decision Processes* 79 (September 1999): 216–47. The classic overview of early overconfidence studies is Sarah Lichtenstein, Baruch Fischhoff, and Lawrence Phillips, "Calibration of Probabilities: The Start of the Art to 1980," in Kahneman, Slovic, and Tversky, eds., *Judgment under Uncertainty* (New York: Cambridge University Press, 1982). Researchers have critically examined how robust the overconfidence bias or phenomenon actually is. A special issue of the *Journal of Behavioral Decision Making* (10, 3, 1997) was devoted to these issues and generally concluded that the overconfidence

bias was real rather than an artifact of the methodology employed. See especially Peter Ayton and Alastair G. R. McClelland, "How Real Is Overconfidence?" *Journal of Behavioral Decision Making* 10 (1997): 279–86.

7. Ellen J. Langer, "The Illusion of Control," *Journal of Personality and Social Psychology* 32 (1975): 322–28; see also Lawrence C. Perlmuter and Richard A. Monty, "The Importance of Perceived Control: Fact or Fantasy?" *American Scientist* 65 (November–December 1977): 759–65. Shelley E. Taylor and Jonathon D. Brown offer an interesting perspective on the positive value of illusions in "Illusion and Well-Being: A Social Psychological Perspective on Mental Health," *Psychological Bulletin* 193 (1988); see also Jane E. Gillham, *The Science of Optimism and Hope: Research Essays in Honor of Martin E. P. Seligman* (Philadelphia: Templeton Foundation Press, 2000).
8. Answers: (1) 39 years; (2) 4,187 miles; (3) 13 countries; (4) 39 books; (5) 2,160 miles; (6) 240 tons; (7) 1756; (8) 645 days; (9) 5,959 miles; (10) 36,198 feet. Adapted from *Decision Traps* by J. Edward Russo and Paul J.H. Schoemaker (New York: Doubleday, 1989) and *Winning Decisions* by J. Edward Russo and Paul J. H. Schoemaker (New York: Doubleday, 2002).
9. Peter Senge defined mental models as people's deeply held images of the world; see Peter Senge, "The Leader's New Work: Building Learning Organizations," *Sloan Management Review* 32 (Fall 1990): 7–23. In contrast, a paradigm is a widely shared mental model that groups use to define their reality: see Thomas S. Kuhn, *The Structure of Scientific Revolutions* (Chicago: University of Chicago Press, 1970). For more on mental models, see Rob Ranyard, *Decision Making: Cognitive Models and Explanations* (London: Routledge, 1997) or C. Marlene Fiol and Anne Sigismund Huff, "Maps for Managers: Where Are We? Where Do We Go From Here?" *Journal of Management Studies* 29 (1992): 267–85. The classic references to mental models and their cognitive functions are: Dedre Gentner and Albert L. Stevens, eds., *Mental Models* (Mahwah, NJ: Lawrence Erlbaum Associates, 1983) and Philip N. Johnson-Laird, ed., *Mental Models,* 2d ed. (Cambridge, MA: Harvard University Press, 1983).
10. J. E. Russo and P. J. H. Schoemaker, *Decision Traps* (New York: Doubleday, 1989), 82–83; see also J. E. Russo and P. J. H. Schoemaker, *Winning Decisions* (New York: Doubleday, 2001), 90–91.
11. O. Huber and R. Wider, "Active Information Search and Complete Information Presentation in Naturalistic Risky Decision Tasks," *Acta Psychologica* 95 (1997): 15–29.
12. Howard Kunreuther, Nathan Novemsky, and Daniel Kahneman, "Making Low Probabilities Useful," *Journal of Risk and Uncertainty* (in press). See also Wes Magat, Kip Viscusi, and Joel Huber, "Risk-dollar Tradeoffs, Risk Perceptions, and Consumer Behavior," in W. Viscusi and W. Magat, eds., *Learning About Risk* (Cambridge, MA: Harvard University Press, 1987); as well as Colin Camerer and Howard Kunreuther, "Decision Processes for Low Probability Events: Policy Mental Models Implications," *Journal of Policy Analysis and Management* 8 (1989): 565–92.

13. Dennis L. Jennings, Teresa M. Amabile, and Lee Ross, "Informal Covariation Assessment: Data-based vs. Theory-based Judgments," in Kahneman, Slovic, and Tversky, eds., *Judgment Under Uncertainty,* 211–30.
14. Daniel Kahneman and Dan Lovallo, "Timid Choices and Bold Forecasts: A Cognitive Perspective on Risk Taking," *Management Science* 39 (1993): 17–31; see also Daniel Kahneman and Amos Tversky, "Prospect Theory," *Econometrica,* 47, 1979, 283–291; Daniel Kahneman, Jack L. Knetsch, and Richart Thaler, "Experimental Tests of the Endowment Effect and the Coase Theorem," *Journal of Political Economy* 98 (December 1990): 1325–48.
15. Robin M. Hogarth and Howard Kunreuther, "Risk, Ambiguity and Insurance," *Journal of Risk and Uncertainty* 2 (1989): 5–35; see also H. Einhorn and R. Hogarth, "Decision Making Under Ambiguity," *Journal of Business* 59 (1986): S225–55. The classic paper on ambiguity is D. Ellsberg, "Risk, Ambiguity, and the Savage Axioms," *Quarterly Journal of Economics* 75 (1961): 643–69, based on his seminal doctoral dissertation, which was recently republished with an extensive new introduction by Isaac Levi as D. Ellsberg, *Risk, Ambiguity, and Decision* (New York: Garland, 2001).
16. P. J. H. Schoemaker, "Are Risk-attitudes Related Across Payoff Domains and Response Modes?" *Management Science* 36, 12 (Dec. 1990): 1451–63. Also see M. Cohen, J. Jaffray, and T. Said, "Individual Behavior under Risk and under Uncertainty: An Experimental Study," *Theory and Decisions* 18 (1985): 203–228; as well as P. J. H. Schoemaker, "Choices Involving Uncertain Probabilities: Tests of Generalized Utility Models," *Journal of Economic and Organizational Behavior* 16 (1991): 295–317.
17. Chris Hsee, "The Evaluability Hypothesis: An Explanation of Preference Reversals Between Joint and Separate Evaluations of Alternatives," *Organizational Behavior and Human Decision Processes* 46 (1996): 247–57. Also see Chris Hsee, Sally Blount, George Loewenstein, and Max Bazerman, "Preference Reversals Between Joint and Separate Evaluations of Options: A Review and Theoretical Analysis," *Psychological Review* 125 (1999): 576–90.
18. J. C. Hershey and P. J. H. Schoemaker, "Probability vs. Certainty Equivalence Methods in Utility Measurement: Are They Equivalent?" *Management Science* 31, 10 (Oct. 1985): 1213–31; see also P. J. H. Schoemaker and J. C. Hershey, "Utility Measurement: Signal, Noise and Bias," *Organizational Behavior and Human Decision Processes* 52 (1992): 397–424; as well as P. J. H. Schoemaker and J. C. Hershey, "CE-PE Bias and Probability Level: An Anchoring Model of Their Interaction," in B. Munier and M. Machina, eds., *Models and Experiments in Risk and Rationality* (Dordrecht, The Netherlands: Kluwer Academic Publishers, 1994), 35–55.

Appendix B: Uncertainty Tool Kit

1. For more details on some of the above tools see Paul Kleindorfer, Howard C. Kunreuther, and Paul J. H. Schoemaker, *Decision Sciences,* Cambridge Press, 1993, and Hugh Courtney, *20/20 Foresight,* Harvard Business School

Press, 2001. Most of the quantitative tools are described in the well-known textbook *Introduction to Operations Research* by Frederick S. Hiller and Gerald J. Lieberman, McGraw-Hill, 2000. Managers may wish to consult the *Harvard Business Review* articles collected in *Managing Uncertainty,* published by the Harvard Business School Press, 1999. For a review of forecasting methods, see J. Scott Armstrong, ed., *Principles of Forecasting: A Handbook for Researchers and Practitioners* (Dordrecht, The Netherlands: Kluwer Academic Publishers, 2001), and the associated Web site http://forecastingprinciples.com

Index

About the Author

Paul J. H. Schoemaker, a world-renowned authority on decision making and scenario-based strategic management, serves as research director of Mack Center for Technological Innovation at the Wharton School of the University of Pennsylvania, where he teaches strategy and decision making. For more than eleven years, he was a professor in the Graduate School of Business at the University of Chicago specializing in strategy and decision sciences. He has also been a visiting professor at CEDEP (INSEAD) and at the London Business School.

Dr. Schoemaker spent an extended sabbatical with the scenario planning group of Royal Dutch/Shell in London, and has since consulted with over a hundred organizations around the world. He is the founder and chairman of Decision Strategies International, Inc., a consulting and training firm specializing in strategic planning, executive development, and multimedia software (see www.decisionstrat.com).

In addition to having written more than seventy academic and applied papers, Dr. Schoemaker is the (co-)author of several books, including *Decision Traps, Decision Sciences, Wharton on Managing Emerging Technologies, Winning Decisions, Peripheral Vision* (with George Day), *Chips, Clones, and Living Beyond 100,* and *Brilliant Mistakes*. His writings have been published in over ten languages and received multiple awards, including the prestigious academic Best Paper Award in 2000 from the Strategic Management Society. His 1995 article on scenario planning is among the most reprinted publications in the fifty-plus-year history of the *MIT Sloan Management Review.*

Dr. Schoemaker divides his time among writing, consulting, lecturing, and investing, and he serves on the boards of several technology-based new ventures. He was born and raised in the Netherlands but completed his university studies in the U.S.A. He has a B.S. in physics from the University of Notre Dame, an MBA in finance, and a Ph.D. in decision sciences from the University of Pennsylvania's Wharton School. He lives with his wife and children in Villanova, Pennsylvania. His hobbies include golf, tennis, and piano. For further details see www.paulschoemaker.com.

Printed in the United States
By Bookmasters